Spring 1997 | Volume 17, no. 1 | ISSN: 0276-0045 | ISBN: 1-56478-153-4

THE REVIEW OF CONTEMPORARY FICTION

Editor
JOHN O'BRIEN
Illinois State University

Senior Editor
ROBERT L. MCLAUGHLIN
Illinois State University

Associate Editors
BROOKE HORVATH
IRVING MALIN
DAVID FOSTER WALLACE

Book Review Editor
GALE RENEE WALDEN

... PAYNE (Vargas Llosa)
STEVE HOROWITZ (Skvorecky)
JAMES GROVE (assistant editor, Skvorecky)

Production & Design
TODD BUSHMAN

Editorial Assistants
LISA ALBAUGH
HAROLD KEMP

Cover Photos: Miriam Berkley (Vargas Llosa), Helena Wilson (Skvorecky)

The Review of Contemporary Fiction is published three times a year (February, June, October) by The Review of Contemporary Fiction, Inc., a nonprofit organization located at ISU Campus Box 4241, Normal, IL 61790-4241. ISSN 0276-0045. Subscription prices are as follows:

Single volume (three issues):
Individuals: $17.00; foreign, add $3.50;
Institutions: $26.00; foreign, add $3.50.

DISTRIBUTION. Bookstores should send orders to:

University of Chicago Press Distribution Center, 11030 S. Langley Ave., Chicago, IL 60628. Phone 1-800-621-2736; fax (800) 621-8476.

This issue is partially supported by grants from the Illinois Arts Council, a state agency.

Indexed in *American Humanities Index, International Bibliography of Periodical Literature, International Bibliography of Book Reviews, MLA Bibliography,* and *Book Review Index.* Abstracted in *Abstracts of English Studies.*

The Review of Contemporary Fiction is also available in 16mm microfilm, 35mm microfilm, and 105mm microfiche from University Microfilms International, 300 North Zeeb Road, Ann Arbor, MI 48106-1346.

THE REVIEW OF CONTEMPORARY FICTION

FUTURE ISSUES DEVOTED TO: Rikki Ducornet, Raymond Queneau, Carole Maso, Wilson Harris, Alan Burns, Curtis White, Milorad Pavić, Richard Powers, Alexander Trocchi, Ed Sanders, and postmodern Japanese fiction.

BACK ISSUES

Back issues are still available for the following numbers of the *Review of Contemporary Fiction* ($8 each unless otherwise noted):

DOUGLAS WOOLF / WALLACE MARKFIELD
WILLIAM EASTLAKE / AIDAN HIGGINS
ALEXANDER THEROUX / PAUL WEST
CAMILO JOSÉ CELA
CLAUDE SIMON ($15)
CHANDLER BROSSARD
SAMUEL BECKETT
CLAUDE OLLIER / CARLOS FUENTES
JOHN BARTH / DAVID MARKSON
DONALD BARTHELME / TOBY OLSON
WILLIAM T. VOLLMANN / SUSAN DAITCH / DAVID FOSTER WALLACE
BRIGID BROPHY / ROBERT CREELEY / OSMAN LINS

WILLIAM H. GASS / MANUEL PUIG
ROBERT WALSER
JOSÉ DONOSO / JEROME CHARYN
GEORGES PEREC / FELIPE ALFAU
JOSEPH MCELROY
DJUNA BARNES
ANGELA CARTER / TADEUSZ KONWICKI
STANLEY ELKIN / ALASDAIR GRAY
EDMUND WHITE / SAMUEL R. DELANY

SPECIAL FICTION ISSUE: Fiction by Pinget, Bowles, Mathews, Markfield, Rower, Ríos, Tindall, Sorrentino, Goytisolo, McGonigle, Dukore, Dowell, McManus, Mosley, and Acker

NOVELIST AS CRITIC: Essays by Garrett, Barth, Sorrentino, Wallace, Ollier, Brooke-Rose, Creeley, Mathews, Kelly, Abbott, West, McCourt, McGonigle, and McCarthy

NEW FINNISH FICTION: Fiction by Eskelinen, Jäntti, Kontio, Krohn, Paltto, Sairanen, Selo, Siekkinen, Sund, Valkeapää

NEW ITALIAN FICTION: Interviews and fiction by Malerba, Tabucchi, Zanotto, Ferrucci, Busi, Corti, Rasy, Cherchi, Balduino, Ceresa, Capriolo, Carrera, Valesio, and Gramigna

GROVE PRESS NUMBER: Contributions by Allen, Beckett, Corso, Ferlinghetti, Jordan, McClure, Rechy, Rosset, Selby, Sorrentino, and others

NEW DANISH FICTION: Fiction by Brøgger, Høeg, Andersen, Grøndahl, Holst, Jensen, Thorup, Michael, Sibast, Ryum, Lynggaard, Grønfeldt, Willumsen, and Holm

THE FUTURE OF FICTION: Essays by Birkerts, Caponegro, Franzen, Galloway, Maso, Morrow, Vollmann, White, and others

Individuals receive a 10% discount on orders of one issue and a 20% discount on any order of two or more issues. Postage for domestic shipments is $3.50 for the first issue and 75¢ for each additional issue. For foreign shipments, postage is $4.50 for the first issue and $1.00 for each additional issue. All orders must be paid in U.S. dollars. Send payment to:

Review of Contemporary Fiction, Chicago Distribution Center, 11030 S. Langley Avenue, Chicago, IL 60628, phone: 1-800-621-2736.

Contents

Introduction: Chased by Life, Politics, Demons: Flying to Fiction 9
Dane Johnson

Demons and Lies: Motivation and Form in Mario Vargas Llosa 15
Luis Rebaza-Soraluz

The Trumpet of Deyá 25
Mario Vargas Lloas

A Bullfight in the Andes 35
Mario Vargas Llosa

Captain Pantoja and the Special Service: *A Transitional Novel* 52
Efraín Kristal

Outside Looking In: Aunt Julia and Vargas Llosa 58
Elizabeth Dipple

Out of Failure Comes Success: Autobiography and Testimony in *A Fish
    in the Water* 70
Alex Zisman

A Mario Vargas Llosa Checklist 76
Alex Zisman

Introduction: The Bittersweet Vision of Josef Skvorecky and a Selected
    Bibliography of Works by and about Him 78
Steve Horowitz

The Last Decade: An Interview with Josef Skvorecky....................................... 82
Sam Solecki

Three Bachelors in A Fiery Furnace, a short story 92
Josef Skvorecky

Authors, Critics, Reviewers, a lecture 98
Josef Skvorecky

Keynote Address on Eastern European Literature in Transition..................... 108
Josef Skvorecky

A Genial Gossipmonger 110
Lubomir Doruzka

The Cowards: Josef Skvorecky and His Contributions to Czech Humorist
    Literature.. 115
Mila Sakova-Pierce

This Thing, *The Bass Saxophone*, Is Anything But Ordinary 120
Josef Jarab

The Engineer of Human Souls: Skvorecky's Comic Vision 126
Edward Galligan

Place and Placelessness in Josef Skvorecky's *Dvorak in Love* 130
James Grove

American Themes in Skvorecky's Work: *The Bride from Texas* 141
Helena Kosek

Josef Skvorecky's Variation on American Themes: *The Bride from Texas* 149
Maria Nemcova Banerjee

A Josef Skvorecky Checklist 157
Robert L. McLaughlin

━━━━━━━━━━━━━
━━━━━━━━━━━━━

The Culture of Everyday Venality: Or a Life in the Book Industry 159
Margeret Wehr

━━━━━━━━━━━━━
━━━━━━━━━━━━━

Book Reviews 167

Books Received 211

Contributors 218

ART AND AFFECTION Criticism

A Life of Virginia Woolf
Panthea Reid
"An important addition to Woolf studies. What especially distinguishes it from other biographies of Virginia Woolf is the large number of unpublished letters and manuscripts Panthea Reid has drawn from to support her analyses of Woolf's complex relationship with her family (in particular her sister Vanessa Bell), her debt to Roger Fry, and her development as a writer. Readers will find themselves continually considering familiar subjects from new, interesting, and enlightening perspectives"—Susan Dick. $35.00, 608 pp.; 64 halftones

ARE WE NOT MEN?

Masculine Anxiety and the Problem of African-American Identity
Phillip Brian Harper
"A thoughtful and provocative meditation on the complex status of the African-American male in American society"—Henry Louis Gates, Jr. "Phillip Brian Harper has an elegant sense of irony, a keen eye for contradiction, and a serious message to convey. These essays on masculinity, race, and homophobia are meticulous, witty, thoughtful, sobering, and absorbing. This is cultural criticism at its best"—Patricia J. Williams. $30.00, 272 pp.

LIGHTING OUT FOR THE TERRITORY

Reflections on Mark Twain and American Culture
Shelley Fisher Fishkin
"Exuberant and provocative.... A fearless and captivating voyage through Twain's many dimensions"—Henry Louis Gates, Jr. "A terrific read, a lively personal narrative that is also dead serious. Her awesome amount of research uncovers fascinating stories that document Mark Twain's anti-racist views and illuminate the durability of *Adventures of Huckleberry Finn*"—Bobbie Ann Mason. $25.00, 256 pp.; 26 halftones

BEQUEST AND BETRAYAL

Memoirs of a Parent's Death
Nancy K. Miller
"Nancy K. Miller counterpoints lyrical introspection about her own grief with critical insight into contemporary memoirs. In the process she produces astonishingly poignant revelations about what it means to live with a dying parent, how it feels to survive after a great loss"—Sandra M. Gilbert and Susan Gubar. Melding the details of her own experience with critical insight into such works as Philip Roth's *Patrimony* and Art Spiegelman's *Maus*, Miller exposes the often tortuous paths of mourning and attachment that we follow in the wake of loss. $23.00, 208 pp.

THE LITERARY MIND

Mark Turner
"Turner's forceful book starts by showing how we use storying and metaphor to understand everything from pouring a cup of coffee to Proust. It ends with the splendidly bold claim that this storying, literary mind comes first, before all other kinds of thought, even language itself. Adventurous and convincing, Turner's work launches a new understanding, not only of literature, but of what it is to have a human brain. To read it is to think about thinking in a way you never have"—Norman N. Holland. $25.00, 208 pp.

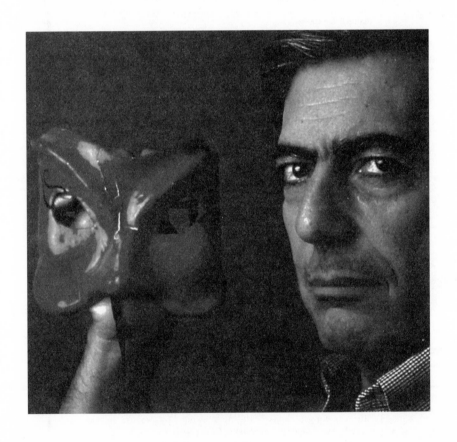

Mario Vargas Llosa. Photograph by Abe Franjndlich (Sygma),
from Vargas Llosa's A *Writer's Reality* (Syracuse University Press, 1991)

Chased by Life, Politics, Demons: Flying to Fiction

Dane Johnson

The Peruvian novelist Mario Vargas Llosa has mentioned many times his "fascination for people who appear to have stepped out of novels" (*A Fish in the Water* 181). His own life could easily fit in this category. Growing up in the 1940s within his mother's warm, extended family in the small Peruvian coastal city of Piura (the setting for several of his novels), young Marito was whisked away one day to Lima "the horrible" (*Fish* 47) by an arbitrary and domineering father whom Mario had long thought to be dead. Upon marrying a divorcée at age nineteen—Julia Urquidi, a woman some thirteen years his senior who also happened to be his aunt by marriage—Vargas Llosa received melodramatic threats from his father—and a wealth of writing material. The courtship and marriage have been depicted three times: as autobiographical realism in the novel *Aunt Julia and the Scriptwriter* (see Elizabeth Dipple's essay), as romantic reverie in *A Fish in the Water*, and, in a twist where the reality part of autobiographical realism suddenly bites back, in Urquidi's own account of their marriage, *Lo que Varguitas no dijo* (What Little Vargas Did Not Say). During this period, Vargas Llosa was in the midst of Zelig-like contortions, holding down some seven jobs, including columnist for several papers, research assistant for a book on Peruvian history, librarian at a men's club, and cataloger of graves in the oldest section of the colonial cemetery of Lima, as well as news director for Radio Panamericana and speech writer for 1956 presidential candidate Dr. Hernando de Lavalle. Vargas Llosa was barely maintaining his studies in Law and Letters at the University of San Marcos while also participating in political activities. His roles ranged from fellow traveler in the clandestine Peruvian Communist Party to one of the young voices within the nascent Christian Democratic Party—all the while trying to live his dream of being a Real Writer.

A man who dreamed to live and who has managed to live most of his dreams, Vargas Llosa made it to Paris in 1959 to fulfill his writerly vision, which, of course, could happen only in Europe. There was the Parisian garret, more odd jobs and allied poverty, the sustaining conversation of a few like-minded souls. His friendship with Julio Cortázar, for example, is summarized in this issue's "The Trumpet of Deyá." Finally—and actually quite quickly—recognition came. Ever since he won the Premio Biblioteca Breve in 1962 for his first novel, *The Time of the Hero*—a bold collective portrait of the Peruvian as a young hoodlum set in a Limeño military academy—Vargas Llosa's status as one of Latin America's premier novelists has never waned.

And like a hero from one of the medieval romances of which he is fond, Vargas Llosa's presence has been legion and controversial: eleven novels, four plays, several books of literary criticism, and seemingly countless literary and political essays in journals and periodicals throughout Latin America, the United States, and Europe. He has even co-directed a movie (a 1976 version of his novel *Captain Pantoja and the Special Service*) and hosted a cultural talk show on television. He has had books burned and books prized. He has been attacked from the Left and the Right. With martyrdom or a Nobel Prize seemingly the only recognition remaining for this protean man, in the late 1980s Vargas Llosa saw himself drawn into a drama as big as one of his novels: he ran for and nearly won the presidency of Peru in 1990. This saga constitutes one half of his memoir *A Fish in the Water* as well as inspiring a separate book by his son and campaign advisor Álvaro Vargas Llosa, *El diablo en campaña* (The Devil on the Campaign Trail).

The adventure of Vargas Llosa's childhood and early adult life, the subsequent peregrinations, the ongoing political and critical activism—all this can distract us from the steady, magnificent labor of a major novelist. Vargas Llosa's work is not marked by the verbal pyrotechnics often associated with experimentation. *Experimentation* is a word that he most certainly would eschew. Still, his novels display an exploration of novelistic form both vast and piercing, a constant questioning of the why and how of stories in our lives combined with an array of riveting tales that explore the trials and tribulations of being a man stuck in the Peru of the last half century (save for *The War of the End of the World*, a historical epic of the Brazilian backlands).

With the presidential campaign now just one part of Vargas Llosa's "life and work" rather than its defining moment (Dipple's and Luis Rebaza-Soraluz's essays underscore the complex relations among these stock terms for a constant but not repetitively autobiographical writer), it now seems necessary to reevaluate Vargas Llosa's vast oeuvre. This issue begins that project with two of Vargas Llosa's own critical essays, one on Cortázar and one on José María Arguedas, followed by a new interview, three critical essays that touch on the range of his career while focusing on less studied works, and a bibliography.

While the essays on Vargas Llosa's work center on *Captain Pantoja and the Special Service, Aunt Julia and the Scriptwriter*, and *A Fish in the Water*, they also engage his presence as an intellectual who intervenes in the public sphere through his novels and other writing—this despite Vargas Llosa's argument in his essays and interview for an inviolable separation between art and politics. In the best general introduction to his work in print at this time, *Understanding Mario Vargas Llosa*, Sara Castro-Klarén summarizes the trajectory of his career as a storyteller: "Having started out as a committed writer, in what he believed was a Sartrean existentialist position, and having later repudiated Sartre's claim to the unavoidable engagement of fiction, in favor of a Flaubertian cannibalism of reality as the mere materials in the making of autonomous fictional worlds, Vargas Llosa deploys in his later novels a narrator involved in direct and polemic political discourse" (225). While not contradicting this summary, this issue suggests that all of Vargas Llosa's narrators raise questions of truth in narration that can be explored but not easily resolved. As a small selection, the critical articles do not engage in detail with every key point in Vargas Llosa's career. We have no essays on his epic novels *Conversation in the Cathedral* or *The War of the End of the World*, for example. But in bringing out the complexities of other narratives and of his artistic vision, our contributors help us to understand the achievement of these grand, complex, somewhat overwhelming texts, as well as Vargas Llosa's genre experiments, like the detective novel *The Death of Palomino Molero* or his erotic "entertainment" *In Praise of the Stepmother*.

"The Trumpet of Deyá" is Vargas Llosa's eulogy for Argentine writer Julio Cortázar, a longtime friend and mentor despite their distance on largely political grounds during the latter years of Cortázar's life. It is also an exemplary display of Vargas Llosa's critical writing, combining a fluid blend of sharp-eyed analysis and personally committed criticism to move gracefully from Cortázar's life to a cogent summary of his literary imagination. It is a homage that makes one want to run to the shelves for Cortázar's work; at the same time, it is very revealing of what is most important to Vargas Llosa. While reflecting on abrupt changes in Cortázar's life and writing brought on during the events of '68, Vargas Llosa brings into nostalgic focus a time when he thought only of writing (like Cortázar earlier, "for whom nothing, outside of literature, seemed to matter, or, maybe, exist"), when he was part of the community of Latin American writers in cosmopolitan self-exile and not placed on the other side of the barricade. Completed after Vargas Llosa's own extended dalliance with (as Cortázar defined politics) "the horrible tendency toward the attainment of useful ends," it is also a wish that we could all return to the magical moment of Deyá, before life and politics shattered the private sanctity of art.

In "A Bullfight in the Andes" Vargas Llosa focuses on the first novel (*Yawar Fiesta*) of Peru's other famous novelist, José María Arguedas. While marking out new territory in Vargas Llosa's longtime engagement with Arguedas by emphasizing Arguedas's status as a literary artist of the first rank (one of Vargas Llosa's first critical pieces was an interview with Arguedas in the 1950s), this close reading of the novel is also a platform from which Vargas Llosa reiterates his beliefs on the status of the real in fiction.

In the interview with Luis Rebaza-Soraluz, "Demons and Lies: Motivation and Form in Mario Vargas Llosa," Vargas Llosa argues for a continuity in his ideas about literature. While the critical essays argue as much for change and specificity, this interview ties together Vargas Llosa's past and ongoing concerns about the nature of the novel and the nature of fiction with his most recent writing: his memoir *A Fish in the Water,* his most recent novel, *Death in the Andes,* and a full-length study of José María Arguedas.

Efraín Kristal's essay, "*Captain Pantoja and the Special Service:* A Transitional Novel," makes the case that Vargas Llosa, partially as a result of reading Euclides da Cunha, partially from his observation of the "failure" of Castro's regime, begins to develop a new character in this transitional novel: the fanatic. Kristal's heady use of changes from one manuscript draft to another—a first glimpse into the intricacies of Vargas Llosa's process of composition—makes a very strong argument for a kind of active transition. The essay also provides insight into a Vargas Llosa novel that is less well known (critics, perhaps put off guard by Vargas Llosa's first humorous novel, have given it short shrift) while placing that text in dialogue with two of his better known novels: *The Time of the Hero* and *The War of the End of the World.* While the focus is on the intricacies of composition and the complexities of narration, Kristal shows that the interplay of politics and art is never far from Vargas Llosa's writing by tying together Vargas Llosa's changes in the manuscript with reading he was doing at the time.

Elizabeth Dipple's "Outside, Looking In: *Aunt Julia* and Vargas Llosa" explicates the complex narrative selves in several Vargas Llosa novels, especially *Aunt Julia and the Scriptwriter* ("the pivotal novel for his acknowledgment of the entire problem of realism"), describing Vargas Llosa as a "self-divided" novelist. While investigating the difficulties brought on by the deployment of a "Mario Vargas Llosa" within this and other texts, Dipple explores the intricacies of Vargas Llosa's commitment to realism—as well as its limits. In some ways her description of a Vargas Llosa constantly representing his failure "at some level to participate" is what is overcome through his presidential campaign and then represented largely as a mistake in his memoir, something from which to fly away.

The focus on *Aunt Julia,* together with Kristal's work on *Captain Pantoja,* reasserts the importance of these two novels for understanding Vargas Llosa's development as a novelist and their worthiness of careful consideration in their own right, not to be seen as mere respite from his big novels (neither has garnered as much attention as *Conversation in the Cathedral* or *The War of the End of the World,* the epic novels that stand as chronological bookends to the two in discussion). In fact, these "less serious" novels achieve what Vargas Llosa set out in *A Writer's Reality* as the highest goal for an author: "something that can satisfy all kinds of mentalities and knowledge and education, and at the same time is creative and artistic and popular" (116).

In the final essay, "Out of Failure Comes Success: Autobiography and

Testimony in *A Fish in the Water*," Luis Rebaza-Soraluz discusses Vargas Llosa's recent memoir, a departure for the author in that it is explicitly an autobiography rather than playing with the name of the author as in many of his novels. *A Fish in the Water* frames Vargas Llosa's career, and Rebaza-Soraluz also refers to key points that are left out of that—the pregnant middle of the "Boom" years. Rebaza-Soraluz brings out the narrative complexity of what on the surface looks like a simple switching from childhood to the near present, for there are actually two distinct types of narration, a kind of war of fictional method that has gone on beneath the surface throughout Vargas Llosa's career. While Vargas Llosa would insist (and does in the current interview) on how the genre of the memoir is distinct from his or any fiction, Rebaza-Soraluz's illustration of the melding of techniques and concerns in this memoir is important. As Rebaza-Soraluz suggests, Vargas Llosa returns again and again to "a good/evil dichotomy combining religious and political rhetoric," a split that is often translated into the pure good possible only in autonomous art and the deceptive evil of anything that smacks of the political.

In all of Vargas Llosa's work we see the constant meditation on writing. The transformation of what is seen (and read, for Vargas Llosa is a long-time historian without title) to words on the page is powerful, a way to truth, but always productively deceitful at the same time. *A Fish in the Water* ends with a description of flying from Lima after losing the presidential election: "When the plane took off and the infallible clouds of Lima blotted the city from sight and we were surrounded only by blue sky, the thought crossed my mind that this departure resembled the one in 1958, which had so clearly marked the end of one stage of my life and the beginning of another, in which literature came to occupy the central place" (522-23).

The wish to separate is strong, the nostalgia for a time of "just literature" palpable. But the complex narrative solutions discussed in this issue and replete in Vargas Llosa's novels show the mix of life, politics, and art to be constant and ever-changing, the yeast for a heady selection of texts. For Vargas Llosa, as he said in the introduction to his play *The Young Lady from Tacna*, "Fiction is the 'complete' man, a perfect blend of truth and falsehood." And despite Vargas Llosa's political interventions (while usually claiming little interest in politics and a combination of fear and repulsion toward power), despite having his life as one of his best roles, it is fiction for which Vargas Llosa lives, fiction for which he will be remembered.

WORKS CITED

Castro-Klarén, Sara. *Understanding Mario Vargas Llosa*. Columbia: Univ. of South Carolina Press, 1990.

Vargas Llosa, Mario. *A Fish in the Water*. Trans. Helen Lane. New York: Farrar, Straus, Giroux, 1994.

——. *A Writer's Reality*. Ed. Myron I. Lichtblau. Syracuse: Syracuse Univ. Press, 1990.

——. *The Young Lady from Tacna*. *Three Plays*. Trans. David Graham-Young. London: Faber and Faber, 1990. 9-76.

Demons and Lies: Motivation and Form in Mario Vargas Llosa

Luis Rebaza-Soraluz

LUIS REBAZA-SORALUZ: In *García Márquez: Historia de un deicidio* (García Márquez: Story of a Deicide), a book whose circulation—if I am not mistaken—you helped minimize, you developed your theories of "inner demons" and the "total novel." What course have these ideas taken since then? Could you summarize your understanding of these ideas and explain how you see them now in relation to your narrative poetics?

MARIO VARGAS LLOSA: I continue to believe that the basic ideas expressed in that book, and in other books or essays I have written about the novel, are valid. They are fairly general ideas that do not explain particular cases but that do explain a certain characteristic akin to the genealogy of novels. The point of departure of the novelistic calling, the vocation of creating with words and with the imagination worlds that are distinct from the real world, is born of a certain conflict, some incompatibility with lived experience, that induces a person, in a generally obscure, nonrational manner, to seek out the alternative offered by fiction. The imagination does not work in a vacuum, it is not a gratuitous movement of the spirit, it operates drawing upon that conflict, trauma, interdict, enmity. . . . That difficult relationship with reality, such as it is lived, can be called many things. In any case it is from this that the imagination constructs that parallel world that is fiction. I call all of this "demons," metaphorically. I did not want to use the word *trauma* so as not to give an orthodox Freudian explanation; nor do I believe that it can be explained as merely stemming from a neurosis. It is a type of conflict that can be infinitely broader than that determined purely pathologically. If there were no basic conflict with reality this vocation would not emerge. This vocation, in my opinion, consists of a rejection of reality and the substitution of another reality re-created in the image of its inventor, drawing from those types of problems or conflicts that I call "demons" because of their obsessive nature. This is a point of departure that establishes an immensely broad common denominator into which practically everything that could create difficulty in adaptation to lived experiences could fit; so you have motives ranging from the most altruistic (the rejection of injustice or social abuse) to the most private or egotistical (not being able to accept an eccentricity or an anomaly) or simply a thirst for the absolute (wanting to live existence more intensely, more fully, going beyond the limits of the human condition). Anyway, that form of rebellion is for me the point of departure for fiction. The originality of a narrative lies not in what it portrays of the real world but rather in what it reforms or adds to it. That is, for me, the specifically literary. The value of fiction is not in its similarity but rather in its dissonance with a reality which it should, nevertheless, represent—in order to obtain recognition, identification with the reader. That is what we call fiction: a reality that, without being reality, being distinct and alternative, asserts itself, in the case of successful narratives, due to its power of persuasion, as the real reality, the authentic, secret reality, reflected in literature. It seems to me that this is a valid explanation for all cases, and yet, of course, a generalization; each particular case represents a distinct method, technique, set of problems, and ambition.

LRS: Returning to the idea of the "added element": in *The Perpetual Orgy*, speaking of Flaubert, you separate description from the anecdote, considering the latter an obligation of novelistic prose. An anecdote is made up of all kinds of experiences, which the author uses unscrupulously. What is important is its organization and its new form; it is here that the "added elements" make the anecdote a fictitious reality, which appears before the reader as a more conceivable reality than the very same reality he himself experiences. Systematically and impersonally exhibiting and withholding information, according to a previously conceived project, make the narrator disappear, who, impassive before what is narrated, does not absolve or condemn. This system leads him to alienate himself from the anecdote to the point of not intervening as a voice, resulting in a broad command of dialogue. Is this your point of view as a fiction writer? Is this your personal idea of realism?

MVL: That is Flaubert's idea, the description of what Flaubert called the impersonality of the narrator: the absolute neutrality that a narrator should maintain with regard to his narrative world. The narrator should be like God, omnipresent and at the same time invisible, an active absence, that is Flaubert's idea. Broadly speaking it is a valid concept, yet not exclusive. There are other versions. There is a very rich narrative in which the narrator is not invisible but rather a domineering, despotic presence, as well as that of an egomaniac. This is the type of narrator most often found in the classic novel. In a novel like *Les Miserables*, which I admire very much, the main character is a narrator who is constantly interfering, pontificating, judging. He does it from beginning to end with such coherence and congruence that he creates an order that in the end establishes itself as acceptable. But as a writer I feel closer to Flaubert's idea of the narrator than to the classic idea of the tyrannical and exhibitionistic narrator. It is very true, and in this Flaubert was extremely perceptive, that although the narrator may be visible, if the fiction does not gain independence, sovereignty, if it does not truly emancipate itself from the reality that serves as its model and has provided it with materials, it does not begin to live, it is ephemeral. Any fiction that needs to be checked against reality in order to justify itself does not attain the category of fiction—it is a document, a testimony. It may have historical or sociological value, but fiction should find justification in and of itself, disregarding its model. This is where a parasitic literature, such as regionalist literature, for example, or literature based on local customs and manners, fails.

LRS: In your article "*Los miserables*: el ultimo clasico" (*Les Miserables*: The Last Classic), published in the magazine *Cielo abierto* in 1983, you call Victor Hugo's work a "grandiose lie." Is the narrator of *Les Miserables* a liar not because he creates fiction but because he wants to make the reader believe that what he says is true?

MVL: That is the ambition of all fiction, to impose itself on the reader as the truth. The raison d'être of all fiction is to be experienced, lived, not as a lie but as truth. Paradoxically, because of its own nature, fiction is and can only be a lie. This lie would never reach recognition, that enthronement as a great literary work, if it did not somehow reveal some truth, if through this lie a truth were not expressed, that can only be expressed through this periphrastic, symbolic, metaphorical path that is the path of fiction. The world is not as Proust, Joyce, or Balzac describes it, because the world is not organized that way, nor does it close up over itself as it does in a novel, where we can follow with absolute clarity the behavior and secret motivations and the reverberations or consequences of conduct. All of this within an order that is not the order of reality, which is fundamentally chaotic. One possible order is that which literature imposes, an artificial, invented reality. There are other orders of course, all of which proceed from culture, religion, and which organize this protoplasmatic chaos that is reality. If in some way it did not reveal something that we identify through our own experience of life, it would be difficult for fiction to gain the approval of the reader.

Let's take a look at an interesting and very explicit example: Kafka. When Kafka writes his stories he has no intention of symbolically re-creating a set of social and historical problems. Absolutely not. He writes stories stemming from a very traumatic and anguished personal experience, stories that he perceives as fantastic, sometimes as pure irreality. He sees this pure irreality as a way of confronting his vital anguish. Kafka's immense prestige has to do with this anguished, absurd world that reflects the instability, insecurity, the orphaning of the individual faced with social forces beyond his control, forces that can destroy him for reasons he cannot fully understand. All of this renders a very graphic expression of a phenomenon that all of Europe and parts of the rest of the world experienced in the era of police states, of totalitarianism—more concretely: Nazism and the persecution and extermination of entire societies. Weighed against this experience, the world of Kafka suddenly takes on symbolic value, and the extraordinary premonitory force of a historic event that the world was to experience. Although it would be completely absurd to say that a novel like *The Metamorphosis* is written to denounce, premonitorily, what would become Nazism, without a doubt an experience like that of the concentration camps, of the Holocaust, does give *The Metamorphosis* tremendously persuasive symbolic value. This is true of all great literature, though it may not necessarily have a direct historical or sociological, moral or cultural or psychological bearing. If we did not identify some aspects of our own experience of reality which, until then, had been obscured, clouded to rational knowledge, literature would reveal itself as a pure game of the spirit, as the creation of a parallel but superfluous reality, and it would not have much validity. All great literature, as distant from historical experience as it may seem to us, is always rooted in lived experience, though that can only be expressed through the lie that is the fabrication of a fictional world.

LRS: In *The Real Life of Alejandro Mayta* the protagonist, as a writer, is carried along in an ambiguous flow of realistic information constantly repeating that what he is constructing is a "lie," a term that is in opposition to the truth. Does he distinguish between lie and falsehood, because it seems to me that he also uses the term *falsehood* in the framework of the interplay of author-character-fictitious reality. Is it this "added element" that differentiates lie from falsehood?

MVL: The theme of that novel, the least understood of all the ones I've written, is precisely the relationship between fiction and reality and between the distinct manifestations of fiction. In this novel there is a political and ideological fiction: that which Mayta experiences, and that experienced by the group of people who, believing they have seen a scientific description of historical reality in ideology, jump into this ludicrous adventure in which they fail. They act, guided by a fiction that is not literary. It is an ideological fiction. The person telling us the story is a narrator who has undertaken an investigation in order to determine all possibly reachable truth as to what occurred, so that he may use it to write a novel, a fiction, a lie, a false re-creation of that reality. What the novel tries to show are two manifestations of fiction: fiction that does not recognize itself as such, that has pretensions of being an objective reading of reality (ideological fiction, which appears very clearly in the novel as a consequence of frustration and violence), and fiction that does not have pretensions of being a scientific description of reality but rather, on the contrary, a visionary, subjective, "lying" re-elaboration of reality. What is surely bothersome is the use of a word that comes with negative religious and moral associations. Nevertheless, *lie* means something very concrete: contrary to truth. A lie is a false truth, it presents itself disguised as the truth. Literature is a lie that presents itself as such, it is a lie that does not pretend, as is the case of ideology, to be a truthful, objective description of reality. It is true that there are many writers who say, "In my novels I denounce a hidden, secret truth"; but what writers say is not as important as what they do. It may be that some really do describe the world as it is, but these are writers who have failed as creators of fiction. The writers who have been successful have not described the world as it is but rather the world as it is with some additions that revolutionize it, transform it, convert it into something very different, and that is what permits us to recognize its originality, a break not only with literary tradition but with the real world as it is.

LRS: And in *The Real Life of Alejandro Mayta,* where might one find the intersection between these two spheres: reality studied scientifically and reality . . . ?

MVL: . . . and reality as it is. Which is of almost infinite complexity because it does not have just one face but rather multiple faces. Even a very demarcated phenomenon can always be approached from another perspective. *The Real Life of Alejandro Mayta* is an attempt to recount, in its minimum expression, what would be a revolutionary movement: the group is very small and the action lasts only a few hours. It would seem that one could know everything about it, due to its minimal dimensions. Yet, this is not so. If one continues to unravel the ball of yarn, one discovers that it is almost infinite, there are psychological factors, social factors, economic, cultural, and geographical factors. Each one contributes a new element to the explanation, the determination of exactly what happened. Literature is a very special form of knowledge, charged with subjectivity and imagination. It is evident that it is not scientific knowledge, not the type the historian or the sociologist, much less the scientist could aspire to. Which does not keep fiction from profoundly impregnating other disciplines or sciences. I find this topic very fascinating. The realm of fiction is much broader than that of literature, the difference being that literature has no intention of deceiving anyone in that respect. Literature is fiction, it presents itself as fiction, and when one reads a novel one does not read it as one reads a biology or chemistry book, or a history or sociology book, because one is obliged to ask these books for something no novelist would accept: a type of photographic compliance with an exterior model. In the field of literature this is totally unacceptable.

LRS: Could you tell us a little about your interest in the historical novel and the historical vision originating from this type of novel? Would it be correct to say that the historical novels that you have written fully express your vision of history? Or is it more a question of a speculative construction as to the most extreme possibilities of a human being in Latin America? The work I have in mind is *The War of the End of the World* and its apocalyptic and atavistic vision. It would seem that prophets and their followers are destined always to engender violence, brutality, and a lack of communication. Also, some of your commentaries and writings on the historic course of Quechua speakers in Peru indicate that, in your view, they too have a destiny similar to the people of Canudos. Would it be correct to say that your historical novels can be read as archetypal commentaries on history?

MVL: I have not written novels in order to spread a conception of history; not in the least. *The War of the End of the World*, which is the most historical novel of those I have written—because it's based on a very precise historical fact, about which there is a lot of literature—and which broadly speaking, only broadly speaking, does follow what happened in Canudos, is not so much a novel to defend a theory of history but rather to show the fiction that theories of history can represent as well, when they have a strong ideological and political charge. That is what happened in Brazil with the republic, with the republicans and their attitude regarding the movement of the people of Canudos. What fascinated me about this story was seeing how political and ideological prejudices succeeded in blinding an entire country to such an extent to the meaning of the rebellion of Canudos, the intentions of the rebels, and the reality of the danger that Canudos represented to the republic.

LRS: Could you also call it intolerance?

MVL: But an intolerance totally conditioned by ideology. Many of the republicans were very generous and idealistic people who had fought for the republic because they very sincerely believed that the republic was going to bring justice, the development of Brazil, and that it was good for the poor. So they simply could not understand why the poor would rise up against something that would be beneficial to them. That is why this whole theory of conspiracy emerges, which is a fiction in the most novelistic sense of the word, stretching from England to the monarchists and the military linked to the Empire, which is assumed to be manipulating the strings of the rebellion in Canudos. The only thing that does not appear is reality; that is, the religious fear of these very primitive peasants, very indoctrinated by fanatical monks with respect to the idea of the republic, which was another fiction as well: a conspiracy of the Masons, agents of the Devil, to do away with Christianity, the true religion in Brazil. What fascinated me about the Canudos phenomenon was how these ideologies, which were totally impermeable to direct experience, managed to blind those two sectors of Brazilian society and bring them to the point of killing each other in that fashion. I was so fascinated by this because it was a phenomenon we were experiencing in many places in Latin America at that moment, those absolutely insurmountable divisions among social groups basically due to ideological and political fictions. The novel is not trying to say that this is history; what it is trying to communicate is that this is not a convincing theory as to what history or society is, nor is it the vision of the Yagunzos or of the Consejero as to what true religion is, which is also a very fictitious and imaginary vision, conditioned by all kinds of prejudices, resentments, rage. That is what fascinated me so much in the case of *The War of the End of the World*. But yes, one could say, in some sense, that it is a novel about the fiction in life, now not only in literature but in history and politics as well. The world of fiction is a protoplasmatic world, it is everywhere; it is in religion without a doubt, and I believe this because, evidently, man cannot live without fiction.

LRS: Is there any common ground, for example, with the Andes of your latest novel, *Death in the Andes?*

MVL: The phenomenon of the Shining Path is present because its members, the Senderistas, appear there. Yes, they represent that form of extreme intolerance, a unilateral division of history, reminiscent of a Jacobin, of a Moreira César in *The War of the End of the World*, and in some way, of a Consejero. But in *The War of the End of the World* there is something more that is not ideological and not at all political, which is a mythology, a religious vision of the atavistic reality that has survived Westernization and the Christian presence and that is somehow expressed in the old Hellenic mythology; that is why I have also re-created this in the case of Dionysus, the world of the Pishtacos, and the world of Andean mythology. This has to do with structures that seem to me to be more permanent than historical or sociological structures. Mythology also has an order that fictitiously imposes itself on the world; myths are literary explanations of the incomprehensible, of that which proves incomprehensible in reality, in nature, and in the human condition. Myths are not gratuitous, they are fictions that, like great novels and great poems, a community recognizes and makes their own, because in some way they resolve a doubt, they appease some kind of spiritual need. That is what I was interested in showing in that novel: how certain myths are perennial, are always there because evidently the types of questions that brought them about have not been completely resolved (they are questions that reappear under certain circumstances); and also how the idea of modernity and progress is such a precarious idea; and how beneath all this lies an atavistic force belonging to a certain tradition that is not easily uprooted. In the event of any collective crisis or insecurity, it erupts with great force and violence. The story of Lituma had been going back and forth in my head for quite some time, but the actual characteristics of the novel were born of the impression that the news of the invasion of Pishtacos in Ayacucho left upon me a few years ago. It provoked a huge commotion in the shantytowns, in the poorest slums of Ayacucho, where the rumor of an invasion of Pishtacos—that hundreds, thousands of Pishtacos were arriving to wrench the body fat off the people to pay the external debt, to export it abroad, so that the government would turn it over to the United States—provoked a phenomena of mass hysteria and even lynchings. Evidently, this was coming from the sediment that had been stirred about and brought up to date, due, of course, to the very particular political and economic circumstances that the region was experiencing. This struck a vein with me that eventually resulted in *Death in the Andes.*

LRS: You have always been very interested in the work of Arguedas, despite some of your concerns regarding his style. You are the two most distinguished Peruvian novelists of this century. What comparison would you make with regard to the issue of style in each of your cases? And as to the form in which you deal with indigenous characters in the novel? You are currently writing a book on Arguedas; on what specific level does Arguedas continue to interest you after so many years?

MVL: I have always had, since I was very young, since the first time I read him, a strong interest in the work of Arguedas, for many reasons. First of all, because his work seems to me to be very rich, very creative, and also because I believe that the world of Arguedas is a world created from a set of problems that any Peruvian writer, so as not to say any Peruvian, has experienced directly (or indirectly) as a central part of his life, because Peru's major problems are the point of departure in Arguedas's work. His case is exceptional because he experienced those problems in his own life: the problem of two cultures; the problem of societies living together without communication under immense tension and violence; the problem of the Indians; the problem of bilingualism; the problem of societies living at different historical levels; the problem of possibilities for the integration of a society with these characteristics; and the problem of the type of literature that could emerge therein. Arguedas took all of this personally, as his own problem. He resolved this creatively in his best moments, in his best books, like *Yawar Fiesta* or *Los ríos profundos*. In the books in which he is not as original nor as creative, even in the books in which it could be said that he failed, he always left a powerful dramatic testimony of enormous authenticity, dealing with the type of conflict in which the literary, the historical, and the cultural all meet. Also, I have always been interested in that process in Arguedas by which traumatic personal experience, the "demons," are raw material for a writer. And how they are used to create a world of fiction. The world of Arguedas is a world of fiction, especially in its better moments, the most creative ones, precisely in the sense of being not a description but an invention of a reality—a reality that he invented based upon a very genuine experience that does not reflect reality as it is, but rather, a reality that has passed through the very delicate, sensitive, and very wounded sieve of a person like Arguedas. That is what interests me about Arguedas, how a person so committed to the idea of justice, to restoring the rights of the peasant, of the Peruvian of the Andes, did, at the moment of creating literature, exactly what good literature does: he invented a world, he did not reflect it, he dismantled it and reassembled it in a very persuasive way, in an absolutely subjective and personal manner. Also, Arguedas is writing within the tradition of the indigenist, regionalist literature which at times conditioned him but which, in some of his better moments, he interrupted. With Arguedas, in some way, indigenism disappeared, despite the indigenist writers who would follow. He creates a kind of literature that puts an end to the characteristics of indigenist literature. The literature of Arguedas is concerned with Andean problems; there are peasants, there are Indians, but it is not indigenist literature.

LRS: In your words, the narrator of *Les Miserables* "judges, excommunicates." In that same article you say "whoever judges and condemns does not listen, he listens only to himself, there is no dialogue, only monologue." Who is the narrator of *A Fish in the Water*? Is he too engaged in a monologue? Is this narrator the most ambiguous, paraphrasing your words, of the characters that Mario Vargas Llosa, the author, creates in the "novel of his life"?

MVL: *A Fish in the Water* is not a novel, it is not fiction; it is an autobiography, it is a book of memoirs. An incomplete autobiography since it covers only two periods of my life. It contains no type of fictitious, literary re-elaboration of reality. It is a document of lived experiences in which there are, of course, very explicit, surely controversial, opinions expressed. In this book there is no fiction, or if there is fiction, it is involuntary fiction, in spite of myself. It is a book in which I wanted to tell what happened and not to use what happened as I do when I write novels: as raw material that I can magnify, add to, or eliminate with complete liberty. The testimony in *A Fish in the Water* is a reliable, truthful testimony, it is not a fictitious testimony.

LRS: Nevertheless, there is a scene in which you reproduce a conversation with your wife about the motives that led you to run for president. At one point you say something to the effect of: well, it is possible that things are not as I present them but rather what I wanted was to create the novel of my life. There are a couple of similar affirmations where you seem to be weighing the possibility of fiction and that of reality.

MVL: One can be truthful and reliable with respect to one's acts. With respect to one's deep-seated motivations, there is always a margin of subjectivity, of error. One thinks one knows oneself, but one only knows oneself based on reason, and we know there is a nonrational part of the human personality that, from that shadow the conscious cannot reach, is always exerting pressure, pushing, inducing, in such a way that we cannot know the most secret motivations behind our acts. It was an act of honesty on my part, an ethical necessity, to say that my wife does not entirely share the reasons I believe to be the ones that induced me to present my candidacy in the elections in Peru. She believes there is also a secret, maybe unconscious, literary reason: the ambition to live a great novel in real life. I don't know, but clearly it is not what I believe led me to be a candidate in Peru.

LRS: Would this be applicable to the motivations behind writing *A Fish in the Water*?

MVL: No, absolutely not. I am basically a writer, and, naturally, a writer is only able to fully understand his experience insofar as he writes about it. I would not say "insofar as he invents it," but yes, insofar as he writes about it. It was important for me to leave this testimony precisely because of the proliferation of lies that accompanied all of my political activities in Peru. At least this way my own testimony on the matter will be on record. I always knew the book would be controversial, but it was also a way to close the file on this experience. Once written—this happens to everyone who writes—this experience somehow distances itself, and one somehow brings it to a close and finishes it off. It is like what happens when one writes a novel, there is always an uneasiness, a restlessness, rooted in those particular experiences that lead one to write a novel. Once the novel is finished, a sort of cathartic effect has been produced; the novelist has expelled that inner "demon." I can say that with A *Fish in the Water*, I expelled the demon of politics, at least of Peruvian politics.

Translated by Luis Rebaza-Soraluz and Larisa Chaddick

The Trumpet of Deyá

Mario Vargas Llosa

for Aurora Bernárdez

That Sunday in 1984, I had just set myself up in my study to write an article when the telephone rang. I did something that even then I never did: I picked up the receiver. "Julio Cortázar has died;" the voice of the journalist commanded: "Dictate to me your comment."

I thought of a verse from Vallejo—"Stupid as a Spaniard"—and, babbling, I obeyed him. But that Sunday, instead of writing the article, I kept leafing through and rereading some of Cortázar's stories and pages from his novels that my memory had preserved so vividly. It had been some time since I had heard anything about him. I suspected neither his prolonged illness nor his painful agony. But it made me happy to know that Aurora had been at his side during those last months and that, thanks to her, he had a sober burial, without the foreseeable clowning of the revolutionary ravens who had taken such advantage of him in his last years.

I had met both of them some forty years ago at the house of a mutual friend in Paris. Since then—until the last time I saw them together, in Greece in 1967, where the three of us worked as translators at an international conference on cotton—I had never stopped marveling at the spectacle of seeing and hearing Aurora and Julio converse in tandem. The rest of us seemed to be superfluous. Everything they said was intelligent, learned, amusing, vital. Many times I thought, "They can't always be like this. They must rehearse those conversations at home in order to dazzle interlocutors with unusual anecdotes, brilliant quotations, and those jokes that, at the opportune moment, burst the intellectual climate."

They tossed subjects from one to the other like two accomplished jugglers. With them, one was never ever bored. I admired and envied that couple's perfect complicity, the secret intelligence that seemed to unite them. I admired, equally, their sympathy, their engagement with literature (which gave the impression of being exclusive and total), and their generosity toward everyone, above all, to apprentices like me.

It was difficult to determine who had read more or better or which of the two said more acute and unexpected things about books and authors. That Julio wrote and Aurora only translated (in her case this *only* means completely the opposite of what it seems) is something that I always supposed was provisional, a passing sacrifice by Aurora so that, in the family, there would be at that moment no more than one writer. Now that I see her again, after so many years, I have bitten my tongue the two or three times I was at the point of asking if she had written much, if she had finally decided to publish. Except for her gray hair, she looks the same: small, petite, with those big blue eyes full of intelligence and the old overwhelming vitality. She climbs up and down the Mallorcan rocks of Deyá with an agility that always leaves me behind with palpitations. She too, in her own way, displays that Cortazarian virtue par excellence: to be a Dorian Gray.

That night at the end of 1958, I sat with a very tall and thin beardless boy who had very short hair and big hands that moved as he spoke. He had already published a small book of tales and was about to re-edit a second compilation for a small series in Mexico directed by Juan José Arreola. I was about to bring out a book of stories too, and we exchanged experiences and projects like two youngsters "who set sail under literary arms." Only upon saying good night did I become aware—stunned—that this was the author of *Bestiario* (Bestiary) and so many texts that I read in Borges and Victoria Ocampo's journal *Sur*, as well as the admirable translator of the complete works of Poe that I had devoured in the two opulent volumes published by the University of Puerto Rico. He seemed to me a contemporary when, in reality, he was twenty-two years older than I.

During the sixties and, especially, the seven years that I lived in Paris, he was one of my best friends and also something like my model and my mentor. I gave him the manuscript of my first novel to read and awaited his verdict with the expectancy of a catechumen. And when I received his letter—generous, with approval and advice—I felt happy. I believe that for a long time I was accustomed to writing presupposing his vigilance, his encouraging or critical eyes over my shoulder. I admired his life, his rituals, his caprices, and his customs as much as the ease and clarity of his prose and that everyday, domestic, and cheerful appearance that he gave the fantastic subjects in his stories and novels. Each time that he and Aurora called to invite me for dinner—first at the small apartment bordering on the Rue de Sèvres, and later at the little house spiraling from the Rue du Général Bouret—it was fiesta and felicity. I was fascinated by his board of unusual news clippings and improbable objects that were picked up or fabricated. I was intrigued by "the room of toys": the mysterious place that existed in their house in which, according to legend, Julio would lock himself up to play the trumpet and enjoy himself like a kid. He knew a secret and magical Paris that did not show up in any guidebook and from which I left loaded with treasures after each encounter with him: films to see, exhibitions to visit, nooks in which to forage, poets to discover, and even a congress of witches at the Mutualité that bored me exceedingly but that he evoked afterward, marvelously, as a jocular apocalypse.

With this Julio Cortázar it was possible to be a friend but impossible to become intimate. The distance that he knew how to impose, thanks to a system of courtesies and rules to which one had to submit to conserve his friendship, was one of his enchantments. It enveloped him with a certain aura of mystery. It gave to his life a secret dimension that seemed to be the source of that restless depth—irrational and violent—that transpires at times in his texts, even the most ragamuffin and cheerful. He was an eminently private man with an interior world constructed and preserved like a work of art to which probably only Aurora had access, and for whom nothing, outside of literature, seemed to matter or, maybe, exist.

This does not mean that he was bookish, erudite, and intellectual in the manner of a Borges, for example, who with all justice wrote: "Many things I have read and few have I lived." In Julio literature seemed to dissolve itself into daily experience and impregnate all of life, animating it and enriching it with a particular brilliance without depriving it of sap, of instinct, of spontaneity. Probably no other writer lent to play the literary dignity that Cortázar did, nor made of play an instrument of artistic creation and exploration so ductile and beneficial. But saying this in such a serious way alters the truth because Julio did not play in order to make literature. For him, to write was to play, to enjoy oneself, to organize life—words, ideas—with the arbitrariness, the liberty, the imagination, and the irresponsibility of children or the insane. But playing in this way, Cortázar's work opened unpublished doors. It arrived to show some unknown depths of the human condition and to graze the transcendent, something that surely never had been intended. It is no accident (or, if it is, it is in that sense of the accidental that he described in *62: A Model Kit*) that the most ambitious of his novels would take as its title *Hopscotch*, a children's game.

Like the novel, like theater, the game is a form of fiction: an artificial order imposed on the world, a representation of something illusory that replaces life. It distracts us from ourselves, serving us in forgetting the true reality and living—while the substitution lasts—a life apart from strict rules created by ourselves. Distraction, enjoyment, fabulation—the game is also a magic resource for exorcising the atavistic fear of humans toward the secret anarchy of the world, the enigma of our origin, condition, and destiny. Johan Huizinga, in his celebrated book *Homo Ludens*, maintained that play is the spine of civilization and that society evolved up to modernity ludically, constructing its institutions, systems, practices, and creeds starting from those elemental forms of ceremony and ritual that characterize the games of children.

In the world of Cortázar the game recovers this lost virtuality of serious activity that adults use to escape insecurity, to avoid panic before an incomprehensible and absurd world full of dangers. It is true that his characters enjoy themselves playing, but many times it has to do with dangerous diversions that will leave them not only forgotten passengers of their circumstances but also with some outrageous knowledge or alienation or death.

In other cases the Cortazarian game is a refuge for sensibility and imagination, the way in which delicate, ingenuous beings defend themselves against social steamrollers or, as he wrote in the most mischievous of his books, *Cronopios and Famas*, "to struggle against pragmatism and the horrible tendency toward the attainment of useful ends." His games are pleas against the prefabricated, against ideas frozen by use and abuse, prejudices, and, above all, against solemnity, the black beast for Cortázar when he criticized the culture and idiosyncrasies of his country.

But I talk of "the" game and, in truth, I should use the plural. In the books of Cortázar the author plays, the narrator plays, the characters play, and the reader plays, obligated to do so by the devilish traps that lie in wait around the corner of the least expected page. And there is no doubt that it is enormously liberating and refreshing to find oneself suddenly, without knowing how, parodying statues, rescuing words from the cemetery of academic dictionaries to resuscitate them with puffs of humor, or jumping between the heaven and hell of hopscotch—all due to Cortázar's sleight of hand.

The effect of *Hopscotch* was seismic in the Spanish-speaking world when it appeared in 1963. It rocked to the foundations the convictions and prejudices that writers and readers had about the means and ends of the art of narration, and it extended the frontiers of the genre to unthinkable limits. Thanks to *Hopscotch*, we learned that to read was a brilliant way of enjoying oneself, that it was possible to explore the secrets of the world and of language while having fun. And we learned that playing, one could probe mysterious layers of life forbidden to rational knowledge, to logical intelligence, abysses of experience over which no one can lean out without grave risks like death or insanity. In *Hopscotch* reason and unreason, sleep and vigil, objectivity and subjectivity, history and fantasy all lose their exclusive condition. Their frontiers are eclipsed. They stop being antonyms in order to become fused. In that way certain privileged beings, like la Maga and Oliveira, and the celebrated "madmen" of his future books, could flow freely. (Like many couples reading *Hopscotch* in the sixties, Patricia and I also began to speak in "gliglish," to invent a private lingo and to translate to its snapping, esoteric terms our tender secrets.)

Together with the notion of play, that of freedom is indispensable when one speaks of *Hopscotch* and all the fictions of Cortázar. Freedom to break the established norms of writing and structuring narrative, to replace the conventional order of the narrative by a buried order that has the semblance of disorder, to revolutionize narrative point of view, narrative time, the psychology of the characters, the spatial organization of the story, and its logical sequence. The tremendous insecurity that, as the novel proceeds, comes to take possession of Horacio Oliveira in confronting the world (and confining him more and more in an imagined shelter), accompanies the reader of *Hopscotch* as he enters this labyrinth and lets himself be led astray by the Machiavellian narrator in the twists and turns and ramifications of anecdote. Nothing there is reconcilable and sure: not the direction nor the meanings nor the symbols nor the ground that one treads on. What are they telling me? Why don't I just understand it? Are we dealing with something so mysterious and complex that it is beyond our apprehension? Or is it a monumental pulling of our leg? We are dealing with both. In *Hopscotch* and in many Cortázar stories, the mockery, the joke, and the illusionism of the salon are often present, like the little animal figures that certain virtuosos conjure up with their hands or the coins that disappear between the fingers and reappear in the ears or the nose. But often, too—like in those famous absurd episodes of *Hopscotch* that star the pianist Bertha Trépat, in Paris, and the one with the plank over the emptiness on which Talita balances, in Buenos Aires—these episodes subtly transmute themselves into a descent to the cellars of behavior, to its remote irrational sources, to an immutable essence—magic, barbarous, ceremonial—of the human experience that underlies rational civilization and, under certain circumstances, rises up to disturb it. (This is the theme of some of Cortázar's best stories, like "The Idol of the Cyclades" and "The Night Face Up," in which we suddenly see a remote and ferocious past of bloody gods that must be satiated with human victims bursting into the womb of modern life and without a continuous solution.)

Hopscotch stimulated formal audacities in the new Hispano-American writers like few books before or after, but it would be unjust to call it an experimental novel. This qualification emits an abstract and pretentious odor. It suggests a world of test tubes, retorts, and blackboards with algebraic calculations, something disembodied, dissociated from immediate life, from desire and pleasure. *Hopscotch* overflows life from all its pores. It is an explosion of freshness and movement, of youthful exaltation and irreverence, a resonant loud laugh in front of those writers who, as Cortázar used to say, put on their collar and necktie in order to write. He always wrote in shirt sleeves, with the informality and happiness with which one sits at the table to enjoy a home-cooked meal or listens to a favorite record in the intimacy of one's room. *Hopscotch* taught us that laughter was not the enemy of seriousness nor of those illusory and ridiculous things that can nestle in experimental zeal when it is taken too seriously. In the same way that the Marquis de Sade exhausted beforehand all of the possible excesses of sexual cruelty, *Hopscotch* constituted a fortunate apotheosis of the formal game to the extent that any "experimental" novel would be born old and repetitive. For this reason, Cortázar, like Borges, has had uncountable imitators, but not one disciple.

To un-write the novel, to destroy literature, to break the habits of the "lady reader," to un-adorn words, to write badly, etc.—all that on which Morelli of *Hopscotch* insists so much—are metaphors of something very simple: literature asphyxiates itself with an excess of convention and seriousness. It is necessary to purge it of rhetoric and of commonplaces, to endow it again with novelty, grace, insolence, freedom. Cortázar's style has all of this, above all when it distances itself from the pompous miracle-working prosopopeia with which his alter ego Morelli pontificates about literature, that is to say in his stories. Those, generally, are more diaphanous and creative than his novels, although they do not display the showy rocketry that surrounds those last ones like a halo.

Cortázar's stories are no less ambitious or iconoclastic than his longer texts. But what is original and groundbreaking in the latter is usually more metabolized in the stories, rarely exhibiting in them the immodest virtuousity of *Hopscotch, 62: A Model Kit,* and *A Manual for Manuel,* where the reader has at times the sensation of being subjected to certain tests of intellectual efficiency. Those novels are revolutionary manifestos, but Cortázar's true revolution lies in his stories. It is more discreet but more profound and permanent because it aroused the very nature of fiction, its indissoluble heart that is the form-depth, means-ends, and art-technique that fiction becomes in the hands of the most successful creators. In his stories Cortázar did not experiment: he found, he discovered, he created something permanent.

In the same way, just as the label *experimental* writer falls short, it would be insufficient to call him a writer of the fantastic, although, without a doubt, if we were to give labels, he would have preferred the latter. Julio loved the literature of the fantastic and knew it like the back of his hand. He wrote some marvelous stories of that sort in which extraordinary events occur, like the impossible change of a man into a little aquatic beast in the small masterpiece "Axolotl"; or the somersault, thanks to intensifying enthusiasm, of a trivial concert into an immoderate massacre in which the feverish public jumps onto the stage to devour the conductor and the musicians in "Las Ménades" (The Maenads). But he also wrote illustrious stories of more orthodox realism: like that marvel "Little Bull," the story of a boxer's decadence, told by himself, that is, in truth, the story of his way of speaking, a linguistic feast of grace, musicality, and humor, and the invention of a style with the flavor of the neighborhood, of the idiosyncrasies and mythology of the people; or like "The Pursuer," which is narrated from a subtle preterit perfect that dissolves into the present of the reader, subliminally evoking in this way the gradual dissolution of Johnny, the brilliant jazzman whose deluded search for the absolute by way of the trumpet arrives to us by means of the "realist" reduction (rational and pragmatic) carried out by a critic and Johnny's biographer, the narrator Bruno.

In reality Cortázar was a writer of realism and the fantastic at the same time. The world that he invented is unmistakable precisely because of that strange symbiosis that Roger Caillois considered necessary for the right to be called the fantastic. In his prologue to the anthology of literature of the fantastic that he prepared, Caillois maintained that the art of the truly fantastic is not born out of the deliberation of its creator but escapes between his intentions through the work of chance or of more mysterious forces. In the same way, he goes on, the fantastic does not come out of a technique, nor is it a literary image, but rather it is the imponderable—a reality that without premeditation suddenly happens in a literary text. From a long and impassioned conversation in a bistro in Montparnasse about Caillois's thesis, I remember Julio's enthusiasm for it and his surprise when I assured him that that theory seemed to me to fit what occurred in his fictions like a glove.

In the Cortazarian world banal reality begins insensibly to crack and to give in to some hidden pressures that push it up to the prodigious without participating fully in it, maintaining it as a sort of intermediary, tense, and disconcerting territory in which the real and the fantastic overlap without integrating. This is the world of "Blow-Up," of "Cartas de mamá" (Letters from Mama), of "Secret Weapons," of "La puerta condenada" (The Blocked-Off Door), and of so many other stories of ambiguous solution that can be equally interpreted as realistic or fantastic since the extraordinary in them is, perhaps, a fantasy of the characters or, perhaps, a miracle.

This is the famous ambiguity that characterizes certain classics of fantastic literature, exemplified in Henry James's *The Turn of the Screw*: a delicate story that the master of the uncertain managed to tell in such a way that there would be no possibility of knowing if the fantastic that occurs in the story—the appearance of ghosts—really occurs or is the hallucination of a character. What differentiates Cortázar from a James, from a Poe, from a Borges, or from a Kafka is not the ambiguity or the intellectualism—which are propensities as frequent in him as in them—but that in Cortázar's fictions the most elaborate and learned stories never die and transfer themselves to the abstract. They continue rooted in the daily reality, the concrete. They have the vitality of a soccer match or a barbecue. The surrealists invented the expression "the daily marvelous" for that poetic reality—mysterious, loosened from contingency and scientific laws—that the poet can perceive underneath appearances by way of dreaming or delirium. This marvelous reality generates books like Aragon's *Paris Peasant* or Breton's *Nadja*. But I believe that no other writer of our time fits this definition as well as Cortázar: a seer who detected the unusual in the usual, the absurd in the logical, the exception in the rule, and the prodigious in the banal. Nobody dignified so literally the foreseeable, the conventional, the pedestrian of human life than he, who, with the juggling of his pen, denoted a hidden tenderness or exhibited an immoderate face, sublime and horrifying—to the extent that, passed by his hands, instructions for winding a watch or ascending a staircase could be, at the same time, anguished prose poems and laughter-inducing pseudometaphysical texts.

Style is the explanation of that alchemy in Cortázar's fictions that fuses the most unreal fantasy with the merry life of the body and of the street, the unconditionally free life of the imagination with the restricted life of the body and of history. His is a style that marvelously feigns orality, the fluent ease of common speech, spontaneous expression, with neither the makeup nor the impudence of the common man. We are dealing with an illusion, because, in reality, the common man expresses himself with complications, repetitions, and confusions that wouldn't work if translated to writing. The language of Cortázar is also an exquisitely fabricated fiction, an artifice so effective that it seems natural, like talk reproduced from life that flows to the reader directly from the mouths and animated tongues of men and women of flesh and blood. It is a language so transparent and even that it blends with that which it names—the situations, the things, the being, the landscapes, the thoughts—to show it better, like a discreet glow that illuminates from within their authenticity and truth. Cortázar's fictions owe their powerful verisimilitude to this style. It is the breath of humanity that beats in all of them, even in the most intricate. The functionality of his style is such that the best texts of Cortázar seem *spoken*.

Nevertheless, this stylistic clarity often deceives us, making us believe that the content of these stories is also diaphanous, a world without shadows. We are dealing with more skilled sleight of hand because, in truth, that world is charged with violence. Suffering, anguish, and fear relentlessly pursue its inhabitants, those who often take refuge (like Horacio Oliveira) in madness or something that appears much like it to escape what is unbearable in their condition. Ever since *Hopscotch*, the mad have occupied a central place in Cortázar's work. But madness begins to appear in it in a deceptive way, without the accustomed reverberations of threat or tragedy. It is more like a cheerful, even tender, impudence, the mani-festation of the essential absurdity that nestles in the world behind its masks of rationality and good sense. Cortázar's madmen are most affectionate and almost always benign, obsessive beings with disconcerting linguistic, literary, social, political, or ethical projects to—like Ceferino Pérez—reorder and reclassify existence according to delirious nomenclatures. Between the chinks of their extravagances, they always leave a glimpse of something that redeems and justifies: a dissatisfaction with the given, a confused search for another life, more unforeseeable and poetic (at times nightmarish) than that in which we are confined. Sometimes children, sometimes dreamers, sometimes jokers, sometimes actors, Cortázar's madmen radiate a defenselessness and a fortune of moral integrity that, while awakening an inexplicable solidarity on our part, also makes us feel accused.

Play, madness, poetry, humor—all become allied like alchemic mixtures in those miscellanies (*Around the Day in Eighty Worlds*, *Ultimo Round* [Last Round], and the testimony of that absurd final pilgrimage on a French highway, *Los autonautas de la cosmopista* [Autonauts of the Cosmopike]) where he overturned his inclinations, manias, obsessions, sympathies, and phobias with a happy adolescent brashness. These three books are other poles of a spiritual autobiography, and they seem to mark a continuity in his life and work, in his manner of conceiving and practicing literature as a permanent impudence, a jocular irreverence. But we are also dealing with a mirage because, at the end of the sixties, Cortázar underwent one of those transformations that, as he would say, "occur only in literature." In this, too, Julio was an unpredictable "cronopio."

Cortázar's change (the most extraordinary that I have seen in any being and a mutation that it occurred to me often to compare with that of the narrator of "Axolotl") took place, according to the official version—which he himself consecrated—in France of May 1968. He was seen in those tumultuous days on the barricades of Paris, distributing pamphlets of his own invention, mixing with the students who wanted to elevate "imagination to power." He was fifty-four years old; the sixteen that remained of his life would be as a writer engaged with socialism: the defender of Cuba and Nicaragua, the signer of manifestos, and the habitué of revolutionary congresses right up to his death.

In his case, unlike so many of our colleagues who opted for a similar militancy but due rather to snobbism or opportunism (a modus vivendi and a manner of social climbing in the intellectual establishment that was, and in a certain form continues to be, a monopoly of the left in the Spanish-speaking world), the change was genuine. It was dictated more by ethics than by ideology (to which he continued to be allergic) and by a total coherence. His life was organized around it and it became public, almost promiscuous, and a good part of his work was devoted to circumstance and current events. This work even seemed written by another person, very distinct from the man who, previously, perceived politics with ironic disdain, as something distant. (I remember the time I wanted him to meet Juan Goytisolo: "I abstain," he joked, "he's too political for me.") In this second stage of his life (as in the first, although in a distinct manner) he gave more than he received. Although I believe he was often mistaken—as when he said that all the crimes of Stalinism were a mere "accident de parcours" of communism—even in those equivocations there was such manifest innocence and ingenuousness that it was difficult to lose respect for him. I never lost it, nor the affection and friendship that, although at a distance, survived all our political differences.

But Julio's change was much more profound and encompassing than that of political action. I am sure that it began a year before the events of '68, when he separated from Aurora. In 1967, as I already said, the three of us were in Greece working together as translators. We passed the mornings and the afternoons seated at the same table in the conference hall of the Hilton and the nights in the restaurants of Plaka, at the foot of the Acropolis, where we went invariably to dine. Together we passed through museums, Orthodox churches, temples, and, one weekend, we visited the tiny island of Hydra. When I returned to London, I told Patricia, "The perfect couple exists. Aurora and Julio have learned how to realize that miracle: a happy marriage." A few days later, I received a letter from Julio announcing his separation. I don't think I have ever felt so misled.

The next time I returned to see him, in London with his new partner, he was another person. He had let his hair grow, and he had a reddish and imposing beard like a biblical prophet. He made me take him to buy erotic magazines, and he spoke of marijuana, women, and revolution as he had spoken of jazz and ghosts before. There was always this warm sympathy in him, that total lack of pretension or of the poses that almost inevitably become unbearable in successful writers when they hit fifty. I should add that he had returned more fresh and youthful, but it was hard to relate him to the man I once knew. Every time that I saw him afterward—in Barcelona, in Cuba, in London, or in Paris, in congresses or roundtables, in social or conspiratorial meetings—I remained each time more perplexed than the time before: Was it him? Was it Julio Cortázar? Of course it was him, but this Julio was like the caterpillar that becomes a butterfly or the fakir of the story who after dreaming with maharajas opened his eyes and was seated on a throne surrounded by courtesans who paid him homage.

This other Julio Cortázar, it seems to me, was less personal and creative as a writer than the earlier one. But I have the suspicion that, to compensate, he had a more intense life and, because of this, was happier than the one before in that, as he wrote, existence transformed itself for him into a book. At least, every time I saw him, he seemed to me young, excitable, game.

If anybody knows, it would be Aurora, of course. I am not so impertinent as to ask her about it. Nor do we speak much of Julio, in those warm days of summer at Deyá. Yet he is always there, behind all the conversations, taking the counterpoint with the dexterity of that time. The cottage, half-hidden among the olive trees, the cypresses, the bougainvilleas, the lemon trees, and the hortensias, exhibits the order and mental cleanliness of Aurora, naturally. It is an immense pleasure to feel, on the small terrace next to the ravine, the decadence of the day, the breeze of nightfall, and to see the sliver of moon appear at the crest of the hill. From time to time, I hear a discordant trumpet. There isn't anybody around. The sound comes, then, from this poster in the rear of the living room where a lanky and beardless boy with a military haircut and a short-sleeve shirt—the Julio Cortázar that I knew—plays his favorite game.

Translated by Dane Johnson

A Bullfight in the Andes

Mario Vargas Llosa

Critics who praise José María Arguedas's first novel share the assumption that there is an essential correspondence between a work of fiction and the reality it "describes," that a novel is successful to the extent that it faithfully represents its model; and so they underscore the similarities between this story's bloody fiesta and life in the Andes. I assume the opposite: that there is an incompatibility between reality and fiction that separates truth from lies (and a hidden complicity that ties them together, since one cannot exist without the other). A novel results from a *rejection* of a real "model," and its ambition is to attain sovereignty, an autonomous life, distinct from whatever appears to inspire it and whatever it pretends to describe. Thus the genuineness of fiction is not that which brings it closer to but rather that which distances it from lived experience: the substitute life it invents—not the reflection of some detached and prior experience but the dream, myth, fantasy, or fable its power of persuasion and verbal magic render as reality. And it is in precisely this sense that *Yawar Fiesta* succeeds as fiction.

In July of 1935 Arguedas became interested in the idea of an Indian bullfight that would function as the center of a conflict facing the social classes and races of an Andean community. Finding himself on vacation in Puquio, he attended a bullfight like the one described in *Yawar Fiesta*. That day, one of the amateur Indian bullfighters—nicknamed "el Honrao" (your Honor), like the character in the novel—was torn to pieces by the bull.[1] Then, in 1937 a work entitled "El despojo" (The Dispossession)— which would figure in the book's second chapter—appeared in Lima. And that same year, the story "Yawar (Fiesta)," a rudimentary version of the book, written a year earlier, appeared in the *Revista Americana de Buenos Aires*.[2] Arguedas's subsequent plan to revise and amplify this tale was interrupted by the year he spent in jail as a political prisoner. He was unable to execute it until the second half of 1940 in Cuzco's province of Sicuani. Recently married to Celia Bustamante Vernal, he had moved there in March of 1939 and served as professor of Spanish and Geography at the Mateo Pumacahua National Men's College until October of 1941. It was after a trip to Mexico in 1940, to attend the Indigenist Congress of Patzcuaro, that Arguedas took advantage of some midterm vacation time and wrote the novel, almost all of it without interruption. As he worked, he sent chapters to the poet Manuel Moreno Jiménez in Lima. The correspondence between the two friends during those months, published by Roland Forgues, minutely documents Arguedas's work on this, his first novel, which, though based on personal experience, as was everything he wrote (as is everything novelists write), was more an act of invention than of memory, a depersonalization of experience that, thanks to fantasy and language, functions to create a fictive world.[3] And in this novel, even more than in the stories of *Agua*, his first book, Arguedas succeeds in creating that axis and infrastructure of all fiction: the narrator.

The Versatile Narrator

The main (though almost always invisible) character of this intense and beautiful novel is not its *mistis* (whites or near whites, the privileged class), nor its *chalos* (*cholos*: *mestizos* or Westernized native peoples), nor its Indians—those collective protagonists who seem to act in unison as though following choreography. Nor is it the pale individual figures who emerge from those collective placentas—the *mestizo* Don Pancho Jiménez, the landowner Don Pascual Aranguena, the subprefect from the coast, the sergeant from Arequipa, nor even Misitu, the bull positioned halfway between the reality of the bullfight and the mythology of the Andes, with vague reminders of the Minotaur. Instead it is the one who either emphasizes or elides them, astutely and skillfully displacing himself from them, recounting some of the things they say and silencing others. He can go back in time to illuminate deeds and events that throw light on the present (the regional mining crisis that brought so many white settlers to Puquio and the agrarian extortion that victimized the native communities and imposed the socioeconomic structure that manifests itself as events unfold in some undesignated year during the thirties). He travels through space, from the Andes to the poor districts of Lima where the *lucaninos* (emigrants from Lucanas province) live. He moves endlessly among the worlds of the whites, the *mestizos*, and the *comuneros* (members of Indian communes), peasants or police, Quechua- or Spanish-speaking, highlanders or coast-dwellers, coming and going between Christianity and animism, reason and magic, with a freedom and ease that no one but he enjoys in this rigidly hierarchical society where, according to his testimony, each and every person is confined to live within his social group, his race, his rites, his beliefs, and his moment in history as though behind bars.[4]

The narrator is the most important character in fiction, whether an omniscient being, external to history—the self-worshiping God the Father of classic romantic tales or the discreet, invisible one of modern works—or an implied narrator, witness to or protagonist of that which he narrates. He is the first character an author must invent to represent him in the made-up story. This is so because his movements, his mannerisms and silences, his perspectives and points of view determine whether what he talks about appears to be true or unconvincing, an illusion that imposes itself as reality or one that stands out as mere artifice. The narrator of *Yawar Fiesta* faces an immense task, because, although he tells a brief story, really a long tale more than a novel, the world he refers to is divided into radically different ethnic groups, into cultures bent on destroying themselves, societies separated by gulfs of hatred and incomprehension. Nevertheless, thanks to his versatility and resourcefulness, he manages to fulfill his narrative assignment, presenting this world as an indivisible though heartbreaking totality.

Who and what is this narrator? There is no doubt that he is a male and from the highlands (because he regards people from the coast as "them" and people from the mountains as "us"), either white or *mestizo*, who feels a psychic closeness to the Indians. He has a deep internal knowledge of them and shares their hardships, fears, and beliefs. He is omniscient and speaks in the present but shifts tenses in order to tell of the whites' arrival in Puquio three centuries earlier, when they laid waste to the surrounding mines, or to recall the Indians' voluntary work on the construction of the Puquio-Nazca road some years before that bullfight that is the central occurrence in the novel, or to evoke the waves of migration of Andean peasants toward the cities of the coast, which that road and others like it made possible.

From time to time he draws near to the mouths of the *mistis*, the *chalos*, the Indians; and by means of a few phrases—an exclamation, a song, an exchange of insults, a speech—he allows them a word, but then quickly takes back control of the story. He has a very sharp visual sense and his observations on the nature of this corner of the Andes—the province of Lucanas, the town of Puquio—are vivid, delicate, and poetic. He is bilingual and when describing the landscape (the rivers, the valleys, the trees, the fields, the mountains) expresses himself in a neutral, elegant, pure Spanish that afterward, as it comes in contact with his characters, becomes *mestizo*-like: peppered with Quechua words or hispanized quechuanisms and colored by the phonetic transcription of the distortions of popular speech.

He has a musical spirit, a superior calling for songs and dances, human activities that he privileges, assigning them a principal role in social life and adorning them with a sacred religious air. He is endowed with a sensitive ear capable of registering all the differences between social groups in terms of tone, accent, and pronunciation; and he possesses a stylistic dexterity that allows him to make the reader know, by means of the distinct music with which they express themselves, when people from the coast (like the subprefect and the sergeant) are speaking (the latter, though a native of Arequipa, talks as though he came from the coast) or when someone else has the floor, be it the members of a Lima-ized elite like Don Demetrio Caceres and Don Jesus Gutierrez, highland provincials like the landowner Don Julian Aranguena and the shopkeeper Don Pancho Jiménez, the literate and politicized *cholos* of the Lucanas Union Center, or the Indians of Puquio's four *ayllus*.[5] This expressive accuracy, this plurality of speech modes that distinguishes *Yawar Fiesta*'s characters, each one expressing himself according to his culture and his rank, has justly been highlighted by critics as one of the novel's artistic achievements; but such praise often misses the point since it applauds the indigenous characters' mode of expression for its authenticity, its genuineness. In truth, this manner of speaking is "authentic" only in a literary sense, not in any historical or sociological way. It is an effective narrative device, but an invention more than a reflection of living language, a creation rather than a linguistic document.

Invented Speech

In a letter to Manuel Moreno Jiménez—who upon reading the manuscript of *Yawar Fiesta* registered certain reservations over the characters' language—Arguedas responded as follows: "I have an idea that anyone who can write about the panorama and life of our highland people from on high and in a refined, controlled Spanish, will, on the other hand, be unable to capture the germinal essence of this world with sufficient force and urgency, a world caught up in a violent and magnificent debate."[6] It was, rather, the reverse. The invention of a language like that spoken by the Indians of *Yawar Fiesta* required not only a mastery of Spanish but a working knowledge of true indigenous speech as well. However, these are both just raw materials that have no capacity to predetermine the final literary outcome: in the hands of a writer less artistic than Arguedas, this language might have sounded as false as that of so many indigenist novels.

In the oft-quoted 1950 article "The Novel and the Problem of Literary Expression in Peru," Arguedas evocatively explains his "long and anguished" search for a style that would allow Indian characters—who in reality communicated among themselves in Quechua—to speak Spanish in a manner that would appear plausible.[7] His aim was to "guard the essence," to "impart the very substance of our spirit to an almost foreign tongue." The solution (which Arguedas calls an "aesthetic discovery") came after multiple attempts "as in a dream" and consisted of "finding the subtle dislocations that would turn Spanish into the proper mold, the adequate instrument." This literary, or, more accurately, rhetorical solution was "to create a language for them [the Indians] built upon a foundation of the Spanish words incorporated into Quechua and the elementary Spanish some Indians managed to learn in *their own villages*." Do actual flesh and blood highlanders talk this way? Argueda's own testimony on this subject is unequivocal: "But the Indians don't even use this Spanish with those who are native Spanish speakers, let alone among themselves! It's fiction."

Yes, this language is fiction and as such implies an unnegotiable distance between itself and the reality, the living speech it pretends to take as its inspiration. It is a semantic fiction, above all musical and melodic, a generic language that dissolves individuals into group categories and makes them express themselves in a depersonalized manner, as though massed together. Now, every generalization is an adulteration; it suppresses the specifically individual in order to foreground something generic, the common quality, the related tendency that marks a group or series. With this device Arguedas creates an effective and expressive verbal object, but one that is autonomous, distinct from Andean linguistic reality. Landowners, *mestizos*, and Indians do not exist simply as masses—classes, races, social strata; they are also individuals with personal characteristics that distinguish each one from the other members of their own ethnos, social group, or collectivity. By suppressing specific differences and registering only common denominators within language modes, the narrator turns away from conventional reality, separates it from the real model, turns it into a representation. Since on stage all the interpreters of a dance, like practitioners of a rite or ceremony, acquire a transitory collective identity, their individual traits become abolished by the gestures and movement of the group to which everyone contributes and of which all are a part.

Yawar Fiesta's fabricated Indian language, with its torn syntax full of quechuanisms and Spanish words disfigured by phonetic transcription, with its abundance of diminutives and dearth of articles, never expresses an individual; it expresses a multitude—one that when it communicates always does so in a plural voice, like a chorus. In contrast to what happens in many other novels belonging to indigenist or regionalist literature, where the figurative language coming out of the Indians' mouths ends up as caricature and destroys the reader's illusions, speech is persuasive in *Yawar Fiesta*; it appears "authentic" not because it is more genuine than that found in other works but because its coherence and the cut of its form—above all, its musicality and coloration—confer artistic status upon it.

The Fantasy of the Social Milieu

It is true that this invented language very effectively helps to give a literary form to one of the most impressive traits found in the novel's Indian society: its collectivism, the community's absolute hegemony over separate individuals. But this does not prevent that language from being a spectacle in and of itself. In other words, it is more than just a vehicle of expression. Breaking forth in rich sonority and plastic originality, it becomes an autonomous reality that engages a reader's attention before any actual message becomes clear. When the novel's Indians speak, their words efface them: language lives, people disappear. This is similar to what happens during a concert when the music's spell makes the music lover forget that what he hears is the product of various instruments and various instrumentalists, or what happens when the perfection of the voices in a chorus vanishes behind the composer's melody. All regionalist writing, constructed at the outset from those "dislocations" of language to which Arguedas refers in his 1950 article, implies a certain aestheticism, a formalism, because it emancipates the form of the narrative matter and establishes the predominance of expressiveness over anecdote. The way characters speak obscures what they have to say. And while they picturesquely chat, this verbal exhibitionism—the deformities, distortions, mannerisms, anomalies, and liberties taken with linguistic norms—comes to be an actual theme of the story. Since a good number of those regionalist stories put social, moral, or ideological goals before artistic ones, the expressive "formalism" they make such a show of, that aestheticism that replaces ideas with the eccentricity and polychromatism of the language that enfolds them, produces a certain incongruity that deprives them of persuasive power, denounces them as fraudulent. In reality, this is the case only—but that *only* is everything in literature—with artistic failures, with an insurmountable breakdown between means and ends.

Why doesn't this happen in *Yawar Fiesta?* Why, even though the Indians' made-up language might be just as fabricated as that of the stories in Ventura García Calderón's *Vengeance of the Condor* or the novel *Tungsten* by César Vallejo, doesn't it give (as in these works) a false impression instead of a true one? Because Arguedas possessed the literary skill to disarrange Spanish artistically, of course, but also because, in *Yawar Fiesta*, a colorful expressive form, offered to readers as a spectacle, doesn't work against but rather coincides with the profound intentionality of a story that was meant not as a denouncement of the social horrors of the Andean highlands, but as a vindication of Quechua culture's right to exist; and it enacts this intention through the medium of one of that culture's most controversial creations, that is to say, a spectacle: that "bloody fiesta" that the book flaunts as its title just so there can be no mistaking the matter.

The Undefeated Culture

Now, unlike so many *costumbrista* novels, *Yawar Fiesta* is not a superficial apology for some local fiesta. In truth, it is motivated by an unbiased intention to stop time, to freeze history. The novel is an argument against the modernization of the Andean community, a subtly disguised yet vigorous defense of what we would call multiculturalism: the separate, autonomous evolution of different cultures and the rejection of any integration that could be understood as the destructive absorption of indigenous culture by Western society. This problem is beautifully symbolized by a forceful and vivid anecdote: the conflicts and incidents provoked by the central government's decision to prohibit the Indianized bullfight. Complete with spectators-turned-bullfighters, dynamite, drunkenness, and packsaddles, the *yawarpunchay* traditionally takes place in the *ayllus* on National Independence Day, July 28; but the authorities try to replace it with an orthodox Spanish bullfight, fought by a professional bullfighter in an enclosed arena.

The narrator presents his story with so much skill that in the end the reader can have no doubts as to what the proper conclusions must be: whoever undertakes to suppress the *yawarpunchay* clearly neither understands nor respects the Indians' culture—their customs, their beliefs, their rites—and, in truth, wishes to deprive them of something precious, their identity. All of the novel's "foreign" characters—the prominent citizens who bow to the subprefect, the "Lima-ized" highlanders, the coast-dwellers who hate anything that smacks of the mountains, the *chalos*, those educated *mestizos* and Indians left confused and culturally detached by life in Lima and the strange doctrines they find there—all share a certain complicity in this anti-Indian pretension.

Even though the bullfight may be an exhibition of savagery, this defense of the "bloody fiesta" is not a defense of barbarism. It is, instead, the defense of a cultural identity that survives and even renews itself despite the secular exploitation, ignorance, and isolation that mark the lives of the indigenous peoples of the Andes, an identity that functions on its own terms, that is, by acclimating the foreign—as it has done in the case of the Spanish practice of bullfighting—to its own magical, collective, animistic Andean tradition, a tradition sharply differentiated from that of its invaders (Spanish, coastal, Christian, white, and Western).

Yawar Fiesta's narrator is a discreet and relatively impartial presence until the fifth chapter; but in the pages that describe the conflict—the prohibition of bullfights without professional bullfighters—he abandons the appearance of neutrality, though without too much show, and takes sides with those who defend the *toropukllay*. He does this by ridiculing the leading citizens who support the subprefect and distance themselves from the shopkeeper Pancho Jiménez. He insinuates that they act out of servility rather than conviction in order to ingratiate themselves with the authorities. Later on, in this same chapter, he shows them at a council session which he invokes in order to foreground racism, since they all seem to believe, along with "the honorable citizen Caceres" that all Indians have "backward minds."[8]

Why does the narrator align himself with those who defend the Indian bullfight? Certainly not because he is unaware of the inherent violence and cruelty that victimize unfortunate peasant bullfighters like Wallpa, whom Misitu disembowels; but rather because the bullfight represents a cultural creation, a symbol of the Quechua people's sovereignty, because the *yawarpunchay*—which at the outset was a colonial imposition—has now been torn from its original culture, transformed, and absorbed into the common property of indigenous practice. The narrator sees *foreign* as a negative concept, something that implies danger, menace, betrayal of the culture to which it attaches itself. And so the narrator ridicules those *mistis* who live on Bolivar Street, who sell their souls so easily, who dare to proclaim: "We need authorities who will come teach us and who will resolve to impose culture from the outside" (102).

Ideology, Acculturation, and Betrayal

These criticisms are not aimed solely at Puquio's Lima-ized, racist elite. They are also leveled against the well-meaning *chalos* who favor suppressing the Indian-style bullfight in order to bring progress to Puquio, a kind of progress that has a clear political and ideological orientation for those *lucaninos* who emigrated to Lima and became admirers of Mariátegui, a promoter of socialism and Marxism. The narrator uneuphemistically rebukes the "literate *cholos*" for taking sides against the native culture from which they came and for aligning themselves—because blinded by an abstract vision of progress—with "the *mistis*" and corrupt authority. It is true that their motives are altruistic: to bring modernity to Puquio, to put a stop to a barbaric celebration in which Indians are disemboweled for the pleasure of the white spectators. But the narrator finds the *chalos'* solution to be a mistaken approach to the problem, a case of simply begging the question, because he denounces a Westernized, "white," anti-Indian assumption about the idea of progress, an idea in which everything that diverges from or contrasts with certain patterns preestablished by a colonizer or conqueror is rejected as an expression of barbarity and backwardness. Were he to accept this conception, the Quechua peasant in pursuit of "progress" would have no alternative but to assimilate the white world and renounce his language, his beliefs, his customs, and his traditions. And for the narrator—the one created by José María Arguedas who wrote *Yawar Fiesta*—to de-Indianize the Indians ("to save the Indians from superstition," as Guzman, one of the literate *cholos* says) would be a crime even worse than exploiting, abusing, and discriminating against them.

The narrator of *Yawar Fiesta* refuses to vacillate between magic and ideology. He chooses the former and thus induces us to share his secret sympathy and respect for the *mestizo* Pancho Jiménez and the landowner Don Julian Aranguena, who, confronting the problems of cultural identity, side in favor of preserving *toropukllay* and thereby demonstrate themselves to be more lucid than the literate *cholos*. Although the first may be a less than scrupulous shopkeeper and the second an abusive exploiter of peasants, at least they both have a refined sense of the land and its customs. They are not ashamed to be what they are. They refuse to renounce their idiosyncracies as provincials and highlanders. They don't aspire to become "foreigners," to Lima-ize themselves, and though in its own way it may be crude and instinctual, they defend an Indian fiesta as if it were their own.

The Male World

They both have yet another outstanding virtue in *Yawar Fiesta*'s viscerally *machista* world: they are brave. In this fictitious reality *machismo* is a totem worshiped by everyone: whites, *mestizos*, and Indians. Oppositions and antagonisms among races, cultures, and regions disappear when it comes to the relation between men and women, since no matter what his education, his background, or his heritage, every man is *machista*, and in such an obstinate and exclusive way that women hardly figure at all in the society described by the novel. That is, when they do appear, always as furtive apparitions, they seem to lack the degree of humanity with which the men are endowed, as though they belonged to some inferior species, halfway between human beings and animals or objects.

All of the men are *machistas*: *mistis*, *chalos*, and Indians, despicable bigwigs like Don Demetrio or prominent would-be rescuers such as Don Pascual, the generous Don Pancho, or that human ruin, the subprefect. All worship physical force and believe in courage. A defiant stance, a disdain for all life (including one's own), recklessness, and even sadism—these represent a kind of bravery. All despise women equally, treating them as presences designed to be beaten so that the *macho* can confirm his own superiority for himself or vent his rage and disappointment. All use the word *womanish* to denote an impoverishment of the masculine condition, something that borders on ignominy. Even the narrator participates in this prejudice, judging by the naturalness with which he presents the men's abusive and despotic attitudes toward women (whereas he always adopts a critical distance when dealing with the extortions and outrages suffered by the Indians). He himself uses expressions such as "even the most womanish" (of the villagers) in a disparaging sense (161).

But woman's extreme condition of inferiority in this world—victim among victims—is made most evident by the narrator's failure to invoke her as either protagonist or actor in events. She appears only sporadically and always as horizon, shadow, or bulk. She moves en masse, a landscape. One could say she exists solely to cry over or pray for men's exploits and tragedies and to allow herself to be shoved, insulted, or mistreated whenever males need to vent their fury on someone. That is what happens to the wife of the *misti* Don Jesus. Furious for having been swindled by the corrupt subprefect, he throws a plate of stewed corn in her face, "because his rage against the subprefect had not yet subsided" (147). And at another point in the story the Indians of K'ayau resort to kicking their women for the most trivial of reasons: so they will remove the children from the neighborhood plaza (154). And when, enraged over the loss of their traditional fiesta, Puquio's Indians hurl insults at the little Spanish bullfighter Ibarito II, they shout "Woman!" (191).

Rage

This conduct is the expression of a more general phenomenon that is characteristic of José María Argueda's world. It is something François Bourricaud, in one of the many fine studies on this novel's *machismo*, calls "the displacement of aggression."[9] In order to vent the rage that grows out of abuse and frustration (but which often seems to arise for no apparent reason), men commit physical violence against someone or something weaker than they are, someone or something incapable of self-defense. Much of the time this means women, but it also includes subordinates—servants, employees, children—or animals, plants, even mere objects. But to interpret this rage in social psychological terms, to see it as a rebellion that wells up in the face of an intolerable state of affairs, as a resistance that is externalized in individual anarchic, irrational outbursts by those exploited, is to miss the way this phenomenon functions in fictitious reality. Characters suffer these emotional explosions—in a transitory yet recurrent way—regardless of race or social position: the exploiters as well as the exploited, people from the coast as well as highlanders. Fury blinds them all and drives them to destroy, injure, torture, or kill. In fictitious reality this sudden rage that possesses individuals or groups and drives them mad, converts them into malignant beasts, is more a magical plague or mysterious inherent malady of the human condition than a Freudian transference of resentment and revenge that inspires the weak to behave as brutally as the strong.

Besides these instances of battered and humiliated women, *Yawar Fiesta* is filled with other examples of the sharp exchanges brought about by the rage in manly souls. After a meeting with Don Pancho Jiménez, one that seems to end on good terms, the subprefect, watching the shopkeeper move off through the shadows of Puquio's town square, suddenly, arbitrarily, and inexplicably orders the sergeant to pick up his rifle and shoot him in the back: "Shoot him! And let him lie there like a dog" (117-18). And if the sergeant had not disobeyed, that would have been the end of the emotional merchant. Don Julian Aranguena, after a frustrated attempt to capture Misitu, first blindly shoots at his own men as they run away terrified by the violent animal and then fires at the sky in a curious mix of exasperation and exultation over his own failure and the impressive power of his bull. The narrator describes this state of mind in an unforgettable way: "He was going to kill it, but kept on firing at the sky, in a joyous rage" (136). Still and all, moments later, this rage mingled with joy impels him to kill the horse belonging to his foreman, the *chalo* Fermin, in order to discharge the remaining fury rising within him.

Collective Deeds

The counterpart to this rage can be found in those affecting outbursts of generosity to which individual characters are occasionally given. This is what we see when Don Julian Aranguena bestows his treasured Misitu upon the Indians of K'ayau or when the bullfighters Honrao, K'encho, Raura, and Wallpa are moved to throw themselves in front of the bull's horns during the *yawarpunchay*. But it is most apparent in its collective form among the Indians, where the individual dissolves into the group, where the private person blends into the social fabric. It is here that these outbursts of devotion and sacrifice reach their highest degree of generosity and selflessness and generate collective deeds such as the competition between the native communities of Puquio and Parincocha that produced a market square in only two months or the Nazca-Puqio road—186 miles in twenty-eight days—constructed by Puquio's Indians. The narrator describes these accomplishments as epic feats that express all that is most positive in the Quechua way of life: its nobility, its idealism. Sometimes these collective deeds have practical benefits for the community—as doubtless is the case with the market and the highway—but their utility does not always determine their moral and cultural value. For example, it would be difficult to establish precisely how the people of Puquio profit from the energy and courage the k'ayaus expend in capturing Misitu, another collective enterprise the novel offers as a model. No, these deeds are valuable in and of themselves, for the simple fact of having been accomplished, for the lack of self-interest with which they are undertaken, because they show the Indians' powerful potential, their capacity for work and sacrifice, the solidarity and will to move mountains that make it all possible. Certain notions of "progress" and "modernization" are at odds with the spirit that governs these collective deeds. The narrator makes this obvious when he describes what happens in response to Puquio's exemplary project of community road building. Throughout the central highlands, this feat unleashes construction fever aimed at opening roads to the coast. The local bosses want these routes to pass by their own haciendas and so road construction turns into a "business," something despicable that denaturalizes a collective effort that started out as a disinterested, "pure" undertaking (121-26).

Degrading Business

In a tentative way, something manifests itself here, a stance that will take on a more precise form in Arguedas's later novels: the rejection of urban civilization, of the market, of the industrial world. Commercial calculation and the love of money are manifestations of egoism and individualism, things that soil and degrade life, phenomena of the city. Human life—even though it may be wretched and seem backward when observed from that urban perspective—only maintains its moral purity in a rural world: there man lives close to Nature, the group prevails over the individual, feelings over figures, and reason has not yet defeated the spiritual, the religious, the magical.

These assumptions are developed far more elaborately in *Yawar Fiesta* than in the novel's prototype, the 1936 short story "Yawar (Fiesta)." A comparison of the two texts shows how much Arguedas's narrative technique has improved and how he has gone on to refine and complicate his literary world in the intervening four years. The short story is full of descriptions of folkways and traditions. The Indians' dialogue sounds like caricature because it has not been reworked in a literary way. The narrator's position is constant and explicit in relation to that which he narrates and his sentimentalism and truculence debase his testimony and undermine the story.[10] In the short story the violence of the *mistis* and the police borders on the improbable. Their amusement over the Indians' blood and suffering could be called demonical. And the Indians, although capable of "collective deeds" like the construction of Puquio's market, fail to personify, as they do in the novel, a rich and ancient culture hidden beneath a surface primitivism. Instead they are a drunken lot with senses dulled by cheap cane liquor, the "poison from the coast." The crazed and greedy native bullfighters throw themselves at the bulls, actually hoping to be gored so they can collect the money Puquio's *señoritas* have stuffed into packsaddles with this corrupt end in mind. The whites' wickedness stems from their individualism and affinity for commerce: "their souls were almost always enemies to one another because they were dominated by the spirit of business, by ambition; but the Indians were not."

The feature that most differentiates one version from the other is the appearance, in 1940, of a new social sector, a wedge between the Indians and the *mistis* that did not exist in the 1936 text: the *mestizos* or *chalos*. They introduce a new dimension of reality: the ideological, the realm of progressive ideas committed to a transformation of society aimed at establishing justice. This is represented by the humble *lucaninos* who emigrate to Lima: Escobar the student, Martínez the chauffeur, Rodríguez the streetcar conductor, Gutierrez the tailor, all those who go to the capital and are progressively de-Indianized and acculturated by the jobs and activities they find there. We see that the narrator condemns such influences because they bring the ingenuous youths, eager for Puquio's modernization, to make common cause with the Indians' exploiters—the subprefect and the *mistis*—in a major crime: the prohibition or, worse yet, the alienation of a cultural creation belonging to the Quechua people.

When they move to Lima's coastal world, the *chalos* begin to lose their ethnic and cultural roots. This clouds their judgment and induces them to become the accomplices of the political authorities and the local bosses. But fortunately, those roots have not disappeared completely, as becomes obvious when we see them, carried away by the spectacle of the Indians bringing Misitu into town, ask the *varayok* (staffbearer, Indian leader) to allow them to help haul the animal in. In other words, if only for a moment, they wish to set reason aside and act out of atavistic emotions and impulses—as the Indians do.

The Defeat of Reason

Reason tells the *chalos* to put an end to the Indian bullfight. For them it is a manifestation of backwardness, a cruel spectacle in which the villagers are gored for their executioners' entertainment. ("Never again will Indians die in Pich'kachuri square just to make those pigs happy!" says Escobar [130].) These ideas come to the *lucaninos* from José Carlos Mariátegui (1894-1930), founder of Peru's Communist Party, a writer and journalist who disseminated Marxist ideas throughout Peru, whose portrait presides over the novel's Lucanas Central Union meetings, and whom the *chalos* respectfully invoke, calling him *"werak'ocha"* and *"taita"* (father and lord) (131). Although Arguedas was never an official member of the Communist Party, he frequently declared that Mariátegui's essays and *Amauta*, the journal he directed, had a decisive influence on his development. What is more, while writing *Yawar Fiesta*, he was relatively close to the communists and his correspondence with Manuel Moreno Jiménez shows him sending articles to the party newspaper, *Democracy and Labor*, and selling bonds to finance it, clear proof that, without being militant, he at least approved of the ideological, rationalistic, modernizing, and Westernizing theories of Marxism in regard to the Indian problem.[11]

But once he began to write the novel—following his natural inclinations, the spontaneous dictates of his spirit—his "demons" turned out to be stronger than his ideological sympathies and ended up introducing a paradox into *Yawar Fiesta*, one to which the story owes a great deal of its dramatic tension. Although the narrator makes an effort to emphasize all the good intentions that guide the *mestizo* ideologues in their plans for modernization, the story he actually tells makes them appear blind and confused when it comes to dealing with the problem of the Andean people. It makes the *chalos* look like the victims of an intellectual mystification that prevents them from approaching this matter in a complete way, makes them appear unable to see it as something more than a fight against the economic deprivation and political abuse suffered by the Indians, unable to see it as a battle for the preservation and defense of the Andean being, his rites, his beliefs, and his customs, which, precisely because they are ancient and tied to tradition, guarantee the identity and perdurability of all that can be called "Indian." By invoking socialism against "magic," the *chalos* stop being a part of their people and become allied with their enemies.

The narrator, on the other hand, when faced with this dilemma, openly chooses the *yawarpunchay* and everything it symbolizes: the originality and force of a culture rooted deep in the past and in the harsh Andean geography—its lofty mountains, brilliant skies, and terrifying chasms, whose secret life of myths and miracles and intense spirituality can be found nowhere else.

Symbolic Victory

Although its presence is suggested throughout the entire length of the novel, this magical and ceremonial, archaic and Andean, Quechua and rural culture bursts forth in all its atavistic force and vividness in chapter 7, "El Misitu." Here the narrator introduces us to the mythic beliefs and magical practices of the Indians of the high plateau, the k'oñanis. They try to prevent the k'ayaus from bringing Don Julian's bull to the ring for the July 28th fiesta. This animal is a legendary and semidivine figure to them: they believe that, endowed with mythical powers, he emerged from the waters of a lagoon (Torok'ocha) one stormy night.[12] In that same chapter we see the narrator blending in with the sorcerer Kokchi while he makes an offering to the k'oñanis' tutelary mountain (Lord Ak'chi) in hopes that he will protect Misitu; and then we see him, from the k'ayaus' perspective, sharing the magico-religious ceremony in which the village Indians ask another mountain spirit (the *auki* or demigod Karwarasu) for help in capturing the bull. In this way an ancestral, animistic, irrational, and magical Indian world appears in full relief, one that coexists, half-hidden, with the more modern and Westernized world of Puquio. And although, like Puquio, it is plagued by divisions and fractures—k'oñanis and k'ayaus disagree over Misitu—it still denotes, despite its primitivism, genuine character. That magical world has an authenticity that the other culture lacks because, besides being degraded through cruelty and servitude, the culture of Puquio bears the appearance of complete bastardization, the appearance of a poor imitation of some remote model inimical to this place in the Andes and to its people, an imitation that culminates in rootlessness. In contrast, the Indians' culture stands out like a natural transcription of that untamed landscape and a faithful copy of the uniqueness of the Quechua people, a culture that flows from lived experience and which, though discriminated against and exploited by white outsiders, still remains uncorrupted because self-interest does not hold sway there, business does not corrode its communitarian and collective social links. Everything is a function of the community, a moral force superior to the individual; and spirituality and religion—the dialogue with the transcendent—continue to preside over human activities.

This dialogue with the other world goes on constantly, through ceremony, music, and dance. They create a milieu in which the human becomes integrated with the divine and the individual becomes integrated with the natural world, a world that has vital and sacred meaning for the *comuneros* because it is inhabited by tutelary gods whose benevolence or hostility determines the success or failure of human enterprises. And so the *comuneros'* capture of Misitu—described in a chapter significantly entitled "The *Auki*"—is not a sporting event but a religious festival, complete with processions and offerings, a sacrifice made by the *lay'ka* (sorcerer), and the music of the *wakawakras*, trumpets made of horn, whose vibrant and dismal sounds, multiplied by the echos of the hills, perform an incantational function, instilling a sense of mystery, terror, uneasiness, and even exultation in the townspeople of Puquio as the hour of the fiesta arrives. It is this context, which gives meaning to the presence of the dancers Tankayllu and Tayta Untu (who reappear in many of Arguedas's fictions, above all in the lovely story "The Agony of Rasu-ñiti"). We see them running through the streets on the eve of the fiesta, tracing their mysterious labyrinth with dance steps and tinkling scissors, like emissaries from the beyond, from a pantheon of gods and spirits of whom the music is a privileged manifestation.

It is this context that explains and justifies the *yawarpunchay*, the barbarous fiesta to which all of these preparatory rituals lead in the book's final chapter. In the end the fiesta imposes its own law—its own irrepressible magico-religious force, bearer of the faith and solidarity of the Indian people—over the fragile intrigues and prohibitions of the authorities from the coast, who, with their court of servile *mistis* and acculturated *chalos*, attempted to replace "the genuine *yawarpunchay*" with that foreign simulacrum, the Spanish bullfight, complete with the little bullfighter from Lima, Ibarito II, whom Misitu, with his strange tricks and turns, drives from the ring. When the native bullfighters, summoned by the screams of the crowd (including those of the *mistis*), come out to face Misitu and the sticks of dynamite go off, and, despite all the *mistis'* entreaties, the bullfight is restored to its traditional Indian style, the narrator, breathing what appears to be a discreet sigh of relief, suspends his narration—precisely at the spectacle's apogee. This ending is not gratuitous: Misitu's death, his chest blown to pieces by the *comuneros'* explosives, is the victory—futile, symbolic—of a culture that, though often beaten down and denigrated by its enemies, renews itself in spectacles like this one and demonstrates its capacity for survival, its unbending will neither to vanish nor to be assimilated.

Despite its indignation and denunciations in the face of the iniquities the *mistis* inflict on the Indians, is it possible to imagine a work of fiction more *conservative* than *Yawar Fiesta?*

Translated by Phyllis Silverstein

NOTES

[1] Letter from José María Arguedas to Manuel Moreno Jiménez, from December 1940, in Arguedas's *La letra inmortal: Correspondencia con Manuel Moreno Jiménez*, ed. Roland Forgues (Lima: Ediciones de los Ríos Profundos, 1993), 101.

[2] "El despojo," *Palabra en Defensa de la Cultura: Revista órgano de los alumnos de la Facultad de Letras de la Universidad* (Lima) 2, no. 4 (1936); "Yawar (Fiesta)," *Revista Americana de Buenos Aires* (Buenos Aires) 14, no. 156 (1937). See also Arguedas's *Obras completas* (Lima: Editorial Horizonte, 1983), 135, n. 11.

[3] *La letra inmortal*, principally the letters from Arguedas to Moreno Jiménez from August 1940 to June 1941 and which contain valuable information on the gestation of the novel, the literary competition at which it was presented and from which it was discarded by the jury (who gave the award to the today completely forgotten *Panorama hacia el alba*, by José Ferrando), and information on the book's publication and the commentaries and reviews that it received. Among these there was one by the historian Luis E. Valcarcel, the father of *"indianismo,"* who was a part of that jury, which, according to Valcarcel, preferred *Panorama hacia el alba* because it embraced "the coast, the sierras, the mountains," while Arguedas's book only referred to one region of Peru and was "unintelligible" to anyone who had not "lived with the Indians" (*La letra inmortal*, 128).

[4] In the original manuscript the story takes place in 1931, but then Arguedas decided to erase the "1 from the date, and put in two ellipsis points," according to what he said to Moreno Jiménez in an undated letter (8 November 1940) (*La letra inmortal*, 94).

[5] *Ed. Note: ayllu* in this case means both a subdivision of the Indian village or community and a kinship group.

[6] Typewritten letter, without a date (October 1940), in *La letra inmortal*, 90.

[7] Published in *Mar del sur: Revista peruana de cultura* (Lima) 9 (January-February 1950): 66-72. There is a version, revised and corrected by Arguedas, that appears as a prologue in the edition of *Yawar Fiesta* put out by Editorial Universitaria, in Chile, in 1968. I am quoting from this last version.

[8] Arguedas, *Obras completas* 2:107 (all citations from the novel are to this edition, which, although not free of errata, suffers from fewer than do earlier ones).

[9] François Bourricaud, "El tema de la violencia en *Yawar Fiesta*," in *Recopilación de textos sobre José María Arguedas*, ed. Juan Laro and Serie Valoración Múltiple (Havana: Centro de Investigaciones Literarias, Casa de las Américas, 1976), 209-25.

[10] "But who cared about this blood? Who pitied this poor cholo, split from top to bottom by the bull's horns?" (135).

[11] *La letra inmortal*, 100.

[12] For Gladys C. Marin, *La experiencia americana de José María Arguedas*, Colección Estudios Latinoamericanos (Buenos Aires: Editorial Fernando García Cambeiro, 1973), 66, magical reality is present from the novel's first chapter, when the narrator, describing Bolivar Street, compares the street of the *mistis* to a snake, the Amaru, an animal that, in the world of Indian mythology, represents evil, destruction, death. In this way, the narrator would be, from the very beginning, subtly classifying the area's leading white citizens as the villains of the story he is going to tell.

Captain Pantoja and the Special Service:
A *Transitional Novel*

Efraín Kristal

Mario Vargas Llosa's reflections on socialism have always informed the themes of his major novels. In the 1960s, when he was an enthusiastic supporter of the Cuban revolution, his novels reflected his conviction that Peruvian society was too corrupt for reform. In the 1980s, after repudiating socialism, his novels explored the dangers of ideology. Unlike the 1960s or 1980s, the 1970s—the period dealt with in this essay—were for Vargas Llosa a time of political ambivalence: he was no longer at ease with socialism, but he did not yet want to give it up.

Even after the Soviet invasion of Czechoslovakia, which he condemned, and the incarceration of dissidents in Cuba, against which he protested, Vargas Llosa was not willing to break with the socialist states. As late as 1974 he was writing articles rationalizing Fidel Castro's policies:

Cruel and pressing economic realities, the scarce resources of a tiny underdeveloped island, and the gigantic, savage blockade imposed by imperialism in order to drown it—all this kept "socialism in freedom" from prospering even initially. Castro's dilemma was to maintain an open socialism in the absence of international support, risking the demise of the revolution by linking its economy and its project to the Soviet model. With his famous pragmatism, Fidel chose the lesser of two evils. Who could reproach him, especially after the death of Allende and the fall of his political movement. . . . Notwithstanding my visceral horror of police states and of the dogmatism of systems that believe in single truths, if I must choose between capitalism and socialism, I bite my tongue and continue to say "on with socialism."[1]

By 1975, however, Vargas Llosa began to reconsider his allegiances to the Cuban revolution and to the Soviet Union. The first half of the 1970s was a period of artistic transition during which Vargas Llosa gradually abandoned the character type most prevalent in his first novels: tragic or innocent victims of a corrupt society, the likes of Ricardo Arana, Gamboa, Santiago Zavala, Jum, and Ambrosio. Vargas Llosa's artistic transition first becomes apparent in *Captain Pantoja and the Special Service* (1973), where he explores, with humor and irony, two themes he had earlier treated with the utmost seriousness and pathos: the depravity of military institutions and prostitution in a society "with a corrupt heart but with a puritan façade."[2]

Captain Pantaleón Pantoja has received a special mission from the general headquarters of the Peruvian armed forces: to establish a secret prostitution service to appease the sexual appetite of those soldiers who rape women near their jungle garrisons. In order to carry out his duties in secret, Captain Pantoja is ordered to live as an ordinary citizen. He is forbidden regular contact with other soldiers and is not allowed to reveal the nature of his clandestine activities to anyone, including the two women he lives with: his wife Pochita and his mother Leonor. The novel's main story line traces Pantoja's adventures and misadventures from the fateful day he receives his orders until his failure and transfer to a humiliating post.

The novel has two types of chapters. Four of them consist of dialogues in which different conversations that took place in distinct times and places are juxtaposed and intertwined, a literary technique José Miguel Oviedo has called "telescoping dialogues."[3] Vargas Llosa gives this technique a twist summarized in his book *A Writer's Reality*: he eliminates the *verba dicendi* (e.g., "he said," "she affirmed with sincerity") and replaces them with the descriptions and observations of a third-person narrator.[4] Instead of identifying Pantoja as the speaker, for example, Vargas Llosa interjects description into his character's transcribed dialogue:

"Because the first time you name me or speak about the Service, I'll throw all fifty specialists on top of you, and let me warn you, they all have long fingernails," Pantaleón Pantoja opens a desk drawer, takes out a revolver, loads and unloads it, spins the cylinder, takes aim at the backboard, the telephone, the rafters. "And if they don't put an end to you, I'll finish you off myself, with one shot in the head. Understood?" (184)

The other six chapters are comprised of letters, notes and reports from the military, articles from local papers, clips of radio programs, and accounts of Pantaleón's dreams.

The contrast between Pantaleón's keen sense of professionalism and the outrageous nature of his operation creates many comic situations in the novel. Determined to carry out his orders and accomplish his secret mission according to strict military protocol, Pantaleón resorts to a series of euphemisms. He refers to his prostitutes as "visitors," and he uses the word *service* to designate the sexual act. With scientific rigor Pantaleón reads books and articles on male sexuality to determine the number and the duration of the "services" each soldier requires per month in order to placate his sexual appetite. For the sake of thrift, he distributes pornographic materials among the soldiers in order to reduce the length of each "servicing." The comedy in the novel arises not only from the unusual nature of the service but also from the way in which it is presented to the reader. For the activities of the service are never narrated from the point of view of either an omniscient narrator or a character but by indirect means such as letters and documents. Panta's official reports use dry bureaucratic language to describe his struggles against unexpected follies: the fury of a soldier who discovers his sister is the prostitute waiting to service him; the cunning of a homosexual who dresses as a woman "to practice his vice with the troops"

(133); the connivances of the soldier who escapes with a prostitute he wishes to marry.

The local authorities are aware of but displeased with Pantaleón's service. Father Godofredo Beltrán Calila, commander and chaplain of the Peruvian Amazon region, resigns his position as a discreet protest against the service; and Scavino, the general in charge of the region, distances himself from Pantaleón and his activities. Pantaleón's mission also creates strains in his marriage: Pochita feels uneasy about her husband's mysterious activities, and Pantaleón falls in love with la Brasileña, a prostitute he takes as a lover. Pochita finds out about her husband's secret service and his infidelity in a letter written by Maclovia, a prostitute expelled from the service who hopes to regain her job by ingratiating herself with the wife of her former boss who she assumes is privy to the whole thing. After reading the letter, Pochita leaves Pantaleón.

In the first draft of *Captain Pantoja and the Special Service*, written between 1971 and 1972, Vargas Llosa created an opposition between Pantaleón and "el Sinchi," an announcer for the local radio station who takes to the airwaves to judge the morality of the local citizens.[5] He is an opportunist who utilizes his radio show to ruin the reputations of those who refuse to surrender to his blackmail. The first draft does not contain the complete development of the novel's plot, but it is evident that "el Sinchi" represented the main threat to Pantaleón's success: he figures out the nature of the secret service and threatens to expose it if Pantaleón does not pay him off.

In the second draft Vargas Llosa began to elaborate a new opposition, more important and decisive to the plot of the novel in its final form: that of Pantaleón and Brother Francisco, the leader of "The Brotherhood of the Ark," a religious order that expresses its spirituality in weird rites that include the crucifixion of insects and small animals.[6] The men and women of the brotherhood must remain celibate. They can "live together, but only as 'brother' and 'sister'; the apostles have to be pure" (152). As their numbers grow, the brotherhood's religious practices degenerate into criminal acts: the members begin to crucify children and adults.

Between the two drafts, Vargas Llosa encountered a book that would have a great impact on his literary career: *Rebellion in the Backlands* (1902) by Euclides da Cunha. Vargas Llosa read it on the recommendation of the Brazilian filmmaker Rui Guerra, who had asked Vargas Llosa to write a screenplay (the movie was never shot) based on some of the historical events that had inspired da Cunha: the Canudos rebellion at the end of the nineteenth century in which a community of humble devotees of Antonio el Consejero—a messianic leader—were massacred by the army of the recently constituted republic of Brazil. In his historical research Vargas Llosa went beyond da Cunha and studied other books on the history of Brazil and on religious messianism that helped him develop the theme of religious fanaticism in other literary projects, including *The War of the End of the World*. The atmosphere of popular exaltation for a charismatic, messianic leader is elaborated in the drafts of the screenplay Vargas Llosa wrote for Rui Guerra. It is the same kind of atmosphere that Vargas Llosa would transpose with black humor in the second and subsequent drafts of *Captain Pantoja and the Special Service*. It is no coincidence that Brother Francisco is Brazilian.

In his early novels, Varga Llosa developed characters such as Gamboa of *The Time of the Hero*, or Pantaleón himself, who are obsessed with the rules of the institution to which they belong. With Brother Francisco, however, a new kind of character will become commonplace in Vargas Llosa's narrative: the fanatic of unyielding convictions, ready to challenge anything or anyone who presents obstacles to his heartfelt beliefs. The model for the religious fanatic in *Captain Pantoja and the Special Service* was clearly Antonio, the counselor from da Cunha's *Rebellion in the Backlands*.

The relevance Vargas Llosa grants Brother Francisco and his brotherhood as the main counterpoint to Pantaleón and his service led him to downplay Sinchi's role as the character who, in the first draft of the novel, was to precipitate the failure of the service. Vargas Llosa decided to water down Sinchi's significance and turned him into a burlesque character with whom he would project onto the Peruvian jungle the amusing epistolary quarrels of medieval knights whose bark is louder than their bite.

One of the ways in which Sinchi attempts to blackmail Pantaleón is through a threatening letter. Here Vargas Llosa is alluding to the letters Joanot Martorell wrote to challenge knights he had no intention of confronting, which Vargas Llosa and Martín de Riquer published (in a book) shortly before *Captain Pantoja and the Special Service*.[7] According to an introductory note by Riquer, Martorell would scrupulously follow the epistolary protocol with which medieval knights accused other knights of an offense and demanded satisfaction. If the addressee denied the charges he should expect a challenge to a duel. Sinchi's epistolary threat fits the pattern:

Accept the reality: the life and death of your millionaire business are in my hands. Until now I have resisted the pressures and I have limited myself, from time to time, to placating the citizenry's anger somewhat, to launching discreet warnings; but if you persist in your lack of understanding and obstinacy, and if, before the end of the month, what is due me is not in my hands, there will be for your enterprise, as well as for its boss and the brains behind it, nothing less than a fight to the finish with neither piety nor compassion, and both of you will suffer the fatal consequences. (124)

Eventually, Sinchi decides to make peace with Pantaleón; he has made enough enemies with his attacks on Brother Francisco, whose influence in the jungle has overshadowed his own. In the course of the novel

Francisco's Brotherhood of the Ark becomes overwhelmingly popular. Several prostitutes abandon the service in order to become chaste members of the brotherhood, and even Pantaleón's mother becomes a follower of Francisco until she finds out that they have crucified a child. The military, which had been indifferent to the activities of the brotherhood, decides to repress the movement when it begins to crucify people. Brother Francisco is captured but escapes with the help of his converts, some of whom are soldiers and officers. He dies a martyr when he orders his devotees to crucify him.

Pantaleón's mission fails after another crucifixion, Brasileña's. The story of Brasileña, like Bonifacia's in *The Green House* or Hortensia's in *Conversation in the Cathedral*, evokes the standard plot of Mexican cinematic melodrama. La Brasileña was a poor child forced into a life of prostitution because of her unusual beauty. Her life as a prostitute leads her to a bloody death (the kind worthy of tabloid journalism), occurring under strange and mysterious circumstances. It is suspected at first that the Brotherhood of the Ark was behind her death because she was crucified in their manner. After other suppositions and conjectures, the case is finally broken: she was murdered by Teófilo Morey, the ex-mayor of a jungle town, and his accomplices, who had plotted to attack a ship of the service to rape the prostitutes on their way to a military outpost. They decided to pirate the ship because Pantaleón had denied them the use of his service. Brasileña's murder was not premeditated, but the criminals crucified her to implicate the Brotherhood of the Ark.

Pantaleón decides to give a eulogy at Brasileña's burial dressed in full military regalia. He does this (as he explains to his superiors) to raise the morale of his female "visitors" following the assault on the ship and threats of further violence. Pantaleón is unable to convince his superiors of the propriety of his action, and the service is subsequently dissolved. Like Gamboa in *The Time of the Hero*, Pantaleón is punished with a humiliating transfer before his actions jeopardize the reputation of the military. The novel ends with a joke. Pantaleón and Pochita have reconciled and are living together in a remote and barren military outpost. Pantaleón is as obsessed as ever with his military duties, but he is still in love with the deceased Brasileña and has become a devotee of the cult to Brother Francisco: "Poor little specialist, oh, how awful, my little crucified girl, my pretty little 'sister' from the Ark" (243)

Although treated in a humorous and ironic manner, the theme of *Captain Pantoja and the Special Service*—the downfall of a well-intentioned military man who fails precisely because he has tried to be faithful to a hypocritical military institution—has an antecedent in Gamboa's predicament in *The Time of the Hero*. But the contrast between Pantaleón Pantoja, as a man obsessed with military discipline, and Brother Francisco, as a religious fanatic ("some guy crucified himself to announce the end of the world" [1]), would reemerge years later as Vargas Llosa developed the theme of his most important novel. In *The War of the End of the World* Vargas Llosa juxtaposes Moreira César, an obsessive general, and Antonio el Consejero, a messianic leader, to explore the nature of violence aroused by fanaticism, be it religious, military, or ideological. In the 1970s, when he published *Captain Pantoja and the Special Service* as well as *Aunt Julia and the Scriptwriter*, he left the political issues in his novels vague and humorous. Vargas Llosa was uncertain about his own political convictions and was therefore not yet prepared to make a decisive connection between fanaticism and utopias or to explore themes that would have clashed with his waning conviction that capitalist society should be eradicated in order to establish socialism.

NOTES

[1] "Un francotirador tranquilo," in Contra viento y marea II (1972-1983) (Barcelona: Seix Barral, 1986), 298-99. The translation from the Spanish is mine.

[2] *Captain Pantoja and the Special Service*, trans. Gregory Kolovakos and Ronald Christ (New York: Harper & Row, 1978), 104; hereafter cited parenthetically.

[3] José Miguel Oviedo, *Mario Vargas Llosa: la invención de una realidad* (Barcelona: Seix Barral, 1977), 127.

[4] "I used the *acotaciones* to present all necessary description in the novel"—*A Writer's Reality*, ed. Myron I. Lichtblau (Syracuse: Syracuse Univ. Press, 1991), 96. Note that Vargas Llosa uses the Spanish *acotaciones* to refer to the descriptions the narrator interjects into the dialogues that replace the *verba dicendi*.

[5] The first draft of the novel can be found in Notebook [E-1], Box 3, Folder 3 of the Mario Vargas Llosa Archive at Princeton University's Firestone Library. According to a note in Vargas Llosa's handwriting, he used the notebook between 1971 and 1972.

[6] Brother Francisco appears for the first time in 1973 and was therefore conceived after Vargas Llosa's first reading of da Cunha's *Rebellion in the Backlands* (Mario Vargas Llosa Archive, Firestone Library, Notebook [E-4], Box 3, folder 6).

[7] Martín de Riquer and Mario Vargas Llosa, *El combate imaginario. Las cartas de batalla de Joanot Martorell* (Barcelona: Seix Barral, 1972).

Outside, Looking In:
Aunt Julia and Vargas Llosa

Elizabeth Dipple

In Mario Vargas Llosa's late 1980s novel *The Storyteller*, his typical and frequent narrator, who is a thinly fictionalized Vargas Llosa, beckons the reader to join him in Florence during an undated stay there, while Vargas Llosa, pursuing his European agenda, reads Dante, Petrarch, and Machiavelli in the tourist-ridden summer heat. The story that he draws us into, after seeing an exhibition of photographs depicting an Amazonian tribe by a recently deceased Italian photographer, is that of a college friend of his, a Peruvian Jew named Saul Zuratas, marked by otherness not only by his Jewish background but also by a huge disfiguring strawberry birthmark that covers the entire right side of his face. Zuratas's subsequent nickname, Mascarita, indicates his life within and behind a mask, his very being altered by the marred countenance he presents to the world.

Vargas Llosa has also posed for the camera with a mask coquettishly held beside his face—an indication no doubt of his disguised persona in the novels. That persona, he argues, is automatically a mask or fiction, although it might call itself Mario, Marito, Varguita, Vargas Llosa. That all too thinly disguised hero dominates the form and function of *Aunt Julia and the Scriptwriter* (1977; trans. 1982) as it later does *The Storyteller* (1987; trans. 1989). My emphasis on the mask would, however, be an inefficient introduction to a brief commentary on *Aunt Julia* if a simple but important semiotic reading were not called into play. Abe Franjndlich's photograph of Vargas Llosa (reproduced on p. 8) depicts the writer in partial three-quarter facial view, the face nervously grim and cropped off at the right border. Held in the subject's right hand is a *carnivale* mask that dominates two-thirds of the photograph and is presented full face to the viewer. The allegorical reading is straightforward: the writer Mario Vargas Llosa dons the mask of literary fiction in order to alter freely the autobiographical self presented. The mask is the fictional representation; the reality behind that mask is inaccessibly other.

The complication that presents itself, of course, is the fact that the face is *not* behind the mask but beside it. Vargas Llosa doesn't don a mask but holds it out at a fair distance and angled away from his face, stressing the separation between the two—and no doubt cautioning critics to beware of the salacious voyeurism of autobiographical commentary. I shall return later to the hauteur of such a warning, but for the moment I wish to contrast it to the lived-in, inescapable mask of Saul Zuratas in *The Storyteller*.

Against all odds, in an extended act of passionate identification, Zuratas sheds his Jewish and Peruvian cultures and becomes a speaker or storyteller among the isolated, uncontaminated Machiguengas, a wandering Amazonian tribe spread through the "unhealthy forests of eastern Cusco and Madre de Dios." Vargas Llosa's narrator describes the *habladores* or speakers thus:

I was deeply moved by the thought of that being, those beings . . . bringing stories from one group of Machiguengas to another and taking away others, reminding each member of the tribe that the others were alive, that despite the great distances that separated them, they still formed a community, shared a tradition and beliefs, ancestors, misfortunes and joys: the fleeting, perhaps legendary figures of those habladores who—by occupation, out of necessity, to satisfy a human whim—using the simplest, most time-hallowed of expedients, the telling of stories, were the living sap that circulated and made the Machiguengas into a society, a people of interconnected and interdependent beings. (93)

Saul Zuratas knows that, marred and masked as he is by his bizarre birthmark, he would not have survived the first culling within the tribe; he nevertheless gives himself, body, life, and soul to them, leaving the Vargas Llosa narrator to puzzle his way through a situation that is alien to him. This narrator can understand Zuratas's hatred of the "intrusion of destructive modern concepts," the longing for "an equilibrium between man and the earth, the awareness of the rape of the environment by industrial culture and today's technology, the reevaluation of the wisdom of primitive peoples, forced either to respect their habitat or face extinction" (242). He can understand that

Mascarita should have decided to turn his back on a bourgeois future and go to Amazonia in search of adventures. . . . He erased all trace of his departure and of his intentions. . . . It is evident that he left Lima with the intention of never coming back, of being another person forever. . . . I am able to follow him this far, though not without difficulty. I believe that his identification with this small, marginal, nomadic community had—as his father conjectured—something to do with the fact that he was Jewish, a member of another community which had also been a wandering, marginal one throughout its history, a pariah among the world's societies, like the Machiguengas in Peru, grafted onto them, yet not assimilated and never entirely accepted. (242-43)

The narrator also accepts that "surely, his fellow feeling for the Machiguengas was influenced . . . by that enormous birthmark that made of him a marginal among marginals, a man whose destiny would always bear the stigma of ugliness" (243).

This limited comprehension, although generous, sympathetic, and rational, also defines even as it haunts Vargas Llosa: the narrator goes on to say that what moves him most in Saul's story and makes him "weave and unweave it a thousand times" is the next stage, which he cannot understand. Taking a giant step beyond conversion, Zuratas in becoming an *hablador* "was adding what appeared impossible to what was merely improbable" (244). Saul has gone beyond the possibilities that Vargas Llosa can imagine as a writer, and it is this knowledge of limitation that makes this novel so crucial, so touching, so important within the career of this self-divided novelist. A translation of Vargas Llosa's own words is useful:

> The rest of the story, however, confronts me only with darkness, and the harder I try to see through it, the more impenetrable it becomes.
>
> Talking the way a storyteller talks means being able to feel and live in the very heart of that culture, means having penetrated its essence, reached the marrow of its history and mythology, given body to its taboos, images, ancestral desires, and terrors. It means being, in the most profound way possible, a rooted Machiguenga, one of that ancient lineage who—in the period in which this Firenze, where I am writing, produced its dazzling effervescence of ideas, paintings, buildings, crimes, and intrigues—roamed the forests of my country, bringing and bearing away those tales, lies, fictions, gossip, and jokes that make a community of that people of scattered beings, keeping alive among them the feeling of oneness, of constituting something fraternal and solid. That my friend Saul gave up being all that he was and might have become so as to roam through the Amazonian jungle, for more than twenty years now, perpetuating against wind and tide—and above all, against the very concepts of modernity and progress—the tradition of the invisible line of wandering storytellers, is something that memory now and again brings back to me, and . . . it opens my heart more forcefully than fear or love has ever done. (244-45)

Years before, after the narrator's first visit to the Amazonian jungle, the idea of the *habladores* raised goosebumps, as it does in the novelistic present in Florence. On the earlier occasion he had explained it to Mascarita by saying that the *habladores* are "a tangible proof that storytelling can be something more than mere entertainment . . . something primordial, something that the very existence of people may depend on" (94). Saul's disappointed response is "Oh, I see. It's the literary side that interests you."

In the terms set up in this novel the limitations of Vargas Llosa's career as a writer are here poignantly and honestly encountered. What interests me principally in this writer's struggle with both the technical and ideological aspects of fiction is the sense, unavoidable within the dynamic bond between writer and critic, that he actively suffers from a fragile sense of not being inside the mask he would don, of failing at some level to participate. His analytical and observational capabilities are exceptional, and, as we learn from his autobiographical narrators, he does his literary homework—he is extremely well read in Western cultural texts and has been thoroughly influenced by his infrequent but profound contacts with the primordial Amazonian forests. Unlike the resolute Mascarita, his narratorial use of the mask is a literary device, not a commitment involving body, soul, life in a single-minded way that denies the temptations of power, the love of women, the wealth and progress of a successful professional. He can therefore tell the story of Mascarita's dedication but must stand uncomprehendingly outside of it, made nervous by it, coming up in goosebumps over a profound path not to be taken by himself as a successful Westernized *écrivain*.

By contrast, *Aunt Julia and the Scriptwriter* presents a more mixed representation within the same contours of a deep problematic in Vargas Llosa's fiction. Here, he offers a version of the fictionist's dilemma within the traditional genre of the bildungsroman. Whereas *The Storyteller* describes a state of affairs, *Aunt Julia* ironically presents a series of obstacles within a complex *mise-en-abyme* framework. *Aunt Julia* and *The Storyteller* share a structure of contrast and balance, tightly conducted in *Aunt Julia* and ingeniously interwoven in *The Storyteller*. A few words about that structuring device are both appropriate and necessary.

Vargas Llosa describes himself as a man driven by obsessions and writing out of them—indeed, he is at pains to convince the readers of his interviews and speeches that he is passionately committed to the very principle of obsession. This tenet, if correct, should verify his absolute insider status in the novels and obliterate most of what I have been arguing through an internal reading of a single text, *The Storyteller*. The actual structure of the novels and the literary problems of realism in the works are, however, more revealing and contradictory.

Formally, Vargas Llosa's tendency is to alternate tales of his own early life and background with the primary subject matter of the text he is writing. He does so in both of the novels I have mentioned and also, interestingly, in the account of his ill-fated political run for election as president of Peru, *A Fish in the Water*. In each case the fixing of his obsession is on his life as lived up to the age of twenty-two; he carries that life farther only in terms of prologue, epilogue, or, in the case of the memoir, as part of an ongoing political exposé. It is as though the passion of obsession was spent early and that his interim years have been spent in analysis, rumination, reworking, fictionalizing, finding a form, thinking about the underlying structures of his art. As *A Fish in the Water* points out, his second wife Patricia saw his political ambition to be president as "the adventure, the illusion of living an experience full of excitement and risk, of writing the great novel in real life."

The key word here is *illusion*, which indicates Vargas Llosa's removal from a firm concept of materiality and belies much of his often stated desire to root his work in reality. There is no doubt that crucial things happened to Vargas Llosa in the world of material existence—his marriages, his exile, his study of European literature, his political ambition; it is equally true that he relives them in the written word in ways that have more to do with illusion than with realistic (i.e., potentially objective) accounts. The very fact that he sees himself as an ex-patriot and a cosmopolitan combines with his hatred of nationalism and the Peruvian rancor he describes in the memoir to help define the primary life decisions that he has made. I am certainly not the first to remind others that his marriages, first to his aunt, the titular Julia of the novel, and then to his first-cousin Patricia, express an extraordinary halt in emotional attachment at a young age, leading him to consolidate his position within the love of his mother's family—the first and best love he knew—and to regain partially the paradise that was lost when his macho father returned to reclaim his wife and make miserable the ten-year-old Mario. Within the boundaries of potential criticism of *Aunt Julia and the Scriptwriter*, the narrator's wanton cruelty to Julia through his casual discarding of her after eight years of marriage and then absolving himself of blame by vindictively citing her expectation of no more than five years, invites a strong Lacanian feminist reading. His illusion that he is presenting a real story is quickly upset.

It seems clear and much more to the point that the experienced world of Vargas Llosa as a writer in the late twentieth century is troubled by the exigencies of both his obsessive autobiographical interest in himself as a young man and his writing fiction in a postrealist period. In some ways the hapless term *postmodern* is worthwhile, if only because its various usages raise the issue of the materiality of fiction, study the appropriation of novels as a commodity through the history of capitalism, and present a perception of fictional literature as parody, while destroying its formerly privileged position of realism.

Although Vargas Llosa began his career as an impassioned defender of the possibility of a totalizing fiction that perfectly balances subjective and objective and high and low culture and presents a whole vision of society, he shortly came to see the idea of the total novel as naive and even demented. That did not, however, reduce his interest in the accomplishments of medieval romance, his interest in melodrama, his admiration of Dumas, his taste for pornography, his study of Flaubert's complex theories of realism, and so on—all of them part of his onetime sense of how a totalizing fiction could be stitched together.

In spite of the extraordinary fecundity of experimentalism in the early novels, especially *The Green House*, *Aunt Julia and the Scriptwriter* is the pivotal novel for his acknowledgment of the entire problem of realism and especially of how he as a writer is affected by it. In *The Green House* the very foundation of the realist enterprise is questioned when Anselmo claims that there never was a green house, with the result that the pastiche of stories and opinions and reportages compiled as a compendium of the tales told by local inhabitants of Piura crumbles. But it is in *Aunt Julia*, eleven years later, that the specific issues of Vargas Llosa's sensibility as a writer within the realist agenda come into direct play. Naively reviled by some as a frivolous novel because it and the preceding novel, *Captain Pantoja and the Special Service*, define the moment when Vargas Llosa says he learned the art of the comic, it is, I think, central to an understanding of this writer's work.

I wish to refer specifically to two moments when Vargas Llosa himself discusses the novel, one in an interview with José Miguel Oviedo just after the completion of the novel, the other in *A Writer's Reality*, a compilation of lectures on his own work. In the Oviedo interview, given on the heels of his having just completed *Aunt Julia*, there is a spontaneity that allows some of the contradictions intrinsic to realism to rise to the surface. Vargas Llosa chose to alternate the fantastic soap operas of Pedro Camacho (based on a real figure he had met in 1953 when he worked for Radio Pan-americana in Lima, Raúl Salmon) with "another story that serves as a kind of counterpoint, that anchors in the tangible, verifiable world the purely imaginary, purely fantastic, mad world of the protagonist and his soap operas" (Oviedo, "A Conversation" 157). Originally, Vargas Llosa saw this other story to be precisely the opposite of the soap operas—"something absolutely objective and absolutely true" ("A Conversation" 157). During the construction of the novel, he learns, or perhaps relearns, the basic lessons of realism:

> my project began disintegrating when put into practice. That is, it was totally impossible to write the chapters in which I wanted to be absolutely truthful and tell only of things which I was absolutely sure had happened precisely so, because memory is tricky and gets contaminated with fantasy, and because even as one is writing, an element of imagination seeps in, takes hold and inevitably becomes part of what one is writing. And at the same time, in the chapters that are supposedly syntheses or paraphrases of the soap operas of the protagonist, there is no "pure invention." There, too, there are foreign ingredients which come from objective reality, which infiltrate little by little. ("A Conversation" 159)

In his 1991 lecture Vargas Llosa is less precise and works harder at the level of theory to differentiate the binary structure of the novel, arguing that "A serious writer is someone who is able to distort reality out of a personal obsession or personal belief, and to present this distortion in such a persuasive way that it is perceived by the reader as an objective description of reality, of the real world. This is what achievement in art and literature is. A good scriptwriter of soap operas is also someone who distorts reality, not out of a personal obsession or personal vision, but out of the stereotypes that are established in society" (*A Writer's Reality* 115). Here, Vargas Llosa tenaciously maintains a distinction that had attracted him years before— Roland Barthes's differentiation between *écrivain* and *écrivante*. For Vargas Llosa, the scriptwriter is an *écrivante* who uses language only as an instrument for the minor task of entertaining, whereas a real writer, an *écrivain*, "is someone who uses language as an end in itself, as something that in itself has justification" (*A Writer's Reality* 115).

I find his earlier sense of the reciprocal flow between the two forms of writing in *Aunt Julia* more creatively and critically interesting than his Barthesian allegiance, which tips him over into the structuralist camp and helps fuel a sense of his separation from the practical function of language as it extends itself into extra-aesthetic realms. Interpreting at a political extreme, one can say that the passage quoted above regarding the definition of a serious writer denotes romantic existentialism and participates in an elitist culture that the experience of reading *Aunt Julia* almost but does not quite encourage.

In speaking of the cultural past, Vargas Llosa claims that "the richest moments in civilization, in history, have occurred when the boundaries separating popular and creative literature disappear, and literature becomes simultaneously both things—something that enriches all audiences, something that can satisfy all kinds of mentalities and knowledge and education, and at the same time is creative and artistic and popular" (*A Writer's Reality* 116). His examples are Dickens, Hugo, Dumas, and Pérez Galdos. Although he could also mention his Latin American contemporaries— Puig, García Márquez, Carpentier, and others—he is typically stuck in the nineteenth century. He overlooks, however, an important quality, especially in the case of Dickens: the lack of contempt for popular culture, a contempt that is irreversibly part of the fabric of his structurally divided novel. This disdain is ideologically dangerous, defining as it does much of the sense Vargas Llosa has of himself as an artist, as a power figure, and as a man. In *A Fish in the Water* he studies not only the vicious political battlefield but also Peruvian rancor. Paralleling to some degree the negativity that García Márquez sees in the idea of *soledad*, Vargas Llosa gives analyses of the deep pain of his background, of his rancorous father, of the various miseries and indignities he suffered at the hands of that tyranny at home and school. He also furnishes a distinction between the concept of *blanco* versus *cholo*, white versus colored, not only seen as racist terms but also in common usage in Peru to indicate where the power lies in any given personal or political situation. As he describes it in *A Writer's Reality*,

We were surrounded by a world of ignorance and prejudice that we took for granted was objective reality.
The divisions in Peru were many. First, racial: there was the Peru of white people, the Peru of Indian people, the Peru of the blacks, and the small minorities of Peruvians, the Asians and the people of the Amazon region. (41)

Given the painful uncertainty of his and his father's status, Vargas Llosa can be understood as a person eager to be symbolically *blanco*, and it is no doubt an essentializing of this that lost him the Peruvian presidency.

It is nevertheless true that in *Aunt Julia* the overriding sense of the superiority of the *écrivain* that young Varguita will become is a double-edged sword. At the level of social materiality, it justifies his prioritizing of writing styles and of readerly competence: young Marito sees his piddling stories as *literarily* more valuable than Pedro Camacho's symbolically *cholo* soap operas, and above both hovers the actual achievement of the mature Mario

Vargas Llosa who has written the text(s) we read. Similarly, Aunt Julia is an unliterary ignoramus who has read only Argentine magazines, trashy books, and two novels, *The Sheik* and *Son of the Sheik* by E. M. Hull: erotically suggestive stuff and no doubt an addition to the comic structure of the novel—but sexist in the extreme and used to arm the snobbish Mario against a continuation of the marriage. Pedro Camacho has read nothing, partly because he has no time and interest and also because he pretentiously feels it would contaminate his style: it is this ignorance that makes him a bad writer. Young Marito reads all the correct literature of the European past, and the assumption is that the mature Mario Vargas Llosa is in clever collusion with the sophisticated reader of *Aunt Julia,* who shares the scale of values presented.

I take little pleasure, however, in the social politics that would render Vargas Llosa's work less interesting than it is. In a recent study M. Keith Booker compellingly argues that a sophisticated metareading of *Aunt Julia* and of Italo Calvino's marvelous *If on a winter's night a traveler* creates an ironic situation in which both naive readers and sophisticated metareaders are finally equivalent in their quasierotic desire to watch the *mise-en-abyme* complexities. Like Vargas Llosa himself, however, Booker is delighted with the idea that the pleasure of the metareader's experience of the novel is heightened by a gentle contempt for the more naive reader (*Mon semblable! Mon frère!*). The charms of ingenuity are intrinsic to the *mise-en-abyme* structure in which endless repetitions of irony upon irony, parody upon parody are called out, as in the novel's epigraph from Salvador Elizondo's *The Graphographer:* "I write. I write that I am writing. Mentally I see myself writing that I am writing . . ." etc. I do not, however, think that the novel's primary justification or interest lies on this side of the *écrivain's* task.

The presentation of the binary fiction, divided between Pedro Camacho's stories and Vargas Llosa's tale of his youthful marriage, is doubly engrossing in that the author seems to me to have chosen the wrong title for the novel. In the Oviedo interview he still, shortly before publication, thought he would give it a picaresque title: *Vida y milagros de Pedro Camacho* (The Life and Miracles of Pedro Camacho). The fact that he changed his mind at the last minute and called it *La tía Julia y el escribidor* foregrounds Aunt Julia but nevertheless tries to balance the two parts of his structure. In doing so, he stresses the unequal tale of the young Marito's marriage to Aunt Julia, which in spite of its sentimental and fantastic elements can be seen as an antifeminist tract unconsciously feeding the male vanity of a callow, ambitious boy who wants very much to take his place within what Adorno called the culture industry.

Critics of Vargas Llosa said that he would get a good book out of the Peruvian presidential election, and so he did, as he did out of the early marriage which, despite its fourteen-year age difference, is not as grotesque or unreal as it is assumed to be within the sexist text. To say that Julia is the mother of his creativity, as Oviedo and others do, is a sleight of hand and not acceptable within social politics; to argue that Vargas Llosa is the victim of his own acquiescence to the social construction imposed by the mainstream culture on his liminally uneasy family is to make him look less intelligent than he obviously is.

The adventures of Pedro Camacho, however, are of riveting significance. Once again Vargas Llosa's narrator, like that of *The Storyteller*, is on the outside looking in and attempting to use a sort of *argumentum ad blanco* to ease himself as writer into a dominant position. I write now from a vantage point beyond the charms of the text, the metafictional games, the sophisticated *mise-en-abyme* and the rigorous self-discipline, analysis, and questioning of Vargas Llosa's extraordinary genius; and I do so in order to try to clarify what the internal workings of the novel reveal about the author's realist agenda. In *Literature and Rationality: Ideas of Agency in Theory and Fiction* the realist critic Paisley Livingston's central argument is summarized in his statement that "assumptions about agency and rationality are in fact essential to all literary phenomena" (5). Vargas Llosa's life of literary discipline has taught him to believe this, in spite of the great amount of experimentation, self-reflexivity, and metafiction that characterize his work. He states firmly and frequently that he has never written fantastic literature and that his is a neorealist agenda. Cerebrally it is, but in the praxis of fiction something else comes out, and that is his deep separation from the obsessions he describes, the commitments he observes, the mad fantastical tricks that others play. Thus, when he proposes to Aunt Julia, her answer and his response ruefully tell all:

"Are you asking me to marry you to show your family you're grown up now?" Aunt Julia asked me affectionately.
"There's that, too," I granted. (242)

Basic eroticism and impressing the family are hardly the stuff of a grand obsession, and indeed the marriage is so curtailed from the beginning by reiterations of its unsuitability and its short-term projection that it is not really in the category of Camacho's parallel fantasies. Aunt Julia says that the marriage of an older woman to a young boy is part of soap opera lore, but as a device, it lacks conviction.

Pedro Camacho's scripts, on the other hand, are so ebulliently told, so bizarre, so full of violence and morbidity, that they transcend their genre and explode on the page. The reader, naive and sophisticated alike, fastens attention onto them and is consistently disappointed by the tepidity and political, moral blindness of the Marito-Aunt Julia text, which functions, at its best, as mere commentary. Vargas Llosa thus achieves something beyond the high crafting that is immediately evident: he manages to widen the base of realism into the realm of the fantastic and to allow Camacho, an essentially naive writer, to become an exemplum of the sturdy (but now nonviable) roots of realism, rather than the merely parodic figure that metafiction would make of him. Why are his alternating tales so much more successful than Marito's story? Not because fantasy is superior to the neorealist experiments presented in the Marito-Aunt Julia line but because, I would venture to guess, Vargas Llosa is more restrained, more inhibited, more uneasy, more self-involved with his own narrator, whereas in the productions of Camacho, his imagination is freed and his creativity is full flow. Oviedo argues (in *"La tia Julia"*) that both lines offer a betrayal and critique of reality: I would go further and say that all realism does this in our time and that Nabokov was right (in his commentary on *Lolita*) when he said that "reality" should always be put in quotation marks.

But whereas Vargas Llosa's narrator is perforce cool, rational, ironic, and restrained, Camacho is not. His scripts bridge the popular and the structurally significant, and his use of language is far above the junk-speak of popular culture. He is also a man dedicated to his task of *écrivante*, obsessed by his work, austere in his life, and endowed with an enormous capacity for work—all qualities instantly recognized and admired by Marito and the mature narrator of the novel. Dedicated to realism even as he plunges in roiling fantasy, Camacho passionately plays the characters he creates, pulling out of his suitcase "an incredible collection of objects: an English magistrate's court wig, false mustaches of various sizes, a fireman's hat, military badges, masks of a fat woman, an old man, an idiot child, a traffic policeman's stick, a sea dog's cap and pipe, a surgeon's white smock, false ears and noses, cotton beards" (134), which he quickly tries on, transforming himself into a rapid succession of characters, and arguing thus: "And why shouldn't I have the right to become one with characters of my own creation, to resemble them? . . . What is realism, ladies and gentlemen— that famous realism we hear so much about? What better way is there of creating realistic art than by materially identifying oneself with reality?" (134-35).

Vargas Llosa contends that he is materially present in the realism of his work but that it is much altered and thereby utterly changed; Pedro Camacho's passionate entry into the reality of his characters involves a masking and costuming of himself, a losing of himself in an unrestrained, joyful act of composition. Vargas Llosa's creation of Pedro Camacho is a triumph; his creation of himself is not. The only way he can justify his central literary achievement in *Aunt Julia and the Scriptwriter* is by praising Camacho's commitment but ambiguously applauding and damning his achievement and status: Camacho's hilarious confusion of his story lines, his certifiable madness, and his subsequent sorry life as a reporter/office boy put him firmly into his place in the ultimate value structure of the novel.

But just as Vargas Llosa is divided against himself, so is this book, where the sense of the author looking from the outside at a verbal star shows how his rational agency is somehow limited by characters that he has met in his life and fictionalized with only a partial view of them. The poignancy of Vargas Llosa as a writer consists in the fact that his work reflects an awareness of his separation—from Mascarita, from Pedro Camacho, from Julia whom he poorly understands, from the Peruvian mainstream.

At the same time, it must be pointed out that his fiction shines brilliantly within the possibilities of genre. Mikhail Bakhtin, stressing the idea of unfinalizability as a mark of major literary works, distinguished between the ideas of context and code: "A context is potentially unfinalized; a code must be finalized. A code is only a technical means of transmitting information; it does not have cognitive, creative significance. A code is a deliberately established, killed context" (147).

Among the many anomalies that characterize Vargas Llosa's *Aunt Julia and the Scriptwriter* is an essential and unresolved problem of genre. Every appearance of serious attention has been paid to elements of this enigma by both Vargas Llosa and his critics, without any firm sense of resolving the problematics of the novel. It is a fiction written under the aegis of realism, participating in postmodernism and metafiction, but it nervously defies definition. It escapes the killed context of code and enters freely and originally into the category of the unfinalized, with the cognitive, creative significance thereby implied. Its importance lies in this haunting unfinalizability, which reaches backward and forward through aesthetic, social, political, and personal categories, without ceasing. If Vargas Llosa were freed further in his creative consciousness, anything might be possible.

WORKS CITED

Bakhtin, Mikhail. "From Notes Made in 1970-71." *Speech Genres and Other Late Essays.* Trans. Vern W. McGee. Ed. Caryl Emerson and Michael Holquist. Austin: Univ. of Texas Press, 1986. 132-58.

Booker, M. Keith. *Vargas Llosa among the Postmodernists.* Gainesville: Univ. of Florida Press, 1994.

Livingston, Paisley. *Literature and Rationality: Ideas of Agency in Theory and Fiction.* Cambridge: Cambridge Univ. Press, 1991.

Oviedo, José Miguel. "A Conversation with Mario Vargas Llosa about *La tia Julia y el escribidor.*" *Mario Vargas Llosa: A Collection of Critical Essays.* Ed. Charles Rossman and Alan Warren Friedman. Austin: Univ. of Texas Press, 1978. 153-65.

——. "*La tia Julia y el escribidor,* or the Coded Self-Portrait." Rossman and Friedman. 166-81.

Vargas Llosa, Mario. *Aunt Julia and the Scriptwriter.* Trans. Helen R. Lane. New York: Farrar, Straus, Giroux, 1982.

——. *A Fish in the Water.* Trans. Helen Lane. New York: Farrar, Straus, Giroux, 1994.

———. *The Storyteller*. Trans. Helen Lane. London: Penguin, 1990.

———. *A Writer's Reality*. Ed. Myron I. Lichtblau. Syracuse: Syracuse Univ. Press, 1991.

Out of Failure Comes Success:
Autobiography and Testimony in
A Fish in the Water

Luis Rebaza-Soraluz

Between the mid-1950s and mid-1970s, Latin America produced an extraordinary number of novels. They were soon recognized, edited, published, and translated by and for European and North American intellectual and cultural markets. The event was called the Boom of the Latin American novel. In 1963 the Boom defined its character and gained definitive access to those markets when Mario Vargas Llosa's *The Time of the Hero* received a prestigious award granted by the publishing house Seix Barral of Barcelona. Some say the Boom ended in 1976, with the well-known violent encounter between Vargas Llosa and Gabriel García Márquez in a Mexico City movie theater.

In spite of being part of these two key moments in the Boom's history, Vargas Llosa has published a memoir that barely touches on any events from those fundamental years in his writing career. Published thirty-one years after Vargas Llosa's international debut, *A Fish in the Water* extensively collects various events from pre- and post-Boom years, favoring recent events in which Vargas Llosa portrays himself as a political and moral leader, the best candidate for the Peruvian presidency, a man—possibly the only Peruvian—of spiritual and material success or, at least, one with an international image constructed as such.

Vargas Llosa's first novel (written at age twenty-three) can be seen as the Boom's first product to obtain European sponsorship and markets. The novel was also part of the massive production and consumption of a vocabulary that would later become the predominant instrument for the political interpretation of Latin America. Within the renewed discussion concerning the social responsibilities of literature during the 1960s, the writer's public acts redefined the Latin American tradition of literature and politics joined by the power of words. For his readers, Vargas Llosa's life became a part of any argument regarding ideologies. As a professional intellectual with a political position, he has exemplified the antagonisms of his time: he has been on both sides of the Cold War, first supporting the Cuban revolution and later distancing himself from any leftist thought.

Vargas Llosa has successfully produced modern fictional images of Latin America. His fame has given his words a powerful platform from which he can be an important essayist producing political imagery. But his fiction and his analytical thought, despite the use of different strategies to persuade and captivate his public, are part of a single verbal world. His memoir combines strategies from both genres like a coin joining two sides, back to back, in apparent opposition, an encounter between fiction and methodical analysis.

A *Fish in the Water*, a five-hundred-page volume, is organized in twenty chapters symmetrically intercalating two different temporal sequences in parallel progression: an itinerary of his short political career in Peru (from 1987 to 1990) and an autobiography of his years as an apprentice writer. The book, subtitled "A Memoir," opens with a fragment of Max Weber's work, chosen, I think, because it embodies Vargas Llosa's major concerns: a good/evil dichotomy combining religious and political rhetoric. Weber writes: "anyone who becomes involved in politics, that is to say, anyone who agrees to use power and violence as means, has sealed a pact with the devil. . . . Anyone that does not see this is a child, politically speaking." After this epigraph, the two narrative threads weave together to form the biography of one protagonist split into two spheres of existence.

The sequence of memories from childhood to youth and the detailed sequence of recent events in the mature writer's life develop their own cause-and-effect relationships. They establish analogies that in the end create a new product by means of their similarities. This final product is the fusing and confusing of both protagonists as the adult writer begins to relive his apprenticeship in an unknown field. Thus his political career turns into a brief new period of childhood and youth where, as a "political novice," he discovers that real politics consist "almost exclusively of maneuvers, intrigues, plots, paranoias, betrayals, a great deal of calculation, no little cynicism, and every variety of con game" (87).

From distant memories, Vargas Llosa chooses episodes of a happy infancy, without a father, in Bolivia; of an unbearable childhood, in "Lima the Horrible" (a name coined during the thirties by the Peruvian poet César Moro) in the heart of paternal tyranny and a dysfunctional family; of a difficult adolescence in a military school resembling Peruvian male society on a smaller scale; of an early adulthood given over to journalistic writing, bohemian promiscuity, and liberation from paternal torment; of separation from the father and from Lima and the subsequent return to the "right path" under the protection of the maternal family and the coastal province; of a young intellectual's explorations as a university student caught between communism and existentialism; of an impulsive adult, adventurous in marriage and literature; of marital ties with the maternal family and their material and emotional support; and of a trip to Paris, ending the narration with the young writer on the threshold of the door to success.

The sequence of recent events deals with topics related to the presidential campaign rather than episodes geared toward narrative climax. The selection of details about Peruvian politicians and the upper class resembles the type of notes taken by foreign travelers more than a century ago concerning "customs and manners." From time to time there are reflections, analyses, judgments, attacks, and defenses. Through autobiography, the narrator and main character form a sole voice, a subjectivity dominating every aspect included in their discourse.[1]

Nevertheless, the nature of those events seems to belong to the public domain: facts that can be traced and confirmed by the objectivity of research. They occur between 1987 and 1990, these boundaries formed by political landmarks: the Alan García administration's attempt to nationalize the banking system, and the last presidential election. The chapters are organized to outline the writer's itinerary in this flow of historical events. His participation consists mainly of speeches at mass demonstrations, the founding of political organizations (such as the Democratic Front and the Movimiento Libertad), and duties required by his presidential campaign in Peruvian territory and overseas. These scenes are surrounded by brief anecdotes and a long annotated list of auspicious and ominous names, woven into the quick ascension and abrupt finale of Mario Vargas Llosa as a public figure in the Peruvian political arena. The level of detailed information reveals documentary and even judicial intentions, giving a sense of settling accounts for an improbable future trial.[2] Because of the amount of information on display that can be corroborated and because of the journalistic, even sociological tone of the language, the political sequence differs greatly from the undocumented facts and intimate tone of the childhood-youth memories. Throughout the former, Vargas Llosa's voice becomes testimonial, the "mouth" of an eyewitness attempting to represent a subordinate group, victim of a political system and an aberrant society, struggling for justice. Two omniscient narrators methodically overlap: one interferes and condemns, the other uses scientific precision to conceal his proximity to the fictionalization of reality. One could say that Vargas Llosa is at his most fictional when he appears most truthful.

Through these and other narrative strategies, the relationships of cause and effect in the recent memory sequence (a plot that claims to be an objective testimony) become the standard by which the sequence of distant events (the most subjective) is arranged and evaluated. Thus one discovers that the writer's formative period was also a political career toward the presidency. At the same time, the episodes of infancy and adolescence extend their emotive forces toward the recent events, fusing the conclusions of both sequences (artistic success and electoral failure) into one structure. When the reader finishes the book, both endings rise up as a single triumphant and heroic story.

In the realms of the nuclear family and nationality the protagonist confronts an identity conflict: whether or not to belong to an order established in terms of patriarchal rules, and how one might overcome these rules. The protagonist belongs to a family and a nation without having chosen them and without being able to reject them. Liberation from father/fatherland is a struggle toward impossible success. To be free from the paternal order is a deception: "That interview . . . marked my definitive emancipation from my father. Although his shadow will doubtless accompany me to my grave, and although at times, even today, all at once the memory of some scene, of some image of the years he had complete authority over me gives me a sudden hollow feeling in the pit of my stomach" (334). Something similar occurs to the links with the fatherland's order: "Although I was born in Peru . . . my vocation is that of a cosmopolitan and an expatriate who has always detested nationalism. . . . [Nevertheless] what happens in Peru affects me more—makes me happier or irritates me more—than what happens elsewhere. . . . I feel that between me and the Peruvians of any race, language, and social status, for better or for worse—especially for worse—there is something that ties me to them in a seemingly invincible way" (42).

The conflict with the paternal order is deferred and then left behind without resolution: "and even though I always tried to be polite to him, I never showed him more affection than I felt—that is to say, none whatsoever. The terrible rancor, my burning hatred of him in my childhood, gradually disappeared in the course of those years" (335). The narrative offers an alternative in order to reduce tension, allowing the story to continue: a trip to seek sanctuary in the maternal family, in the coastal province or in a foreign land. But family and state overlap: "Perhaps saying that I love my country is not true. I often loathe it, and hundreds of times since I was young I have promised myself to live a long way from Peru forever and not to write anything more about it and forget its aberrations. But the fact is that it is continually on my mind, and whether I am living in it or residing abroad as an expatriate, to me it is a constant torment" (43).

In this scenario of paternal *patria potestas* one can see the concealed coherence of his political discourse, where modern national and electoral problems are explained as being a result of "racism, ethnic prejudice, social resentment" (498). Those are the same factors that cause the collapse of his family—a social nucleus: "But the real reason for the failure of their marriage was not my father's jealousy or his bad disposition, but the national disease that gets called by other names, the one that infests every stratum and every family in the country and leaves them all with a bad aftertaste of hatred, poisoning the lives of Peruvians in the form of resentment and social complexes" (5).

In the story of Vargas Llosa's life his father's marriage fails. In the story of Vargas Llosa's political career the country fails, confined to a cyclic and invariable plot: "We always used to talk politics whenever we were together, and each time, somewhat cast over with sickly melancholy, we wondered why everything in Peru always tended to get worse" (37-38). A strong reason for this failure is what he calls a Third World (*tercermundista*) disposition: "One of the most damaging myths of our time is that poor countries live in poverty because of a conspiracy of the rich countries, who arrange things so as to keep them underdeveloped, in order to exploit them. There is no better philosophy than that for keeping them in a state of backwardness for all time to come" (44). Vargas Llosa insinuates that this *tercermundismo* is pre-Columbian and essential to the "ancient realm" that is Peru because it fuses with the "social resentment" which (he feels) "existed in Peru since before the arrival of Europeans" (498).

On the other hand, a detailed and extensive discourse offers political and economic solutions for the country:

> The recurrent theme of my three speeches had been that the way out of poverty does not lie in distributing the little wealth that exists but in creating more. And in order to do that markets must be opened up, competition and individual initiative encouraged, private property not be fought against but extended to the greatest number, our economy and our psychology taken out of the grip of the state, and the handout mentality that expects everything from the state replaced by a modern outlook that entrusts the responsibility for economic life to civil society and the market. (41)

Here it seems inconsistent to argue resentment in a technical analysis of the origins of national problems. The novelistic strategies of the fiction writer and the technical reasoning of the former presidential candidate's discourse interlace successfully because of a strong structure of analogies—a solid base for an artistic construction that persuades through polysemy and ambiguity.

Mixing "urgent letter" and "memorandum" styles, the book closes with an epilogue in which the perspective of the author-narrator (with respect to his private and public life) and the events of historic reality converge. Vargas Llosa imposes the successful conclusion of the young writer story onto the story of his political career. He only appears to have failed and thus his misfortune gains novelistic intrigue. The book's plot has no proper conclusion; the epilogue closes the book by endowing "real" events—those not organized by the memoir—with a sequence that coincides with the writer's story. While Peru fails, Vargas Llosa's *truth* succeeds: "Early in the morning on April 6, 1992, I was awakened by a telephone call from Lima. Alberto Fujimori had just announced on television, to everyone's surprise, his decision to close Congress. . . . In this way, the democratic system reestablished in Peru in 1980, after twelve years of military dictatorship, had its very foundations destroyed yet again, by someone whom, two years before, the Peruvian people had elected president" (525).

In *A Fish in the Water*, with the honesty of a fiction writer, Vargas Llosa brings together major problems being discussed in contemporary literature. Alongside the truth, if it exists, his realism, verisimilitude, autobiography, testimony, and sociology become as ambiguous as our perception of reality. This book creates a solid possible world, which is why, in my opinion, it functions as a novel. The book is the novel of his life, and therein lies its success. The problem presented by a book such as *A Fish in the Water*, which claims to be sociological truth, is its ambiguity with regard to the validity of a subjective interpretation of the Peruvian political situation, given its apparent neutrality. This problem of blurred borders has led to the mishandling and manipulation of Vargas Llosa's work and public life.

NOTES

[1] These strategies bring to mind Vargas Llosa's description of those Victor Hugo creates in *Les Miserables*, a gigantic presence interfering in the flow of events, judging, anathematizing: "he who judges and sentences does not listen, he listens to himself; he does not dialogue, he speaks only to himself" (*"Los Miserables:* el último clásico" 34; my translation).

[2] This recalls Vargas Llosa's study of Flaubert's techniques: "one of the most effective tactics for concealing the existence of the omniscient narrator is to make of him an impartial and meticulous gaze, eyes that observe the fictitious reality from a distance that never varies and a mouth that relates what those eyes see with scientific precision and total neutrality. . . . [T]he verisimilitude of what is recounted depends on this invisibility" (*The Perpetual Orgy* 227-28).

WORKS CITED

Vargas Llosa, Mario. *A Fish in the Water.* Trans. Helen Lane. New York: Farrar, Straus, Giroux, 1994.

——. *"Los Miserables:* el último clásico." *Cielo abierto* 23 (Jan.-Mar. 1983): 32-40.

——. *The Perpetual Orgy: Flaubert and "Madame Bovary."* Trans. Helen Lane. New York: Farrar, Straus, Giroux, 1986.

A Mario Vargas Llosa Checklist

Alex Zisman

Fiction

Los jefes. Barcelona: Editoral Rocas, 1959. Rev. ed. *Los jefes. Los cachorros*. Barcelona: Seix Barral, 1980. *The Cubs and Other Stories*. Trans. Gregory Kolovakos and Ronald Christ. New York: Harper & Row, 1979.

La ciudad y los perros. Barcelona: Seix Barral, 1963. *The Time of the Hero* Trans. Lysander Kemp. New York: Grove, 1966.

La casa verde. Barcelona: Seix Barral, 1966. *The Green House*. Trans. Gregory Rabassa. New York: Harper & Row, 1968.

Los cachorros: Pichula Cuéllar. Barcelona: Lumen, 1967. Rev. ed. *Los jefes. Los cachorros*. Barcelona: Seix Barral, 1980. *The Cubs and Other Stories*. Trans. Gregory Kolovakos and Ronald Christ. New York: Harper & Row, 1979.

Conversación en La Catedral. Barcelona: Seix Barral, 1969. *Conversation in The Cathedral*. Trans. Gregory Rabassa. New York: Harper & Row, 1975.

Pantaleón y las visitadoras. Barcelona: Seix Barral, 1973. *Captain Pantoja and the Special Service*. Trans. Gregory Kolovakos and Ronald Christ. New York: Harper & Row, 1979.

La tía Julia y el escribidor. Barcelona: Seix Barral, 1977. *Aunt Julia and the Scriptwriter*. Trans. Helen R. Lane. New York: Farrar, Straus, Giroux, 1982.

La guerra del fin del mundo. Barcelona: Seix Barral and Plaza y Janés, 1981. *The War of the End of the World*. Trans. Helen R. Lane. New York: Farrar, Straus, Giroux, 1984.

Historia de Mayta. Barcelona: Seix Barral, 1984. *The Real Life of Alejandro Mayta*. Trans. Alfred MacAdam. New York: Farrar, Straus, Giroux, 1986.

¿Quién mató a Palomino Molero? Barcelona: Seix Barral, 1986. *Who Killed Palomino Molero?* Trans. Alfred MacAdam. New York: Farrar, Straus, Giroux, 1987.

El hablador. Barcelona: Seix Barral, 1987. *The Storyteller*. Trans. Helen Lane. New York: Farrar, Straus, Giroux, 1989.

Elogio de la madrastra. Barcelona: Tusquets, 1988. *In Praise of the Stepmother*. Trans. Helen Lane. New York: Farrar, Straus, Giroux, 1990.

Lituma en los Andes. Barcelona: Planeta, 1993. *Death in the Andes*. Trans. Edith Grossman. New York: Farrar, Straus, Giroux, 1996.

Nonfiction

La historia secreta de una novela. Barcelona: Tusquets, 1971.

García Márquez: historia de un deicidio. Barcelona: Barral, 1971.

La orgía perpetua: Flaubert y "Madame Bovary." Barcelona: Seix Barral/ Madrid: Taurus, 1975. *The Perpetual Orgy: Flaubert and "Madame Bovary."* Trans. Helen Lane. New York: Farrar, Straus, Giroux, 1986.

José María Arguedas: entre sapos y halcones. Madrid: Ediciones Cultura Hispánica del Centro Iberoamericano de Cooperación, 1978.

The Genesis and Evolution of "Pantaleón y las visitadoras" and Panel Discussion. Ed. and trans. Raquel Chang-Rodríguez and Gabriella de Beer. *The City College Papers* 12 (1979).

"Cómo nace una novela." *Américas* 31 (March 1979): 3-8.

Contra viento y marea (1962-1982). Barcelona: Seix Barral, 1983. In 2 vols. as *Contra viento y marea, I (1962-1972)* and *Contra viento y marea, II (1972-1983).* Barcelona: Seix Barral, 1986. *Contra viento y marea, III (1964-1988).* Barcelona: Seix Barral, 1990.

La verdad de las mentiras: ensayos sobre literatura. Barcelona: Seix Barral, 1990.

A Writer's Reality. Ed. Myron I. Lichtblau. Syracuse: Syracuse Univ. Press, 1991.

Carta de batalla por Tirant lo Blanc. Barcelona: Seix Barral, 1991.

El pez en el agua. Barcelona: Seix Barral, 1993. *A Fish in the Water.* Trans. Helen Lane. New York: Farrar, Straus, Giroux, 1994.

Josef Skvorecky. Photograph by Andrej Barla

The Bittersweet Vision of Josef Skvorecky

Steve Horowitz

Critics commonly regard Josef Skvorecky as one of contemporary Czecho-slovakia's finest writers. His successes and scandals under the Communist regime are well known in his native country, and his works in translation have given Western eyes a glimpse of Czech life during the Nazi and Communist eras. He has also written about Czechs in exile, including those who fought in the American Civil War, the musical genius Anton Dvorak, and the refugees who defected after the 1968 Soviet invasion.

Skvorecky himself is one of those post-1968 émigrés, which has led to a curious phenomenon. Although Skvorecky writes in the Czech language about Czech characters, he has become one of the most respected authors in Canada, his adopted country. He was appointed to the Order of Canada in 1992 and has won the Canadian Governor General's Award. He also received (with his wife, Zdena Salivarova) the Order of the White Lion in 1990 from Czech President Václav Havel, the highest award given to *foreigners*. Certainly Skvorecky's largest audience reads him in translation rather than Czech.

Despite having lived over twenty-five years in the New World, Skvorecky remains quintessentially European in his choice of language, topics, and characters. He has always maintained a Czech sensibility, which filters his perceptions of America. Consider the previously unpublished short story "Three Bachelors in a Fiery Furnace" he has generously donated for this issue. The influence of Ernest Hemingway on his use of dialogue and descriptive style is clear. Yet the story is distinctly Czech, not only in its setting and characters but in its bittersweet vision of the world. Skvorecky discusses his experiences as an East European writer in the changing world in two previously unpublished lectures: his address to the Fourth World Congress for Soviet and East European Studies, and his Keynote Speech to the conference on Eastern European Literature in Transition.

In contrast, no one has done more than Sam Solecki to reveal Skvorecky's accomplishments as a *Western* writer. His book on Skvorecky, *Prague Blues* (1990), brilliantly delineates Skvorecky's constant evolution as a fiction writer. For this issue Solecki has interviewed Skvorecky, their discussion focusing on Skvorecky's more recent work, primarily *The Bride of Texas*. The fresh information provided suggests Skvorecky's increasing Westernization. Indeed, the two essays here on *The Bride of Texas* approach this same idea from distinct perspectives. Helena Kosek's "American Themes in *The Bride of Texas*" and Maria Nemcova Banerjee's "Variations on American Themes: *The Bride of Texas*" both reveal the development of

Skvorecky's American concerns and sensibilities, as evidenced in this latest novel.

Tracing a career for most authors is easy, but not for Skvorecky. The details of Skvorecky's early life are simple enough. He was born in Nácod, Bohemia, Czechoslovakia, in 1924. He graduated from Charles University in Prague in 1949 and earned his Ph.D. in 1951 with the thesis "Thomas Paine and His Significance Today." At this point, following Skvorecky's career quickly becomes confusing. In terms of his writings there are usually three key dates: when the work was originally written; when it was published in Czech; and when the English translation first appeared. But the translations have not come out in chronological order; they sometimes precede the Czech publication and even appear in French or Polish first. For example, *The Republic of Whores* (English translation,1993) was originally written in 1954 in Czech. A Czech edition printed in 1969 was destroyed by the Communist regime. So a Czech edition was not available until 1971 and then from Skvorecky's own Canadian publishing house, although there was a French translation published in 1969.

But while the details of Skvorecky's literary biography are complicated, a quick sketch can situate the works discussed in this issue. Skvorecky wrote his first novel, *The Nylon Age* (1946), while a university student, but it went unpublished for over ten years because his writing did not meet the favor of the Communist Party censors who controlled the printing presses. When *The Cowards* was published in 1958, he lost his editorial position at the Czech literary journal *World Literature*, and the editors and directors responsible for the book's publication were also fired. *The Cowards* concerns the liberation of a Czech village from the Nazis at the end of World War II. Skvorecky's characters did not fit the heroic mold of the socialist-realist fiction demanded by the Communist Party. *The Cowards* did not appear in English until 1970.

"The Bass Saxophone" was originally written in 1963, the same time the changing political zeitgeist led to Skvorecky's rehabilitation by the authorities. Its treatment of the artist, in this case a musician, under an authoritarian regime appears analogous to the problems Skvorecky himself was facing. Then came the Prague Spring, the Russian invasion of Czechoslovakia, and Skvorecky's defection to the West. *The Engineer of Human Souls*, written in 1977, specifically reflects on what happened in his world during the previous four decades. *Dvorak in Love*, written in 1983, again deals with a seemingly autobiographical situation, that of a Czech artist living in the New World. Skvorecky's 1996 novel, *The Bride of Texas*, concerns the same topic from the perspective of immigrants.

I once asked Skvorecky, while drinking shots of Canadian whiskey from little hotel refrigerator bottles, why he wrote autobiographical fictions instead of autobiography. He looked at the darkening blue sky over the Cedar Rapids landscape: numerous train tracks, a slow, thick, brown river, and the glowing neon sign of the Quaker Oats factory. He said: Why limit yourself to the truth, when you could improve on real life? In fiction you can make up something better. The landscape below could have been modern Bohemia with its mix of the agricultural, industrial, and commercial. Indeed, the largest ethnic minority in the area were descendants of Bohemian immigrants. Skvorecky and the townspeople weren't going to accept things as they were. They aimed to enhance their existence.

An Interview with Josef Skvorecky

Sam Solecki

SAM SOLECKI: *The Bride of Texas*, appeared in Czech two years ago and in English last year. Could you tell us something about it?

JOSEF SKVORECKY: It's a historical novel, set during the American Civil War, and deals with a group of Czech soldiers serving in General Sherman's army in the campaign in Georgia and the Carolinas until the final victory at the Battle of Bentonville. As far as I know, and I did a great deal of research for the novel, this story about Czech-American soldiers has never been told. With the exception of one individual, all of the characters are real.

SS: Why did you make an exception for the one?

JS: Well, I needed someone who could bind the various stories and episodes together. Many of the stories, by the way, are based on narratives written by the soldiers themselves which I found in old Czech-American almanacs published throughout the second half of the nineteenth century.

SS: As with several of your earlier novels, *The Bride of Texas* has a subtitle, "A Romantic Story from Reality." *Dvorak in Love* had "A Light-Hearted Dream."

JS: In this case, the "romantic story" that runs through the novel came from a nineteenth-century romantic story, a Czech story published in the United States and written by a writer who is now completely forgotten. It involves the very beautiful daughter of a poor family in Moravia who becomes involved with the son of a prosperous local farmer. As you can guess, the father is opposed to his son's involvement with the girl, but the boy persists and eventually he and the girl try to elope to America, but they are caught. In the end the father decides that the best way to break up the romance is to have the girl and her family emigrate to America. He pays the bill for the entire family, and so the young girl, Lida—which she changes to Linda in the United States—ends up in America.

Unfortunately, when she arrives in America she is already pregnant. Anyway, she has the baby and decides that having tried love, she will now try to find a rich husband. She becomes involved with the son of a rich plantation owner who, like the Moravian farmer before him, is predictably opposed to his son's involvement with a poor, though beautiful, immigrant. They elope to Savannah, Georgia, and that's where they come into direct contact with the Civil War as General William Tecumseh Sherman's army overruns the city.

She's no fool, and she realizes that a Northern victory signals the end of her fiancé's wealth, so she immediately leaves him and catches a young officer in Sherman's army.

SS: So far it sounds like a modern romance novel with a very resilient and capable heroine.

JS: It is, or at least one aspect of the novel is. The other involves the soldiers I mentioned who are all folksy characters who spend a lot of time telling stories. They're not much different from the soldiers in Hašek's *The Good Soldier Švejk* or in my own novel *The Republic of Whores*. It's probably the one thing soldiers in all armies and at all times have in common: they spend a lot of time telling stories.

The central character here is Sergeant Kapsa, a real figure whose story I found in my research. He was a real soldier, a professional, who joined the army before the Civil War started. He was in the Thirteenth Battalion with five other Czechs, and the commander was Sherman, then just a colonel. The archives don't explain why there were six Czechs in this particular unit, but my theory is that they were all probably deserters from the Austrian army, which at that period conscripted soldiers for a seven-year term. And this meant that you had to say goodbye to whatever life you had when you entered the army. If you had a girlfriend, she probably wouldn't wait until you got out.

I have a hunch that the deserters who made it to America probably found out that it was easier to join the American army than to do anything else because after so many years of soldiering, they didn't know anything else. And since they were professional soldiers or at least had some experience in the military, some of them made very capable drill sergeants.

SS: Did the documents indicate whether Sergeant Kapsa was a deserter?

JS: No. But in my story he accidentally kills his commandant in a fight over the commandant's wife, with whom Kapsa has been having a love affair. If he'd stayed, he would have been tried for murder, so he ran. It's a romantic story like many of the stories I ran across in the Czech writing of the period. These stories are not "great" writing, but they are often very moving.

What I try to do in the novel is to tell the story of the war, of Sherman's March, through the eyes of these soldiers who also were a part of great historical events even though their story hasn't been told yet.

The bulk of the novel is composed of five chapters between which are sections that I call the writer's intermezzos, and these are narrated by a successful woman writer who has had an interesting life. For example, she disrupts her wedding by leaving the groom, the future General Burnside, at the altar and running away. Incidentally, this part of the story is true; Burnside's fiancée did run away from the altar. The rest is fiction. She changed her mind because she received a letter from a publisher who wanted to publish her first novel. Given a choice between marriage to a soldier and a career as a writer, she opted for freedom.

SS: This section at least sounds like a contemporary feminist novel.

JS: She ends up as a very successful writer, a best-selling author of novels "for young women" that are similar to the Harlequin Romances. At the same time she dreams of writing a serious novel, and she begins one at the start of the war when she herself becomes indirectly involved by hiring an escaped slave. She decides to write the story of the black woman who, after the war, unfortunately, ends up as a very successful madam of a very successful brothel in Chicago. Instead of a tragic heroine, she is faced with a real-life successful entrepreneur.

What I find fascinating is how often reality is as funny as any fiction. For instance, before the war, there was a militia in Chicago, organized by the Czechs, which called itself the Lincoln Slavonic Rifles. I found the letter in which they ask for permission to use Lincoln's name. Their main concern seems to have been about what sort of uniform to wear and how to keep out anyone who was not of Slavic origin. Unfortunately, when the war broke out, few of them wanted to serve and they found various excuses for avoiding combat. So the Slavonic Rifles gradually became full of Germans—only twelve Czechs remained—and the name of the unit was changed to Lincoln's Rifles.

SS: How does a Czech-Canadian writer find himself writing about the American Civil War? In other words, how did *The Bride of Texas* begin?

JS: It began when I was doing research for *Dvorak in Love*, which was published in 1986, and I ran into some narratives and stories dealing with the war and with Czechs and Slovaks who had fought in it. They were often told in a very naive way, and, as you would expect, they were full of Victorian coincidences; but they showed an aspect of history that many people, including many Czechoslovaks, weren't aware of. One of them, by the way, was a novel by a woman who became a courier for Thomas Masaryk during World War One. She traveled back and forth between Prague and the United States until the latter entered the war.

One of my favorites is the story of the Czech soldier who met two slaves in North Carolina who spoke Czech. What happened was that they had been raised by a childless Czech couple who brought them up speaking Czech. They are probably the first two blacks in history to speak Czech.

SS: Is this a true story?

JS: Oh yes, yes. And in the archives and almanacs and Czech publications of the period you find other similar ones.

SS: This is one thing that *Dvorak in Love* and *The Bride of Texas* have in common. They're both grounded in a great deal of research in historical documents. In fact, in the Czech edition each comes with a lengthy bibliography and an authorial note explaining the extent to which the novel is historical and factual. I can't think of many other novels that make as explicit a claim for their historicity. Each also has many period photographs of the people and places referred to in the novel. It's as if you don't want the reader to forget that these novels have a slightly different cognitive status from novels in general. The photos and the bibliographies also create the impression that these books have an indeterminate generic status somewhere between fiction and history; they take the claims of history seriously without necessarily giving historical discourse primacy over the fictional one.

JS: Well, you know I designed the books that way—with photographs and etchings—because I think they enhance the novel's period flavor. They also help the readers visualize the characters better—how they look, how they dress and so on. I must admit I'm disappointed that the photos and etchings don't appear in the English translation of *Dvorak in Love* because they are an important part of the novel. As for the bibliographies, I know that there are several novels written about the Civil War which have them as well, as a kind of documentation for the fiction, so I'm not the first to do that.

You know, in Prague I was congratulated on the bibliography in *Dvorak in Love* because it contained some pieces that, though not very important, were not very well known. By the way, the bibliographies are also important because I could be accused of plagiarism.

SS: Like D. M. Thomas in *The White Hotel*.

JS: Yes. So I protected myself by listing my sources and letting my readers know what the origins of the novel were. *The Bride of Texas* also has a postscript that contains a brief history of the Civil War because Czech readers won't be as familiar with it as Americans.

SS: Listening to you describe *The Bride of Texas*, I'm struck by the fact that even in a war novel, you have strong central female figures. And this is also true of *Dvorak in Love*; there at least three of the most important and most fully developed characters are women—Josephine, Adele Margulies, and Jeannette Thurber. Would it be fair to say that there's a significant turn toward strong women characters in your later fiction?

JS: No, I don't think so. I think that if you look carefully at the early work, you will see that the adolescent and teenage girls have independence and strength, though perhaps different from what today's feminists look for in a woman character. Don't forget that Danny is almost always a victim of the women he pursues, in *The Cowards*, *The Republic of Whores*, *The Swell Season*, and others.

I've always loved that book of Virginia Woolf's, *A Room of One's Own*, where she explains about the androgynous nature of people and especially of the writer. And I must admit I find it exciting to write in a female voice, from inside a female character. Some radical feminists may disapprove and maintain that it is impossible for a man to write from within a woman's viewpoint. I think that's nonsense. Two of the greatest novels we have, *Anna Karenina* and *Madame Bovary*, are the result of a man writing about a woman. And as I said, I enjoy doing it, trying to speak in the voice of a Jeannette Thurber or Lorraine, the writer in the new novel.

SS: We've talked about the fact that the photographs are missing from the English edition of *Dvorak in Love*, but that's not the only thing that is different between the Czech and English versions. If you read the novels side by side, you notice that the order of the chapters has been changed significantly, and the last chapter in the Czech version is now the penultimate one. My own impression is that the novel is much darker, almost tragic, in the English version than it is in the Czech.

JS: You're right, of course. There is a difference. Even the title is different. My American publisher suggested that no one would know what *Scherzo capriccioso* meant, and so they came up with some alternatives, including *Dvorak in Love*. As for the ending, the Czech ends with Adele Margulies boarding a train and leaving Dvorak after having failed to persuade him to return once again to America and the Conservatory. In the English the novel ends with a much darker chapter dominated by death, especially the inevitable death from cancer of Sissieretta Jones, "the black Patti."

SS: And there's that lovely and poignant image of "the white patch of the boat" surrounded by "the black, black darkness."

JS: You know, I like the changed ending.

SS: I'm not suggesting that it's better or worse, but it changes the mood of the close and makes for a slightly different novel.

JS: Well, I'm not the first novelist to have a novel that exists in two different versions. There's Fitzgerald's *Tender Is the Night* and James's *The Aspern Papers*.

SS: And Dickens's *Great Expectations* and Lawrence's three versions of *Lady Chatterley's Lover*. As Joyce said about the allusions in *Ulysses*, this is something that will keep the critics and professors busy for a long time.

I just want to turn back for a moment to the research you did for the last two novels. Did this change how you write a novel? I mean with *The Cowards*, *Miss Silver's Past*, and *The Swell Season* you didn't really need anything beyond your memory and your imagination in order to create. But with *Dvorak in Love* and *The Bride of Texas* you did a large amount of preliminary research and then had what must have been folders of material that had to be used, adapted, and referred to if the novel was going to be accurate in a historical sense.

JS: As you know, before *Dvorak in Love*, I had never written a historical novel, and so I had to develop my own techniques. The main difference between *Dvorak in Love* and *The Engineer of Human Souls* is that with the latter, when I had my outline, I could fully immerse myself in my memory and imagination; and I could write eight hours a day without having to consult any books or documents. It was all in my head, and I just kept on writing. With *Dvorak in Love* and *The Bride of Texas* on the other hand, I just couldn't do that because I can't keep all that information, all those dates and places and names, in my head. I would be writing, and then I would suddenly realize that I had forgotten something that might be important, and I had to stop writing for an hour or more while I looked it up. Only when I was doing the second draft could I write without interruptions, because I didn't need to consult the sources anymore. You know, before I attempted to write a historical novel, I hadn't appreciated how difficult and complicated a process it was.

SS: With *The Bride of Texas* your novels now cover nearly a century and a half of Czech life and history. There's not much about the first three decades of this century, but otherwise your body of work is almost a fictional chronicle of the life of a people.

JS: Well, it may sound old-fashioned to confess this, but one of the reasons I wrote *The Bride of Texas* is the patriotic one of offering a sort of tribute to the Czech soldiers who fought and in some cases died in the war. Their names are in the novel and they are real names, as are the names of the battles in which they fought.

SS: I don't think there's any doubt that the last two novels represent a significant departure for you, and it's certainly one for which there's little to prepare us in the earlier fiction. But I suspect that most of your reviewers and critics—from Helena Kosková to Paul Trensky—would agree with me if I said that your novels have been permeated by history from the start. *The Cowards*, after all, deals with the closing days of the Second World War, *The Republic of Whores* shows Czechoslovakia in the closing years of Stalinism, and *The Miracle Game* re-creates the Prague Spring and is a political and historical roman à clef with portraits of various individuals prominent in the period, from Václav Havel to Pavel Kohout.

I'm not trying to suggest that something new doesn't enter your fiction with *Dvorak in Love*. I'm simply saying that there also seems to be a certain continuity as well. In fact, I also wonder whether there isn't a natural progression between the two kinds of historical novels in your body of work, both of which are ultimately rooted in realism and concerned, though in different ways, with history.

JS: I think you're right in saying that I've always been concerned with history; being from Czechoslovakia it was hard not to be. In almost all my novels the action takes place against a historical background. The stories do have a context within which they take place and which influences the characters and their lives in some way. You could probably say the same thing about the Boruvka stories up to a point; the things Boruvka can do and cannot do are determined by the kind of society he lives in. And if you read them in the order they were written, you can see the different periods or phases of life in Czechoslovakia since the 1950s.

I once planned a series of five mystery novels with my friend, the poet Jan Zabrana, each of which was to have a different historical period for its setting. The first was going to be set during the Great Depression, another during the Second Republic (1938–39), the third during the war, the fourth after the war, and the fifth in the Stalinist era. Anyway, I never wrote the last two because I had to leave Czechoslovakia. For some time, I even contemplated writing the fourth one and sending it to Zabrana who could submit it under his own name. It was tempting and the series was very popular.

SS: The books were published under Zabrana's name, weren't they?

JS: Yes, I was still under a political cloud because of the scandal over *The Cowards*. We plotted the stories together, and then I would write the novels and Zabrana would take them to the publisher. Zabrana and I also collaborated on a children's novel called *Tanya and the Two Gunmen*, which is both an adventure novel and a sort of Russian language textbook. It has a Russian girl, a tourist, lost in the woods, who meets two young Czech boys and sort of teaches them to speak Russian by correcting their imperfect Russian.

SS: I find this interesting because language or languages seem to me to have always been a central concern in your novels. In *The Cowards*, for example, there are at least four major languages spoken as well as a couple of dialects, and this is also true of works like "The Bass Saxophone," *The Miracle Game*, and *Dvorak in Love*. And several of your critics have commented at some length on your ability to differentiate characters by how they speak. You seem to have a very good ear for dialects and dialogue. When you write dialogue, do you try it out by speaking the lines out loud?

JS: No, no. I just write it out as I hear it in my head. But it's interesting because when I was a young man and trying to write fiction and poetry—every young man writes poetry because for that you don't need experience, just feelings—my fictional dialogues were just awful—the dialogue was wooden and just a vehicle for information. I could feel that every character spoke in the same way. And then I read Hemingway's *A Farewell to Arms*, and I could see what could be done with dialogue. I also learned from other American writers I was reading at the time—Faulkner, Ring Lardner, Damon Runyon, and Mark Twain, of course, and even some of the predecessors of Mark Twain.

SS: Why were you so interested in the American writers?

JS: Well, I was very interested in American folklore; in fact, Lubomir Doruzka and I put together and had translated a huge anthology of American folklore. It must be one of the largest ever put together in Europe. But to return to your question about dialogue, I can't say that I have ever been aware of or self-conscious about paying attention to how people speak. And I have never studied language or linguistics. There are certain mysteries in writing, things that the writer can't explain.

SS: I want to worry the topic just a bit longer, because it seems to me that one of the ways that you keep the novels from being monologic or monophonic, even when they are narrated by Danny Smiricky, is by your ability to let the other characters have their say in voices that are absolutely distinctive. And I would argue that this freedom increases between *Miracle in Bohemia* and *Dvorak in Love*. The former offers various narratives, discourses, and ideological stances, while in the latter each chapter is narrated by or focused on a different character. The final effect is polyphonic, in Bakhtin's sense, as the reader is surrounded by various viewpoints expressing often conflicting interpretations and systems of value. Even in *The Engineer of Human Souls*, though the novel is narrated for the most part by Danny, the students' views are given a full hearing and his disagreements with them are part of a novel-long dialogue about ideologies and some of the topics mentioned in the novel's subtitle.

JS: Well, as you know, I have never been inspired by any ideologies, and I believe that there are novels that are completely devoid of ideologies—unless you agree with Marxist critics who tell you that everything is ideology or ideological, and I don't. There is a tremendous difference between the not-binding ideology of a liberal democracy and the mandatory totalitarian ideologies of political correctness. Some of the worst novels ever written were written for ideological reasons, and no one reads them now.

SS: But as anyone who had read *The Republic of Whores*, *Miss Silver's Past*, or *The Miracle Game* realizes, socialist-realist novels, ideological novels, have been the source of some of your liveliest humor and satire.

I want to return to the question of language for a moment. I wonder whether your most radical gesture in language, and perhaps your riskiest, doesn't occur in those stories and novels in which you have Czechs who have emigrated speak a Czech heavily inflected with English. I almost have the feeling that the ideal reader for these—and these include *The Engineer of Human Souls* and *Dvorak in Love*—is a bilingual reader, or at least one with some awareness of both languages, someone who can get the wit, whether it originates in Czech or English, and who can appreciate the energy of these bilingual portmanteau words.

JS: Yes, but you know English is such an international language now, that there are few Czech readers who wouldn't understand the words either from the context or just because they know some English. I suppose they will get the gist of it.

SS: Looking at this from another point of view, these passages must be a translator's nightmare, in the same way that some of the names in your fiction are. The villain of *The Republic of Whores* is nicknamed "Malinkatej dabel" in the Czech; in François Kerel's French this becomes "le P'tit Mephisto," while Paul Wilson christens him "the Pygmy Devil."

JS: There was the same problem with Dotty's name and the way she spoke in *The Engineer of Human Souls*. I once had a letter from a Czech woman who said she enjoyed that novel but didn't like the sections in which Dotty appeared because she found the way she spoke incomprehensible.

As for the problems some of these things cause for a translator, all I can say is that some aspects of a novel simply cannot be translated; something is always lost.

SS: Is it Valéry who said that literature is what is lost in the translation?

JS: It is unavoidable.

SS: Since we're speaking of translations, in *The Republic of Whores*, as was the case with *Dvorak in Love*, we have a novel that is substantially different in certain parts from the Czech original. This is particularly true of a couple of rather raunchy scenes and of two chapters that have been very skillfully conflated into one. Again, textual scholars will have a field day some time in the future comparing editions.

One of the scenes that I'm referring to shows a group of soldiers forming a sort of guard of honor or gauntlet for a female military prisoner on her way to the toilet. As she passes, they "present arms" by dropping their trousers and saluting her with their erections. In the English this is changed to a "rigid salute" and a swelling in their trousers. It's not quite the same thing. What happened?

JS: I have a very good editor, and she suggested that some repetition could be eliminated by intercutting the two chapters, and she told me that the night scene in the jail would get me attacked by all the feminists—it was simply too strong. So I changed it, toned it down. In the Czech film based on the novel they retained the scene as it is, and the film has been very popular. I don't know.

SS: The Czech text has the subtitle: "A Fragment from the Period of the Cult."

JS: Yes, that was because I originally planned the book as the introduction to a long novel or a long introductory chapter to a much longer book dealing with Danny's return to civilian life, but I never wrote that. So that's why I called it a fragment, though I dropped the subtitle from the English version. That's also why it has this loose structure which some people have criticized as episodic.

SS: But there are some threads holding the chronologically arranged episodes together. There's the focus on Danny, his last weeks in the tank corps, and the love affair with Jana, the officer's wife.

JS: I think that what a reader needs to ask about the book is whether or not it stands on its own despite the episodic structure or form. It's not meant to have the form of a more conventional novel, and each of the stories is intended to be both self-contained and related to the others.

I wasn't sure for some time whether or not to publish the novel in English, but what finally convinced me to do so was its immense popularity in Czech.

SS: Your wife once told me that she thought it is the most popular of all of the novels published by Sixty-Eight Publishers.

JS: That's true, but I should add that it's popular mostly with male readers, most of whom have had similar experiences when they were conscripted into the national army; very few women like it. Still, in the Czech Republic, a nation of eleven million people, it has sold over 250,000 copies.

SS: What are you working on now?

JS: I am writing a script for Czech television based on Edgar Allan Poe's "The Mystery of Marie Roget." I have been fascinated by Poe for a long time, and I can't explain why, but perhaps it has something to do with the fact that he is the father of the detective story.

SS: You recently wrote an article on Poe for *Světová literatura* in Prague.

JS: Yes. The dramatist Helena Slavikova read the essay and asked me to write something for television. The script is a drama that focuses on Poe at a time when his wife is sick, dying, and it also develops some of the ambiguities surrounding the death of Marie Roget, especially the possibility that she may have been made pregnant—maybe even killed—by the owner of the cigar store in which she worked. There is a suggestive sentence in the coroner's report in Poe's story: "The medical testimony spoke confidently of the virtuous character of the deceased." The script develops the possibility that—but since this is supposed to be a mystery story, I won't disclose the solution now.

Authors, Critics, Reviewers

Josef Skvorecky

The soundest advice ever given to a writer is Hemingway's: a writer should never read his critics. If he believes them when they praise him, he must believe them when they say he is no longer good. That undermines his self-confidence, the prerequisite for a job well done.

It is excellent advice but very few writers were able to take it to heart and act accordingly—although some were. There is a story in the émigré Czech novelist Egon Hostovsky's memoirs, *Literarni dobrodruzstvi ceskeho spisovatele v cizine* (*Literary Adventures of a Czech Writer in Foreign Lands*, 1966), about an experiment conducted by Faulkner's editor at Random House, R. N. Linscott. *A Fable* had just come out in France, and the author, in New York at the time, had an appointment with his editor who wanted to introduce Hostovsky to him. As they waited for Faulkner's arrival, Mr. Linscott, to Hostovsky's puzzlement, covered his desk with clippings of French reviews of the new novel and arranged them in a certain pattern. "Let's remember the pattern," he told Hostovsky, "so that we can see whether he touched them." When Faulkner entered his office, Linscott excused himself and the Czech writer for ten or fifteen minutes since, he said, they had some business to attend to. Linscott told the novelist to take a seat at his desk and, in their absence, to amuse himself by reading the reviews. A quarter of an hour later, when they came back, they found Faulkner sitting in the editor's chair with the pattern of reviews undisturbed.

In the end, Hemingway did not follow his own rule and literally devoured reviews of his books during the last and bitter phase of his life when reviewers were almost unanimous in their opinion that the star of the twenties had written himself out. After several years of reading, the star of the twenties blew away his head with a shotgun.

It is simply dangerous to read one's reviews. But then, until the arrival of modern American democracy, where even defecating on the Stars and Stripes is permitted, writing had always been a dangerous profession. Increasingly so in our own century, and in that part of our world known until recently as the Evil Empire.

However, some specifications should be made.

You may have noticed I used the word *critics* only when I paraphrased the quotation from Hemingway: otherwise I talked about *reviewers*. That is, of course, a very basic distinction to be made if one wants to discuss what happens to the mind of an author contemplating things written about his artifact. Only the negative verdict of a critic should be deadly: the reviewer's scathing remarks the writer should dismiss as irrelevant.

Should, but very rarely does.

In my vocabulary a critic is someone who does his homework. He won't write about an author until he has familiarized himself with at least the most important parts of his oeuvre, until he has spent some time thinking about it, and only then has come up with an opinion. If that opinion includes no redeeming qualities and passes the unequivocal verdict of "No good at ALL!", then the writer should reach for his shotgun. But such situations, these days, are fortunately rare, at least in the West. Since the times of Marx there have not been too many critics filled with enough Marxian meanness peppered with heavy irony and caustic sarcasm to invest the long hours of work and great amounts of mental energy necessary to write a substantial book of criticism as a scathing attack on a novelist they dislike. Most critics, fortunately, seem to share Anthony Burgess's feelings about their profession: "in my capacity as critic," wrote Burgess, "I never stab anybody, for I know how life-denying it is to be stabbed. Writing a book is damned difficult work, and you ought to praise any book if you can."

Therefore, nowadays critics pose little danger to the novelist.

Theoretically, reviewers should pose even less danger. They work in haste; they base their judgment on a first impression rather than on at least a pretense of analysis; often they have not read anything else by the author but the book under review; and how thoroughly they've read even that one work is open to question judging by the frequent misquotations and interpretational contortions one reads about in Letters to the Editor. The tendency to show off, moreover, to demonstrate the brilliance of the reviewer's mind at the expense of the misquoted author is also well known. All in all: authors really should not read reviews, and if they must, they should dismiss their opinions as mostly inadequate, often ridiculous, sometimes malevolent, and generally invalid. After all, there have been too many categorical dismissals of great books by reviewers to bother about the views of those frustrated and underpaid gentlemen. The man, for instance, who wrote about *Madame Bovary*'s author that "Monsieur Flaubert is not a writer" could not have spent too many hours reading the book, or else he was devoid of any sense of aesthetic beauty and of any understanding of life. Similarly, the reviewer for the *Odessa Courier* who searched in vain for "a page that [contained] an idea" in *Anna Karenina* and labeled the book "sentimental rubbish" was hardly qualified for his job. And so, since it is another well-known fact that negative reviews do not affect sales, and if they do then—more often than not—positively, the author should not lose one minute of sleep over bad reviews.

He should not, but—

Many years ago I wrote a short story, "The End of Bull Macha." In 1953, to be precise. I'm still quite proud of that story, although being proud of my literary efforts is usually not one of my sins. However, I had good reasons to be proud of this one. At a time when almost everybody wrote social-realistic fairy tales, I concocted a story about a zoot-suiter who, at a Sunday matinee dance, tries to do a jitterbug, is led off the dancing floor for "eccentric dancing," and when he protests the treatment which, he says, insults human dignity, the cop makes him show his identity card, takes down his name and address, and throws him out of the premises. I'm sure those of you who have "been there," to paraphrase Mark Twain, or have studied the times, will agree that whatever else this story is, it is not a fairy tale.

In the early fifties I showed it to a good friend, Dr. Ludvik Svab, a psychiatrist and the guitar player of the Prague Dixieland Band of classical fame, who liked it. He liked it to the extent that, in a private apartment somewhere on Pohorelec, he read it aloud to a midnight gathering of underground intellectuals. There was a literary critic present; I did not know who he was and never found out since. But he must have been one of us, the unsung dissidents of the early fifties when the word didn't even exist: otherwise he would not have been there, and Ludvik would not have dared to read my highly subversive stuff to the gathering. When Ludvik finished reading, the company remained quiet for a few minutes which I happily interpreted as a symptom of the deep impression my story had made on the circle of the like-minded. Then the critic got up and asked Ludvik whether the author was present. Before we went to the gathering, we agreed that Ludvik would not identify me as the bloke responsible for "Bull Macha," and so he said: "No." "In that case," said the critic, "I can be frank." And he launched into a improvised but fluent diatribe against "Bull" which, I felt, lasted an eternity. He dissected and aborted my brainchild without mercy and with what seemed to me great scholarship and deep critical acumen. In his final remarks he compared my, in his words, "shapeless and aimless attempt at literature" to a story by, of all writers, Jack London, a favorite of the Stalinists. And yet he was an underground critic. Or was he a police spy just posing as one of us? In any case, the comparison demonstrated that, unlike London's, my story was a complete artistic disaster for it failed to produce an unpredictable climax. And sure enough, he was right. The consequences of jitterbugging in the fifties were quite predictable. Many years later I learned that London used to buy ideas for such stories from Sinclair Lewis, for hard cash. I also realized that the tale was a typical example of the rather debased genre known as twist-in-the-tail.

But on that terrible night so many years ago I had no such knowledge. Ludvik, the good friend that he was, sensed the catastrophic state of my mind, and he walked me home, all the way from Pohorelec, which is on the hill west of the Hradchin castle, to my sublet room on the hill above Smichov, although he lived in Mala Strana, only about fifteen minutes of a brisk walk from Pohorelec. He tried to give my badly punctured ego a boost. Without any success at all.

That nocturnal literary execution felt like the end of my life, and I did not recover from it for about a year. I was young, oversensitive, overuncertain, too deeply submerged in writing for anything—friendship, love, praise from friends—to give me the tiniest of consolations. Those were most certainly the darkest, most hopeless, utterly horrible months of my life. I'm sure you will not consider this an exaggeration. You certainly know about the history of literature so you know about the many similar sufferings over the immaterial stuff of letters penned on a page of paper.

I wanted to begin this next paragraph with the words *strangely enough*, but then I thought better of it. There is nothing strange about the fact that the avalanche of vicious criticism that followed the publication of my first published novel, *The Cowards*, was not nearly as pernicious to my soul as the midnight verdict of the unknown underground connoisseur of Stephen Crane's "clever school of literature." The explanation is easy, and it has to do with the second distinction I'd like to make here.

The first distinction, if you remember, was between critics, whose bad opinion hurts, and reviewers, whose acerbic stabs should be dismissed as unimportant. The second distinction is between aesthetic and ideological condemnation. The first can be, and sometimes was, fatal to the writer's soul: after the disastrous reception of *Moby-Dick*, for instance, Melville fell silent for nearly forty years. Ideological condemnation can be, and far too often was, fatal to the writer's social status, financial fortunes, well-being, and even physical survival. Surely I do not have to mention the tragic fates of many writers in the Evil Empire. But as far as the writer's soul is concerned—his artistic self-confidence, his sleep—ideological criticism is harmless; it may even boost the ego rather than puncture it.

The nocturnal underground critic almost killed me and caused me months of beastly suffering. Something similar, though not nearly as drastic, happened to me shortly before the Party gave orders for launching a campaign against *The Cowards*. I had read my friend Karel Ptacnik's new fiction *Mesto na hranici* (The Border Town) and the experience threw me into desperation. Compared to what seemed to me a rich, panoramic, and superbly knowledgeable description of a very complex social situation, peopled with a stunning number of finely drawn characters, my own simple transcript of a week's adventure at the end of the great war in a small Bohemian town seemed insignificant, light stuff, telling the reader nothing about the complexities of life and society: in short, an embarrassing failure.

I was utterly desperate. It was not jealousy, which is usually the word used to describe the state of mind of the writer who feels that his colleague and rival has written a better book than he. Jealousy is a form of envy. But this is no envy. It has nothing to do with your colleague's brilliance and success. It has to do with your feeling of inferiority, not hatred. It is not temptation to commit murder, but a veritable dark night of the soul. I do not believe that Salieri killed Mozart. He only went mad.

It's a platitude to say that authors are the worst judges of their own work, and I can only hope that the platitude is correct. In any case, the extremely well-orchestrated campaign against my novel pulled me out of the abyss of desperation and made me feel that, perhaps and after all, I was not such an entirely lousy novelist as I thought myself to be.

Why?

Because the ideological critics of the Communist Party of Czechoslovakia put me into very good company indeed and painted my characters in colors I very much wanted to display in real life but never quite managed to. I was an introverted, shy youth who was unable to step knowingly on an ant and who always offered his seat on trains to the elderly and to what was then known as the weaker sex. But to the distinguished Party poet-reviewer Josef Rybak, writing in the Party daily *Rude pravo*, I was a "cynical photographer" who has "shown his own low moral character better than anyone before him." Surely, this was quite some praise in a field that was the playground of some very famous cynics known to the Czech literati in translation. And sure enough, their names popped up in connection with mine. Another Communist critic, Vaclav Behounek, commented disapprovingly that my hero and alter ego Danny Smiricky "reads like a latter-day Sanin," the hero, of course, of Mikhail Artsybashev's novel, or like Smerdyakov from *The Brothers Karamazov*. The book, Behounek opined further, was of the category of "Céline's *Journey to the End of Night*."

Could there be a better praise? Yes, there could. Céline was invoked also by Rybak who compared *The Cowards* to *Death on the Installment Plan* which, he wrote, was a book so despicable that *Journey to the End of Night* "was by comparison harmless reading for girl guides." The dear old man! And what about the following wonderful assessment from the pen of one Frantisek Kejik, the reviewer for the Army daily *Obrana lidu?* "*The Cowards* is the methodological handbook from which the remnants of the Golden Youth draw their means of expression rather than, as was believed until now, getting them from the penny dreadfuls, the illicitly distributed pornography, and the even more illicitly circulating trashy American novels." The last category was made specific by the Slovak socialist realist Vladimir Minac who, in *Kveten*, named Hemingway, Faulkner, Dos Passos, Joyce, Kafka, and Proust as the alleged and dubious models for me and the likes of me.

And so on. As I said, I was in good company. They crowned me the spokesman of the zooters who, in my mind, pleasantly associated with an old article in *Der Neue Tag*, the Nazi Party daily in the Protectorate of Bohemia and Moravia, in which they were held up for contempt as cynical and decadent American jazz fiends. The "humorous" Party weekly *Dikobraz* printed a rhymed satirical poem about me of which the first line—spoken by a Prague lady snob—stuck in my mind: *Ten autor nudu zahani*, or "This author dispels boredom." One of my innermost ambitions, since my days on the tenor sax, was to become a good entertainer. Well, perhaps I had become one.

So the smear campaign, although I lost my job, gave me at least some shaky confidence in my abilities as a fiction writer. It almost annulled the lingering dark night of the soul, the aftermath of that midnight on Pohorelec so many, many years ago.

This paper was originally read at the Fourth World Congress for Soviet and East European Studies in Harrogate, England, 21 July 1990.

Keynote Address: Eastern European Literature in Transition

Josef Skvorecky

It is an honor and a pleasure to have been asked to deliver the keynote address at this symposium. We should have an interesting and hopefully useful exchange of opinions, at a time when literature in the former Evil Empire is—as some believe—in a state of crisis. True, censorship, the mortal enemy of art, is gone, but the age of ruthless commercial interest, another, if less deadly enemy, has set in. Judging by articles I read, some people over there are close to desperation. The fact, for instance, that in Bohemia the biggest best-seller of 1991 was Margaret Mitchell's old potboiler *Gone with the Wind* equals, in some minds, a death knoll for serious Czech literature.

I do not share that desperation, and I hope this gathering of learned and creative people won't share it either. More than forty years ago, shortly after socialist realism, on orders from the Communist Party, throttled Czech literature, I—emulating Joseph Conrad—attempted single-mindedly to render the highest kind of justice to the cultural policy of that Party. Walking down Wenceslas Square one night with my dear friend Zdeněk Urbánek, I was mulling over the question whether there was anything good the Commies had done to Czech literature. In my naïveté—which is a polite word for stupidity, I guess—I told my friend: "Well, they destroyed everything else but we must concede one thing to them: they put an end to trash; to all those saccharine weekly romances and mechanical Westerns." With a touch of sarcasm in his voice, my friend said: "Is that so? I think they have just replaced one kind of formulaic trash with another. And anyway—this seems to be almost a natural law: if you don't have trash on the market, you don't have Joyce in bookstores either."

I never forgot this nocturnal lesson of the master, and to this day it has been filling me with stubborn optimism. Because it means one thing: seek freedom and everything else will be given to you. An absence of freedom is much more dangerous than any other danger, and since we, writers from the former Communist states, now possess freedom, we can survive anything: even the poisonous, though so well-written, melodrama of the late Miss Mitchell. So let's take courage and let's celebrate, at this symposium, the precious possession which had been missing from the world of art in our homelands for so long.

This is my second invitation to the symposia sponsored by the School of Slavonic and East European Studies of the University of London. I couldn't attend the previous one, held in September 1989; this time I was able to make it.

The organizing committee of both symposia sent the participants a list of topics for discussion. At the previous one, they were to assess the view held by the organizing committee according to which "prose fiction published in Czechoslovakia . . . had been underestimated. On the other hand, Czech literature published abroad had often been overestimated." Funny: when I read this sometime in the summer of 1989, it struck me as being pretty much the same as the recurrent thesis of the now defunct cultural establishment in Prague. It is quite remarkable how two groups of literary critics, working in totally different milieus and divided by the now-lifted Iron Curtain, could come to almost identical evaluations of literary affairs. For instance, Jan Kozak, the chairman of the former Writers' Union, writing in the amusing English language propagandist magazine *Panorama* sometime in the mid-eighties, voiced the same criticism and supported it by statistical data: whereas during the past five years, he pointed out, "459 English and American literary works, 217 German literary works, and 314 books from the French-speaking world" were published in Czechoslovakia, Czech writers "did not meet with the same attention" in the West, although in the same period of time they wrote "1242 new original works." A two-page map of the world was attached to these findings, with names of Czech and Slovak writers inscribed over the countries where their works appeared in translation. I don't remember the names on the map of the United Kingdom, but I recollect the two colleagues who represented Czech writers on the map of the United States: my old friend Josef Nesvadba, and one Helena Smahelova, whose work I'm unfamiliar with. Apparently she wrote a novel, *Dora Abroad,* in which the heroine visits the place ever popular with people who don't like America: the Bowery in New York City. She observed that nothing like that—I guess she meant alcoholics—could be seen in Moscow. She apparently never visited the Writers' Union Club in that city.

Inspired by Mr. Kozak and by the opinion of the London organizing committee, I've produced some amateurish statistics of my own. It seems that, in the period under scrutiny, only some twenty-eight books by eleven Czech authors came out in the U.S. alone. Naturally, this does not detract from Mr. Kozak's veracity since none of these eleven writers was among the authors of the "1242 new original works" published in Czechoslovakia. Apparently, they have been underestimated by Prague publishers, and since, by American publishers, they have been overestimated, it makes, in fact, for a nice balance.

Interestingly enough, this year's invitation shows further similarities, this time affinity in terminology. In the view of the organizing committee, "The Aesopian language of antisocialist writing, so long fostered by sanctioned as well as banned writers, has become as dead as the square-wheeled bicycle." If I'm not mistaken, "antisocialist" is Party Newspeak for "critical of Communist society" and, of course, Aesop's method may indeed be dead by now, since censorship went to hell along with Communist society. What the committee, perhaps, had in mind was that contemporary interest in such writings of and about the past has vanished. That may be true, I'm afraid. Of course, somebody once wrote something to the effect that people who know nothing about the past are in for a big surprise in the future. But my rehash of the original quotation may be inaccurate and, anyway, wisecracks are just *bon mots*, nothing more.

The organizers further speak about "the dangers of a lack of political constraint leading to a lack of artistic restraint." For me it is interesting to find such sentiments in a letter signed by Professor Pynsent. Judging by the little I read of his opera, I would think that he has a high opinion of modern literary experimentalists, and they, in my mind at least, rarely associate with any sort of artistic restraint. In a self-critical piece charmingly entitled "A Fool in London," published in the Prague weekly journal *Tvars*, Professor Pynsent has, for instance, words of high praise for *Finnegans Wake*. That book may be described in various ways—Evelyn Waugh, for example, saw it as proof of Joyce going mad with artistic vanity—but my characterization of it would most likely not be that it's a work of "artistic restraint." Our host says about it: "If a maid or a poor black woman in some southern state in the U.S.A. had a chance to hear some paragraphs from *Finnegans Wake*, she would understand them just as well as a much more educated and research-minded man like you and me." (He is addressing his interviewer). This strikes me as another intriguing closeness of views: of a Western literary scholar, and an Eastern propagandist-poet. Those of us who were in the University when Vladimir Mayakovsky was considered the King of Poets will remember his celebrated lines about art believed by some to be incomprehensible to simple folks. The concluding verse of that Marxist piece of idealism asserts that these simple folks do not have a lesser understanding of great art than you and me.

Another topic on the list calls for a "redefinition of trash." From that I gather that trash was defined at the previous symposium which I was unable to attend, and consequently I don't know the definition that is to be newly defined at this symposium. *Trash* also seems to be Professor Pynsent's favorite critical term. In an essay which appeared about a year ago in the Slovak weekly *Literarny tyzdenik* he made the observation that, being British, he was unable to "distinguish between Tatarka's and Mňačko's trash." Neither am I, since I don't know the current definition that is to be redefined. In these circumstances, I have to resort to standard dictionary definitions. These make *trash*, in the literary sense, synonymous with *kitsch* which, in turn, is defined as "a pejorative word for a work which is of little merit; a mere potboiler; something 'thrown together' to gratify popular taste." Professor Pynsent, being a scholar, surely arrived at his assessment of the two Slovak authors through meticulous analysis with which

I am unfortunately not familiar. I only read the two authors for my enjoyment, and they didn't strike me as fitting the above-mentioned definition of trash. But I always trust a scholar's judgment, and so I should regret having published two kitschy books by the late Dominik Tatarka.

It's only human, I guess, to be eager to know what the same scholar thinks about my own work. After reading the results of his analysis of Mňačko and Tatarka, I confess I was a little apprehensive of his verdict of me. But a passage in his *Tvar* piece reassured me. There he says: "I find only one thing that makes good literature good literature, and that is ambiguity (which also means humor in the English sense of the word, and irony in the romantic sense) but I would add that a great work of art must have something in it which is there potentially for everybody, a philosophical system, let's say, even though only a post-Kantian can understand it critically, but at the same time it must have some power of an inner experience through which it arouses compassion." I apologize for this ad hoc translation of Professor Pynsent's Czech into English, but I pondered this quotation a long, long time, and eventually I felt even more encouraged. True, I wasn't sure whether I ever used ambiguity except, perhaps, in the ending of my novel *Miss Silver's Past*, where it's left to the reader to decide whether Mr. Leden will rape Miss Silver or not. Neither was I sure if I used humor in the British sense for I didn't quite know what it meant. Hobbesian humor, perhaps? Or humor according to the theories of Herbert Spencer? In any case, most readers, including Professor Pynsent, as I found later, think of me as a humorous writer. On the other hand, I was mildly certain that the term *romantic irony* may be applied to my way of writing. According to my dictionary, "romantic irony occurs when a writer builds up a serious emotional tone and then deliberately breaks it and laughs at his own solemnity." That, I guess, comes pretty close to what critics in America describe as "mixing tears and laughter" and apply it to my technique. So I felt even more confident. A setback made me less so—when I realized that I probably had no philosophical system, let alone a post-Kantian one, guiding my pen. I was, however, slightly emboldened again by the demand of the "power of inner experience" which arouses "compassion." Some critics—even a few British critics—and a larger number of jazzmen—even some British jazzmen—found precisely that, i.e., "the power of inner experience," in my novella "The Bass Saxophone," among them—if I may brag a little—the great Alice Babs, the immortal Duke of Ellington's favorite singer. And though I wasn't sure whether my inner experience led anybody to compassion, I felt, on the whole, confident that in Professor Pynsent I would find a friendly and appreciative critic. My self-esteem rose accordingly.

Well, I was in for a surprise. In another essay, "Social Criticism in Czech Literature of the 1970s and 1980s Czechoslovakia," I, at long last, found the professor's opinion of me. I am a "well-intentioned trashist" writing "in the Salingeresque sentimentalizing style" which I "introduced to Czech literature at the end of the 1950s."

Luckily, following the advice of Hemingway and the practice of Faulkner, who rarely read his critics, and having been through all kinds of troubles, some of them considerably more serious than mere literary rebuffs, I have developed a rhino hide. So I took Professor Pynsent's remarks for a friendly gibe, also because there are some faltering insights in the *Tvar* interview. My books, it is said, are "swell entertainment" and they "often duplicate your and my own experience." This pleases me to no end since I have always desired to be a good entertainer: first as a nightclub saxophonist, later, when I realized that I couldn't do it, and suffered long enough because I couldn't, a writer-entertainer; an author of potboilers "every copy of which would travel from hand to hand, from hands marked by pinpricks and corrosive laundry detergents, reddish with kitchen cleansing powder, soiled by ink spots, into hands bruised by some other kind of hard life, until finally the title page of all copies would become lost and nobody would know anymore who the author was. And it would be unnecessary to know, because everybody would find himself in the book." Well, I see I must be a trashist all right, letting myself be carried away by the words of a master-trashist, the "Czech seller of banalities" in the words of Professor Pynsent, the purveyor "of the worst petty bourgeois pussyfooting," Karel Čapek. On the other hand, it may also mean that I've always had the ambition realized in *Finnegans Wake*, as it has been demonstrated by the professor on the example of the Southern Negress's—sorry, black lady's—sorry, African American woman's literary taste.

So back to the serious critical stuff: my books "often duplicate your and my own experience," says the professor. He, however, questions, whether they "tell us anything real—except that we should stay on the surface, that it is better not to dig deep into the emotional intestines." Well, I confess I never do that. Mea culpa. Instead of following Dr. Freud, I uncritically accepted some views of T. S. Eliot concerning Shakespeare, as diluted by some popular Yankee authors, and I most likely misinterpreted even those since, on my way to emotional bowel movements, I managed to penetrate only skin-deep.

In the *Tvar* piece Professor Pynsent describes himself as a teacher of "intellectual decency." Apparently that's why, in the last analysis, I do not fare too badly with him. "I have nothing against [Skvorecky's] books," says he. "As you know, I'm deeply interested in trivial literature." In North America we use a different term: we call books that folks like to read pop-literature. In any case Professor Pynsent's interest is heartwarming. Especially since, as Mr. David Short, also of this school, states in the bibliographical work *Czechoslovakia*, which he has compiled, I'm largely my own publisher, and, though this has not always been so, in our age self-publishing authors are deemed unworthy of the attention of serious criticism. But, perhaps, I'll be allowed to note in my defense that it is extremely hard to convince publishers in the West that they should bring out Czech originals of one's works. Since my books, just like Kundera's, Havel's, Grušas's, Klíma's, Kriseova's, Kotrla's, Vaculík's, Kresadlo's, Benes's, Salivaroa's, etc., were turned down by Czechoslovak publishing houses for not being up to the standards for literature by authors like Mr. Husak's Foreign Secretary, Mr. Chnoupek, whose work Professor Pynsent translated into English for the late Mr. Maxwell, I most regretfully had to resort to the shameful practice of cottage-industry publishing and even to self-publishing. Therefore I'd like to use this occasion and thank here publicly those Western publishers who overestimated the efforts of me and my friends to the point of publishing them in various languages although, regrettably, not in Czech. But I and my wife—we had no editors—made up for that neglect and published, under the label of Sixty-Eight Publishers, Corp., some 225 titles. I know that most of these books do not meet the high artistic demands of the London School of Slavonic Studies. However, I comfort myself with the thought that, at least, by publishing them we brought some fun into the gloomy lives of exiles and the only slightly sunnier lives of people at home. Now that any conceivable political prejudices against Czechoslovakia have become dead as a square-wheeled bicycle, I see a good chance with the Western publishers for authors of higher aesthetic stature than the ones I and my wife published, although, until now and in this part of the world, they have been underestimated.

Why, actually, was that so? Judging by Professor Pynsent's essay mentioned above, books published in the 1970s and the 1980s in Prague constitute one uninterrupted line of harsh social criticism of the conditions of life in Communist Czechoslovakia. That should have been the sort of stuff antisocialist, capitalist publishers would jump for and bleed one another to the point of bankruptcy, fighting for Western rights at auctions. Why didn't they? The essay provides an insightful hint: "Generally speaking, social commentary is stronger now than it was in the 1960s, even if political [stress is mine] commentary . . . is weaker." This observation is well worth paying attention to: given the discriminatory practices of capitalist publishing companies, one can safely assume that it was precisely this lack of political commentary which led to these authors' underestimation.

That, I guess, is easy enough to see. But *why* were these ferocious social critics so feeble in their *political* criticism? I searched for an answer over many a book I borrowed from the Robarts Library of my university but I confess, I couldn't find one. Why?

Tired of hard thinking, to which I'm not used, I stared at the reproduction of an artifact by Jiri Kolar which I keep on the wall over my desk. It had been made by a technique invented by Kolar which he calls "zmizik," or "disappearing act." My reproduction is called "Bonjour, Monsieur

Gauguin," and even people only as slightly familiar with French impressionism as I am will identify it as a work of the said Gauguin. There is the wooden fence of the front yard, there is the colorful background—but something has happened to M. Gauguin. He disappeared from the picture! The artist somehow completed the background hidden in the original painting by M. Gauguin's now missing body.

Suddenly, in my mind, everything fell into place. Why this is precisely the technique Vladimír Páral, the writer I have always taken for the most accomplished technician of the contemporary Czech novel, had been using up till 1968. He captured the social aspects of living in the 1960s with a pen worthy of a true master while, at the same time, he managed to make the Communist Party perform a truly Kolarean disappearing act. Not only is it never mentioned in the series of his pre-1968 novels, its presence and the presence of the less savory institutions created by the Party are not even felt. And yet, these works give the impression of an almost photographic rendering of Czech life. I take my hat off to such an accomplishment.

This disappearing act, it seems to me, to a greater or lesser degree, was performed by a whole literary movement in Czechoslovakia in the 1970s and 1980s. For lack of knowledge of how its participants called themselves or how their critics described them, I will take the liberty, if I may, of labeling the movement Czech neonaturalism. I'm probably wrong or at least inaccurate, but I was struck by one aspect of these writings which the Czechs, it seems to me, had in common with the old American muckraking naturalists. Like the latter, they loved to wallow in a wide assortment of societal ills such as virulent alcoholism, prostitution (the hard-currency variety: an improvement on the pre-Communist soft-currency whoring which was accessible to simple folks, not just to American tourists), further drug pushing, embezzlement, privilege seeking, inventive bribery, money laundering, etc. If we are to believe these novels, various mafias operated in actually existing socialist Prague, preselling apartments of moribund people to underworld racketeers who earned money in cahoots with smuggling highway truck drivers from the West—well, Professor Pynsent gives an exhaustive catalog of these topics.

Only a few of these writers, however, approached the old naturalists' conclusion, and they never formulated it *expressis verbis:* that man is doomed to senseless tragedy, and that the world is a stage not for just class-conflict but for a Manichaean struggle between Evil and Good, in which Good always loses, no matter what social system happens to be the status quo.

Classical naturalists had all sorts of theories that explained the sorry state of man and society. The pessimistic mood and the muckraking gusto of their novels were firmly rooted in what they believed was a scientific analysis of reality, an analysis that revealed the *causes* of the tragedy of both society and human existence. In their novels these causes were *always* demonstrated: occasionally through direct comment, more often by means of imagery, story development, metaphor. Based on Darwin and Spencer, later on Freud and Marx, the great novels of European and American naturalism were, in fact, artful novelizations of philosophical and scientific theories.

The Czech neonaturalists were supposed to write with a background of Marxist knowledge which was to operate in a way similar to the theories of the old boys. But any analysis, Marxist or other, would discover that, in a society sporting a total monopoly of power, the ultimate source of social, moral, and political no-no's is the failing not of individual subjects of that power but of the power itself, in the case of Czechoslovakia, the power of the atrophied Communist Party. In fact, one didn't have to work out an elaborate analysis to come to this conclusion. All that was necessary was to live in Czechoslovakia. The neonaturalists lived there. But unlike the classical naturalists who identified the ultimate source as they saw it, their Czech followers could not diagnose the source of all evil in the actually existing socialist world—that is, if they wanted to see themselves in print rather than in jail. So they wrote in what resembles the naturalist mode but without its philosophical underpinning. They performed the disappearing act en masse.

But still—even if they refrained from identifying the villain—how come they could get away with so much muckraking? I don't pretend to know the answer because I lived elsewhere at the time. Professor Pynsent attributes this remarkable liberalism to the Third Congress of the Association of Czech Writers in 1982 where "criticism was given Party blessing by the Central Committee secretary Josef Havlin who called on writers to fight 'Schlamperei,' poor morale at work, opportunism, indifference and the petty bourgeois mentality." I'm not so sure. Party calls for sharp criticism of such things were nothing new in 1982; in fact, the Party had always officially "encouraged" what it called "positive criticism," and even "audacious artistic experiments" ever since the late Stalinist Vaclav Kopecky in the 1950s coined the term *suchari* (dry biscuits) for writers who toed the line but produced unexciting "dry" works, lacking the "juice of life," etc. In fact, distinguishing between "social" and "political" criticism, as Professor Pynsent does, comes pretty close to the old Party separating "positive," i.e., acceptable criticism from "negative," i.e., "antisocialist" criticism. The former, labeled ever since Minister Kopecky launched his campaign against dry literature, *komunalni satira* (which should be translated, I guess, "criticism of symptoms"), attacked precisely the *Schlamperei* Comrade Havlin condemned again in 1982. What the neonaturalists did, when compared to the old practitioners of "communal satire," was that, sensing the tired state of the Party, they pushed their criticism of symptoms much farther than their predecessors. Their printing success was simply due to the method of attributing evils of the system to individual sinners, even sinning Party members. Doing this, they deviated from Marxism, of course, and came close to Christian explanations of societal malignity. But they got away with that, too, since, in their works God Himself performed the disappearing act.

My hypothesis may be off target, but if it is, then only by a slight margin. The lack of underpinning was apparently felt by the few honest and yet published critics in Prague. Thus Jan Lukes wrote in *Prozaicka skutecnost* (Prosaic Reality) in 1982: "A literature that must first, in endless variations convince itself that character and morality weigh more than power, fame and profit . . . instead of attempting to capture the deepest social roots of the phenomena described . . . only as cosmetic flaws of individuals, cannot fulfill its avant-garde social function."

But still—thinking about the clever methods of the neonaturalists—I can't get rid of the gnawing suspicion that the absence of philosophical underpinning may not have been the only reason why capitalist publishers ignored them. Professor Pynsent, apparently, harbors a similar suspicion when he writes: "The essential failing of recent Czech literature is . . . a lack of style. The period has produced no prose stylists, only very few stylish poets, and I have not yet read a single drama of merit." I understand that he limits his observations to the period from 1970 till 1986, when his article, from which I quoted, was printed. Therefore he excludes authors known already in the 1960s who cannot be seen as *products* of the two decades under scrutiny. Indirectly, however—if I understand him correctly—he acknowledges that there *were* good stylists in the previous period as, indeed, it seems to me, to be the case. Harbal, Fuks, Scotola, Páral, Vaculík, Havel, Kundera, Grušas and others, all meet, I gather, the criterion of "prose stylists," with the exception, perhaps, of Václav Havel, of whom Professor Pynsent doesn't think too highly. He believes, for instance, that Havel is "an incestuous writer" which, I must confess, surprises me. I know Havel and his literary and some other escapades pretty well, but I don't think they include this particular sin. Havel is also "an escapist who overstresses the importance of language to such an extent that he becomes a victim of his own language-consciousness." This comment is too learned for me, but it would seem that Havel, as a man obsessed with language, must be *some* sort of stylist. But, of course, he is outside the time category specified by Professor Pynsent. He began having his plays produced in the 1960s, and he stopped having them produced—although not in Great Britain—in the 1970s; so he doesn't count. The same is true about most of the above mentioned stylists. Nevertheless, within temporal, geographical, and social limits, in which Professor Pynsent is discussing the literary crop of the previous two decades, it is certainly fair to say that Czech neonaturalism produced no Stephen Crane.

At long last, the regime that forced writers to unnatural magicians' tricks is now gone, and a new era is dawning. Even neonaturalists will now be able to call a spade a spade, and the others use styles and methods that would have shocked the now-defunct censor. This era, I understand, is to be the subject of this symposium.

So I'll stop here. I apologize for my rambling speech, focused mostly on problems of the past which, these days, interest only a few people. I know it was not much of a keynote address but most likely just a piece of well-meaning academic trash. There is, however, quite a lot of such stuff being written everywhere so that mine will, hopefully, escape attention. Ladies and gentlemen, I wish you fun at this conference. I feel you will help to clarify, in papers and discussion, the intricate problems which literature faces in the post-Communist world.

Keynote speech delivered at the "East European Literature in Transition" conference at the School of Slavonic and East European Studies, University of London, 4 December 1992.

Three Bachelors in a Fiery Furnace

Josef Skvorecky

On Saturday evening in the spring, the girls appeared in sensational short skirts and cinnamon coats, and the unblemished whiteness of their petticoats shone in the rosy evening. During the week the girls worked hard, but Saturday evening was a holiday.

In the morning they would usually hurry without breakfast, for girls want to be slim, and I would see them early in the morning, fleeing through the fog to the spinning mill. They came back in the afternoon, in a procession which flooded the town, as soon as the sirens would go off. They would vanish into the scratched gate of a cracked house, in the entrails of which they would devote the rest of the day to some secret female activity.

But on Saturday evening they were Kocandrlovic women, Mary and Magdalene, and they would set out on a pilgrimage along the town's promenade, on a walk leading nowhere, just to swing those skirts on stiff petticoats and defiantly shine their lace into the twilight of our youth.

Meduna, Schultz, and I had been swaying up and down the street from six o'clock on, and the rosy spring, which didn't really belong to us anymore, was destroying us. Meduna, a stout locksmith with a not very active imagination, dressed in an intensely elegant jacket of checked spring fabric, with a good-natured face hidden by a Styl hat, and placidly lit by an Orient cigarette. Schultz, a thin old pal from the tobacco store, with bright, beautiful eyes which nobody noticed, and a Mongol face full of trust; an aging hunter from the distant prairies of childhood.

A few people walked by, even girls, and Meduna's eyes hunted among them. But I saw them coming on the opposite sidewalk, Moroccan collars under cheeks like dog-roses, with sky-blue skirts, and stiletto heels tapping out small, tender periods after their hopes. It is awful what kind of wall there can be between people because of sheer misunderstanding, a mere difference in age and intelligence, what a misfortune. The most artful Irene, the prostitute from Holesovice, talked about such girls—just to talk. But I was venturous. I mulishly believed that if I had at least one more opportunity like the one during the winter, everything would be different, and Mary or Magdalene, it didn't matter which, would talk like Sapfo, like our beautiful, sweet Bozena Nemcova.

"Let's go," said Schultz.

"Wait," I said. The gold swan on the apothecary building shone in the evening's rosy light. The incredibly pink, sticky, slowly flowing light was dripping down the front of the building like watered-down blood onto the sidewalk, and they were approaching on it.

"Good evening, camellias," I said quietly. But they didn't answer. Their little heads like black-thorns drifted through the pink lemonade like two sweet stiff necks. Perhaps they didn't know whether it was plural or singular. I didn't know, either. And I didn't care. Plural, singular, dual, it's all the same.

"So let's go!" I said to Meduna. And we went. Oh hell. My heart was aching. That pink syrup onto the pavement of the street. Ah, camellias! Ah, ladies, ah, my friends from the spinning mill, afflicted with obstinacy where I'm concerned, you made a mighty bad wreck o' me.

When I looked back, they were already far away, and only the white tips of their lace were sending out luminous signals to the rosy gray of evening. But these signals were not intended for me. I didn't make it with them, but these novices in Texas Levis had not yet learned Morse code. Nobody will learn it. Not until it is already late. Not until it is no good anymore.

"Let's go somewhere where there's music," said Meduna.

"Let's go to the Graf," suggested Schultz.

So we headed for it, but when we got there I didn't want to go in. Hadinec had just come from there.

"Ahoy, Hadinec," said Meduna.

"Ahoy," said Hadinec. And then, "Don't go there. It's really dead."

"Are there any girls there?" asked Schultz.

"No."

"No girls at all?"

Hadinec shook his head.

"So let's go to the Sport," said Meduna. We went. The sky grew dark, and rosy streaks were interwoven through it like angels' swords banishing people from Paradise. This may be the last spring. Day after day is dropping from the calendar of our life, and those beautiful girls, Mary and Magdalene, will soon be married. Maybe even within a year. We may no longer even be on the earth in a year. I was really sorry about it.

We reached the Sport Hotel and stopped; we looked at each other uncertainly, and Meduna nodded. Silhouettes behind the milk-glass door stirred and opened it. A little table with an empty saucer for money and a fresh pad of admittance tickets, a man with a delightfully inviting smile, and a deserted, bare corridor to the underground bar appeared. We were petrified, and in silence looked at the cool, bottomless corridor. The smile on the man's face lingered for a while. Then it faded away. Then he closed the milky door. Meduna turned around and fixed his eyes on the dark sky over the station, where the cold and damp stars were oozing through the rosy flames. Schultz swore. Meduna's eyes had filled with a vast male weariness. I grew awfully sad, right to the point of dying. Meduna, looking somewhere in the direction of the spring stars, said in a tired voice, "Everywhere they are enticing, and everywhere."

A *Genial Gossipmonger*

Lubomir Doruzka

In 1992 an ingenious Czech film director decided to shoot a TV feature on Josef Skvorecky. Proposing to show him through testimonies of some of his best friends, he asked them the same question: "How did you like your portraits in Skvorecky's novels?" Some of them—including Václav Havel, president of the Czech and Slovak Federal Republic, and the Oscar-winning film director Jiri Menzel of *Closely Watched Trains*—admitted that when they first read a clandestine copy of *The Miracle Game* during the Communist period, they did not find "their portraits" in this novel very flattering. However, this did not prevent them from appreciating the book as a whole and in no way endangered their personal relations with the author. Their responses, in fact, reflected an intellectual wisecrack of the 1970s which stated that in *The Cowards* Skvorecky upset everyone in his native town, while in *The Miracle Game* he upset all of the nation. Since *Náchod* (the author's birthplace) and *narod* (Czech for nation) rhyme, the wisecrack enjoyed great popularity. Finally, Skvorecky's tendency to upset people continued in *The Engineer of Human Souls*: this time a great many Czech exiles not only in Canada and the United States but elsewhere. Their common lot, regardless of where fate may have blown them, gave rise to some idiosyncrasies that they all shared and they "recognized" themselves—or, rather, the way they would react to certain situations—in characters that Skvorecky may have drawn from quite different models.

All Skvorecky's novels up to *Dvorak in Love* are located in realistic contemporary settings. However, with the passage of time, these settings have gradually become historical so that today some of the younger readers may read *The Miracle Game*, for example, as a historical novel, which can hardly do without some well-known historical figures. These characters—sometimes the primary movers of the main story, sometimes appearing only marginally to add a special coloring to the atmosphere—are often modeled after real persons, therefore tempting some readers to try to figure out Skvorecky's crossword puzzle of twentieth-century Czech history. This game especially drew Czech readers to Skvorecky's novels, while often remaining outside Western readers' awareness. Still, this sense of scandal, so limited to his country, is finally a secondary attribute, as shown by the fact that his works can be (and are) appreciated by people to whom this game remains unknown.

More interesting, even to his readers abroad, is the question of to what extent Skvorecky borrows from reality. And this does not concern only his characterizations: this also relates to the question of how he fictionally uses real incidents, which often contribute to the development of his characters. That is, he may tell us something about what a person looks like, he may even endow him or her with some characteristic gestures or phrases. But he does not dare to penetrate into his character's thinking or feeling (except occasionally when telling the story in the first person). He prefers to show, from the outside, how his heroes behave under certain conditions and in certain situations that are based on fact.

A Czech reviewer called Skvorecky—without any negative intention—a genial gossipmonger. In fact, his books are gigantic collections of stories, jokes, or humorous hard-to-believe incidents that nevertheless are rooted in historical reality. Sometimes these actions really happened to the historical characters that Skvorecky has co-opted for his fiction. Sometimes, Skvorecky takes an incident and appropriates it to affect his fictional characters. Sometimes it happens to somebody quite different. Sometimes he creates episodes that combine scraps of real events happening at various times and in various places to various people. Sometimes these episodes are more imaginatively based on a sound historical estimation of what might or might not have happened to his characters if they had been living during a certain era.

Not very long after the original Czech edition of *The Miracle Game* was published in Toronto and began to be smuggled to socialist Czechoslovakia, I sat in a small café with Karel Srp, chairman of the Jazz Section of the Czech Musicians' Union (he was later sentenced to eighteen months in jail after a spectacular trial). The place was crowded and we could get seats only at a table for four. Our neighbors were a couple of teenagers, probably a Czech student with his date. He seemed to be fully absorbed in conversation with his companion, so we talked shop without any reservations. After some time I had to leave the table and when I returned, our neighbors were gone. But Karel Srp told me with a gleaming face: "Just imagine what that boy told me. He apologized for overhearing our conversation—which he could not avoid, sitting so near us at such a small table—and then he added: 'I just couldn't help identifying your friend. We're leaving now, but when Lester comes back, please tell him I wish him all the best.'" As I said, this was soon after *The Miracle Game* was published in Canada. There were not too many copies in Czechoslovakia, and possessing one and lending it to somebody else could be classified as antisocialist activity. People were sent to prison for lesser charges. Yet, as this story indicates, Skvorecky's book—despite its limited access in Czechoslovakia—had a profound effect on readers in his homeland. This shows the role that Skvorecky's books played in his homeland—a role of which his readers in the West were hardly aware.

Lester, in truth, is a very minor figure in the novel—he appears in two scenes only. He has a moustache, which should suffice to identify me as a model for this character—there were not many mustached jazz writers in the country at that time. Also, some other characteristics fit me like a glove. For instance, Lester would simply sit through boring meetings, signing nothing, and not involving himself in the counterrevolution. Skvorecky may have been just exercising poetic license in writing that Lester's flat voice, along with his moustache's expressionist waggle, were symbols of a movement we all belonged to. But regardless, these scraps of description taken together were enough for the student, who obviously had some knowledge of the Prague jazz scene, to send his best wishes to me, a proto-type of one of the characters in this prohibited book.

So now what about the situations Lester finds himself in? Are they based on reality, too? The first episode involving Lester, where he and the narra-tor record a program in a broadcasting studio, is indeed based on fact. Skvorecky and I did produce a radio program of this kind, though not with live guests. But when Skvorecky develops this into a series of incidents lo-cated at different times, the connection with reality becomes much looser: it becomes a fictional reminiscence of what might have happened, a remi-niscence depending on the dramatic climaxes so infrequent in everyday life.

The second scene with Lester is quite different, as he and the narrator emcee a concert by Bert, a progressive American folksinger and banjo player. Most of the audience does not care (because they do not under-stand) what he sings about. For them, he is simply an American star, one of the very few who has come to Prague, and he gets an enthusiastic welcome. Bert is enthralled by his success, so he adds a political, anticapitalist song and asks Lester to translate its lyrics, word by word, before he sings it. Lester advises him against this, but Bert is adamant. Lester obliges and treats the audience to a pastiche of leftist propagandistic phrases that they know all too well from the local Party press and publications. The singer, up to now wildly acclaimed, meets with a frozen silence.

This episode, as far as my memory goes, never happened this way. The model of the singer is obviously Pete Seeger, the only folksinger associated with the American leftist movement who ever got to Prague during the 1950s and 1960s. Neither Skvorecky nor I acted as interpreter for him. But both of us, as well as many of our colleagues, had experienced very similar situations in meetings with leftist writers, journalists, or playwrights, who came to Czechoslovakia with a political vision and who found it difficult to understand that something had gone wrong, right from the beginning, with the realization of their socialist dreams in our country. This was a typical situation, although hardly ever so dramatic as in Skvorecky's fictional treat-ment of it. Skvorecky simply takes a representative situation, lets it be en-acted by his characters (disregarding where, or when, or to whom some-thing like this really happened), and makes the characters react as they might have reacted in real life.

Sometimes it may seem that Skvorecky is overblowing such situations.

Readers in the West may find the atmosphere of *The Republic of Whores*
(the Czech title is "The Tank Corps") too Rabelaisian, although in depicting the absurdities of army life it hardly goes farther than Joseph Heller's
Catch-22. But again, despite its exaggerations, the novel's stories are deeply
rooted in reality. It is dedicated to Stanislav Mares and me, "the reserve
NCO's who were there." The three of us (including Skvorecky) served in
different units in different places and partly at different times, so that our
varied experiences were complementary and mutually enriching, and
Skvorecky's use of them is revealing, as evidenced, for example, in the absurd scene of the Fucik badge examination. In the second year of my
twenty-four-month military service, I participated as a member of the ex-
amining board in many such sessions that featured details even more exuberant and unbelievable than those appearing in *The Republic of Whores.*
But none of these sessions had the dramatic and climactic development
that Skvorecky created from the material he had experienced, gathered, or
invented. Still, the book catches the atmosphere of army service at the beginning of the fifties; it is a collection of multiple individual experiences
told by an author who was able to transform collective experience into a
work of art.

Yet another example of how Skvorecky cannot pass up a real story if it
suits his fictional purposes comes from *The Engineer of Human Souls.* At
the time when it was in manuscript and being partly typeset in that cozy
setting room of Sixty-Eight Publishers in Toronto, I went on a music business trip from Prague to Latvia. I arrived in Riga just in time for a composer
friend to take me to a fishing cooperative on the Baltic beach for a great
traditional celebration of the longest day, the summer solstice. There I saw
a long line of beer drinkers, moving like ants to a single place in a great
open meadow, where it was possible to relieve their bladders behind a huge
poster of Vladimir Ilyich Lenin. This sight was fascinating, and I wrote
about it to Skvorecky when I returned home. He liked the story so much
that he expertly inserted it into the finished manuscript, so that it would
enrich the novel's comical atmosphere.

The Czech critic's bon mot about Skvorecky being a genial gossipmonger
indeed contains much truth. Certainly Czech readers may better appreciate the characters, stories, and situations as they have been part of their
own experiences. But nobody who has ever read even the most hilarious of
Skvorecky's works would mistake him for just a jolly storyteller. There is
always a deeper, more profound note within his stories. It is not by chance
that a collection of his crime stories is called The Mournful Demeanor of
Lieutenant Boruvka.

This narrative stance falls within the tradition of the crime story—specifically in some of the crime stories by Karel Čapek. Some of Čapek's crime
stories show a deep compassion with the villains—if his perpetrators, simple

human beings caught in a web of circumstance that does not allow them to act otherwise, can even be called criminals. A similar approach can be seen in some crime novels by Ruth Rendell where the perpetrators are sometimes more pitied than condemned.

Čapek transferred this compassion from his crime stories to serious novels. At least two of them, *Hordubal* and *A Plain Life*, show ordinary, decent people reacting to situations and conditions they can hardly master or influence. Skvorecky's gossip collecting is something very similar, for behind his stories, behind his characters' efforts to confront and cope with their comically bittersweet lives, one hears that famous shriek of Clark Terry's trumpet as he enacts the role of Puck in "Such Sweet Thunder," the Shakespearean suite by Skvorecky's beloved Duke Ellington: "Lord, what fools these mortals be!"

Of course, Skvorecky's view of the human condition changes over time: there is a process of ripening in his art. When he was young and "innocent" in his native country, everything seemed clear to him, as it does to Danny, the teenage hero of *The Cowards*, "The Bass Saxophone," and "Emöke." However, he begins to doubt whether everything is really so clear and simple, and *The Miracle Game* reinforces this idea of change when the narrator portrays life as "that badly written whodunnit in which the perpetrator is the truth but can never be run down." And, later in *The Engineer of Human Souls*, Skvorecky recognizes the difficulty—if not the impossibility—of explaining to people growing up under different conditions and in different surroundings matters about your own country and life that you find clear and self-evident.

At the same time, even as Skvorecky confronts the idea that it may be impossible to make your personal experiences truly understandable to others, he continues to affirm that you must keep on trying to connect. And if you can do this most efficiently by collecting and retelling the gossipy stories about others—a favorite human pastime since Chaucer's *The Canterbury Tales*—then you do it. It may not be such a bad way of confronting the problem of explaining yourself through fiction.

The Cowards: *Skvorecky's Contributions to Czech Humorist Literature*

Míla Šašková-Pierce

In the Czech Republic Josef Skvorecky is famous for his role in helping Czech literature and culture to prosper in exile, despite the stiff censorship of the post-Prague-Spring government. But this rebel of Czech literature also deserves credit for his other contributions to Czech culture.

As a translator of English literature, Josef Skvorecky became for the Czech reading public a mediator of new ideas, works, and trends developing in the Western world. Besides being a theoretician of English mystery and detective stories, he was a member and later a supporter of dissident intellectuals who produced the nonofficial philosophy and literature that defined the achievements of Czech literature. His real conspiratorial life started when (together with the writer Zdena Salivarová-Škvorecká) he defected to Canada and began to support Czech dissidents from abroad. As a partner in his wife's publishing house, Sixty-Eight Publishers, he disseminated works that would have been suppressed by the Czech Communist Party and remained hidden in many writers' desk drawers.

Skvorecky is also a jazz theoretician and this knowledge plays a great role in his fiction. He describes his involvement in the Czech cinema in *All the Bright Young Men and Women,* in which he underlines the fact that the lucid and irreverent creativity of the intellectuals who fought the brainwashing experience of Stalinism was responsible for producing the New Czech Cinema of the sixties. Skvorecky belonged to the semiunderground debate clubs, which defined the culture of the post-Stalin times. The members (aspiring writers, filmmakers, and other Czechoslovak artists) helped stimulate the ensuing cultural thaw of the sixties.

Skvorecky's greatest role, however, was as a writer. Despite the threat of imprisonment, loss of work, and denied access to education, his admirers copied and distributed his works, allowing millions of readers to enjoy the liberating laughter his books offered. There are numerous reasons for his popularity. First, Skvorecky created the ideal anti-Communist literary hero. Apolitical and highly intelligent, Danny Smiricky represented the cynical, intelligent individuals who were able to make it through the system without having to compromise themselves. Danny, originally a character taken from real prototypes, became a hero for Czechs to model themselves after.

Second, Skvorecky created a specific language, coining a number of neologisms and reestablishing the legitimacy of colloquial Czech in literary works. He abolished the taboo against a sexually connoted lexicon, gracefully using vulgar and erotically charged words. His playful mastery of the spoken language, which constantly demonstrated his knowledge of world culture, starkly revealed the Communists' empty lingo. Composed of lofty, little received sayings and pseudohumanistic slogans expressed in a halting and wooden Czech, the Communists' ideological jargon appeared in the mouths of Skvorecky's characters with a vengeance, mocked by its own idiocy and degraded by the brutish actions of the people who use it. In contrast, while the Communists batter high literary language with unintentional barbarisms and mindless content, Skvorecky's heros, especially Smiricky, use the creative pliability of colloquial Czech to express perceptive and intelligent views. This is especially true in *The Cowards*. In fact, many of the neologisms, such as *Bibenka* (little idiot), coined by Skvorecky have entered the lexicon of the Czech language and helped define the antiestablishment's intellectual expression.

Skvorecky has in many ways been a rebellious innovator. He exploded onto the post-World War Two Czech literary scene with his novel The Cowards. While the novel itself does not contain anything objectionable by Western standards, it did violate the rules of the dominant Czechoslovakian Communist literary genre, socialist-realism. Furthermore, Skvorecky boldly treated the subject of the Second World War, which had already become a sacred text of the official literature, inaccessible to the comic writer. In The Cowards Skvorecky offered a new look at life under German occupation, ironically depicting the May Uprising in a small Czech town. The book intentionally pokes fun at the timid "heroism" of middle-aged patresfamilias and other participants in the five-day uprising at the end of the war, occurring just before the Allied armies arrived.

The timing of the uprising, as portrayed by Skvorecky, is ironic. During the Nazi occupation, the townspeople have tried to survive without compromising themselves too much, without openly rebelling, and without provoking the occupying administration. They fear the terrible penalty any act of disobedience might cost the civilian population. However, when the victorious outcome is assured, the town organizes a cautious uprising. The town's adolescent boys realize their hopes; they are drafted, although, given their lack of training, they are not allowed to carry weapons when patrolling the town, and therefore they fail in their exhibitionistic heroism.

Skvorecky describes the complex motivations of the participants: their fear, fatigue, hunger, and eroded courage. Danny, as hero and narrator, appears for the first time in Skvorecky's canon as an adolescent eager to perform heroic deeds, although motivated mainly by the nonheroic factors of girls and desire. When the novel was first published, this antiheroic presentation was correctly perceived by the majority of readers as a mockery of the official history. They did not find an exalted and romantic uprising, as it would be presented in the heroic prose of the socialist novels. Thus *The*

Cowards and the works that followed need to be assessed against the background of the officially sanctioned program of socialist-realism. Only by seeing Skvorecky's novels in this context can one understand the negative reaction of official criticism, why the authorities censored and ultimately banned his books.

The socialist-realists' fictional world is an orderly place. As it describes the often violent revolutionary transformation of a capitalistic society into the communist utopia, it offers calm and morally monochromatic characters. These heroes take part in the socialist struggle for a better future by sacrificing all their individual, personal goals. At the end of a socialist-realist work there are no unresolved loyalties, moral dilemmas or ambiguous characters. All conflicts are synthesized into a final state of perfection, which underscores the undisturbed flow through time of a single governing ideology. The historical dialectic of Marxist theses and antitheses comes to rest in a postrevolutionary happy synthesis. The tormented individualistic "I" is absorbed into the monochromatic and mighty "We."

Sex and sexual yearning have no legitimate place in this dialectic. Sexuality is represented essentially in two forms, either as positive romantic love among Communists or as a perversion among class enemies. If a comrade is misled by lust, other comrades help him return to the proper path. The true socialist hero controls his desires. He is a saint/eunuch ready to sacrifice his individual pleasure, excising his biological flaws for the well-being of the collective. Although Freud's concept of compensation of sexual energy could be, at least in theory, used by the authoritative directives of socialist-realism, it is not. For despite the parallel between the asexual sacrifice of the revolutionary and the concept of compensation, Freud's works were among the *libri prohibiti* by the socialist authorities.

In reaction *The Cowards* flaunts socialist-realism's sexual prudery, undercutting the linear rendition of unidimensional heroism and the preplanned pedagogical resolution of all conflicts. Smiricky deconstructs the premises of the compensatory mechanism and concentrates on its causes. Skvorecky deconstructs the socialistically validated outcome of compensation into its primary impulses and, as a result, provides us with a cynical view of human motivations. As perceived by the adolescent Smiricky, the world is a mating dance for a number of distinct individuals who could never merge into the collective "We." Males are preoccupied with love and sexual conquest, while females play little games to impress the males. Consequently, heroism is primarily the outcome of chance, not the result of intelligent contemplation or moral motivation.

As a result, Skvorecky is the foremost humorist of antisocialist-realism. He satirizes the degradation of idealism in the socialist-realism canon, the hollowness of its ideological slogans, and its idiotic meanness. *The Cowards*, along with *The Republic of Whores* and *The Miracle Game*, introduced new comic and satirical forms that were later used by other Czech writers.

The humor in Skvorecky's works is thus based on the incongruity between original ideological ideas and their repetitive and defective verbalization by morally and intellectually impotent members of the Communist Party. Specifically, Skvorecky portrays—often with sexual undertones—an ordinary humorous situation and comments upon it by irreverently exposing the inappropriate postulates of the abstract Communist jargon. In *The Republic of Whores* Danny masters the role of the false friendly intellectual who, by using ideological slogans in a creative way, reverses their meaning and takes the arguments away from his superiors. After all, committed Communists cannot publicly acknowledge that their ideology could be untrue, unbelievable, and blatantly false. Skvorecky's books therefore are manuals about how to vanquish the primitive logic of Communist politics, while letting the authorities remain convinced of their intelligence and the invulnerability of their power. Having invented this ruse, he can manipulate the powerful and transform them into benevolent mentors.

Danny is a sarcastic intellectual who does not believe in idealism any more than his Communist tormenters. But unlike them, he sees through the paradox of power and uses his insights to obtain whatever he wishes. His behavior constitutes a collection of intellectual exercises that provide him with a reasonable degree of success with women and offer him a way to succeed through bluff and sarcasm. Like every Czech national, Danny is defined by the political circumstances as a reactive individual. Inevitably, then, the whole Czech nation has been able to identify with his struggles and his attempts to use cynicism to rise above any intellectually emasculating compromise with the unintellectual brutality of the Communist slogans.

Skvorecky has been often considered by Western literary critics to be a direct descendent of Hašek, the famous Czech humorist and author of *The Good Soldier Švejk*. Skvorecky himself, however, rejects this comparison. He doesn't believe that he has much in common with the cowardly and immoral creator of Švejk, nor does he see much of the knowledgeable and educated Smiricky in Hašek's hero. Certainly Skvorecky's novels have a leaner narrative than Hašek's intentionally ornate, digressive narration. But what the authors do share is a realistic description of characters nested in the everyday: we find an unchanging climate of drinking, unfaithful wives, impotent men, intellectually incapable leaders, stupid bureaucracy, and pervasive sexual yearnings. Whenever there are heroic actions, they result less from true human motivation than from pure chance or brutal necessity.

Unlike the idealized proletariat of socialist-realism, the working class in Skvorecky's fictional world behaves as a class of workers—real men trying to provide for their families, to live day to day and from pleasure to pleasure.

Without the props of ideology, these uneducated people use simple and sometimes foul language, and when they speak about the future order of the world, they naturally emit ignorant and funny opinions. They do not sound like Karl Marx's idea of the proletariat. They cannot resolve all social problems, which, of course, according to Marxist doctrine, they should be able to do by virtue of their class origin. In Skvorecky's works the young people have commonplace adolescent concerns. They are not absorbed in the fight for the classless future of humanity, but rather they're absorbed by sex. The girls are also earthbound, caught up in looking for a good marriage and a financially attractive situation.

Against Skvorecky's concrete world, the abstraction of socialism is a laughable game as long as those laughing at it do not get caught. Through the author's subtle manipulation, the reader is drawn into becoming a conspirator, one who *knows*—a member of the club of the initiated. The enemy remains the Communist Party, with their grasping for power, their stupidity, and their cruel charades, which we readers can see through very easily. Our shared view of the Communists is validated by Smiricky's erudition and his keen and poisonous perception.

Skvorecky's voice, tone, and intonation reflect an aspect of the cultural reality of life lived under a totalitarian regime. He is sarcastic, cynical, and angry. The cathartic experience of writing and reading, of laughter and bitter anger, becomes a cleansing metacommunication about the paradoxicality and illogicality of existence while playfully offering a means of dissociating oneself from one's tormenters. Skvorecky's language also fosters power because turning the Communist world upside down forces Communism to collapse, leaving every individual free to find a renewal of the soul. Is it surprising, then, that Skvorecky stimulated the whole nation's quest for unity against this oppressive ideology? Or that his fiction lives on in the post-Communist world? If anything can, Skvorecky's ironic wit will continue to aid the Czechs in shedding their harsh, heavy, and uncompromising Communist past.

This Thing, the Bass Saxophone, Is Anything but Ordinary

Josef Jarab

Josef Skvorecky's fascination with jazz is no new story for anyone who knows the author or has read his work. His writings and his private perception of the genuinely American musical phenomenon made it only logical and proper that he should be present at the Reduta Jazz Club in Prague during Bill Clinton's visit in January 1994, when the president of the United States brought his idea for a project called Partnership for Peace and was given by the Czech head of state, Václav Havel, a shining brand-new saxophone in return. The American statesman showed his appreciation by playing the instrument not only in Prague but later in the Kremlin for the president of Russia. All participants in this political game gave jazz a role as an opener of doors needing to be unlocked. I daresay that for Skvorecky, the jazz-loving Czech-Canadian fiction writer, it must have been exciting personally to witness these bits of history, if only to enjoy the importance of that jazziest of musical tools, the saxophone, which he himself used to play.

For Skvorecky, jazz has never been just entertainment. Like most of the musicians whom he has admired since his youth, he always found the music "an elan vital, a forceful vitality," and he believes, indeed knows, that its effect can be cathartic. This notion was of true relevance to the author and his own generation as much during the Nazi war as it was during the Communist regime in the decades after the takeover in 1948. Having watched closely and covered widely, in the American and Canadian press all through the seventies and eighties, the dramatic story of the Jazz Section in his former country after the Soviet occupation in 1968, Skvorecky has had good reason to believe that jazz retains some of its original vitality. In a recent interview, during his visit to the Czech Republic, Allen Ginsberg expressed the daring conviction that African American culture in general and jazz in particular may have contributed to the ending of the Cold War, and I believe that his old friend Josef Skvorecky would not, in principle, disagree; Skvorecky certainly knew and wrote about many Czechs and Slovaks "who liked syncopation more than their government" and behaved correspondingly.

The world of Josef Skvorecky and of his fictional alter ego, Danny Smiricky, is, in fact, unthinkable without jazz, and for the latter, as he was first introduced to us in *The Cowards* in 1958, the history of our civilization even falls into two ages, "before and after jazz." Profane as this may sound, it reflects accurately the nature of Danny's appreciation of jazz as something divine, something ideal and omnipotent. However, it was in the no-vella "The Bass Saxophone" that Skvorecky's passion for this kind and mode of music was expressed most eloquently and elegantly.

Although the narrator remains nameless in this long monologue, no-body would be surprised at his identification as Danny Smiricky; he men-tions the tantalizing Irena who was the lady of his heart, he speaks of the same friends, Benno and Lexa, with whom he played in the local jazz band, he lives in the same small town of Kostelec, located in German-oc-cupied Bohemia, and we hear of the same Messerschmitt airplane factory that was located there. The young man who, like Danny in *The Cowards*, was "seventeen eighteen" at the time of the story, shares some of the emo-tions and views of the protagonist in Skvorecky's first novel, including the conviction that the life experience that is most real feels "like a movie." Paradoxically then, this extreme dreamer can call himself "an absolute re-alist." And consequently, the narrator's story in "The Bass Saxophone" is more than real, it is surreal; it is a vision of the world that the ostensibly existing "Kostelec would not believe." The man's statement that he "was a person strictly of this world" is meaningfully qualified with his after-thought, "and my only myth was music."

But it was exactly this myth that made the story happen and helped shape it into one piece. The desire to perceive the music, to hear jazz, which is always so evocative of freedom, enhanced the will of this Czech youth to play it, even with a German band, and thus to partake of its poten-tial. It is obviously the author himself who strongly believes that the lan-guage of jazz can do more for communication and understanding of indi-viduals and groups, even those cast by history into mutually hostile worlds, than any other language. In the story the young German, Feldwebel, who seems to be infatuated with the narrator's sister, never manages to reach out to her, nor does she dare to show any recognition of his courting; his affec-tion, unfulfilled, may have ended with his life somewhere near Tolbukhin or Stalingrad, while she, unmarried, has "died of cancer before she turned thirty." The notebook with his love poetry perhaps "sank through snow to the earth, slipped into the river, the river carried it to the sea, it dissolved there, turned into nothing." And the only thing left is a Rilkean line from the notebook that has stuck in the memory of the narrator. No gratification, no catharsis. Unlike the jazz story, in which the scream of despair is over-powered by the sound of music, and the fear is conquered by the will of the musician to join other players and be in rapport with them, this challenge finds its symbolic and literal embodiment in the unusual object of the bass saxophone.

It is the enormous size of the instrument and its rareness that makes the narrator sense it as something "mythical," even "mysterious." And it must have been the young musician's enchantment that makes him ask the un-necessary question, whether the bass saxophone was what it indeed was; the force the object exerted must have helped him cross the line between the two nations, a line that was both an expression of mutual hostility and a sign of national and racial taboos introduced by the war. The youth's defiance gains a (grotesquely) mythological dimension after he is asked by the German whether he would like to try the instrument and play it; the bass saxophone becomes the biblical apple and he is Eve, or else the old man, who speaks "like the Serpent," is also "a miserable, hideous Eve with one bad eye," and the young man is Adam. When he later holds the huge instrument in his hand, it feels to him "like the tower of Babel," and it would be difficult not to notice the sign of aspiration to unconfound the languages humans use, a visionary project worth another attempt, however unrealistic the undoing of the biblical story might have been. After some deliberation and reasoning between his own voices as a playful and innocent child and a rational grown-up, the young man decides that "there are two tongues within every language," in fact suggesting that one, and only one of the two, is capable of communication beyond individual languages and nations.

Considering the historical situation, this in fact amounts to a rebellion, which is not only an "unreasonable" act but could also prove dangerous, if not fatal, for any of the parties involved. The courage to transcend fear and reason and animosity comes from the power of music, from the vitality and spontaneity of jazz, which travels from soul to soul and across borders with such ease. A German officer who has wanted the narrator to help the old man carry the case with the bass saxophone does not give orders but appeals for assistance with a reminder, "you are both musicians." Indeed, this common feature creates fertile ground for the use of the common tongue, which is capable of overshadowing the existing differences. Not only does the young man grant his help, he also tries the instrument and eventually consents to sit in for the band's disabled saxophone player in a public performance. It is natural then that, when he takes the place at one of the music stands in the Lothar Kinze *Unterhaltungsorchester*, he feels "transformed into one of them." One of whom, we may ask. One of the musicians or Germans or grotesques? As a matter of fact, each or all of these categories would, in a way, hold.

But what did it mean to be a grotesque in the Third Reich? And what, indeed, was normal under those circumstances? As in every totalitarian state, the official authorities and their ideologies and propaganda machines decided what was normal and what was not; and individuals by their public behavior determined whether they would fit in the ranks or fall out into a pool of the unwanted whom those in control, possessing nearly absolute power, could declare grotesques or freaks.

The history of jazz in Nazi Germany, the Soviet Union, and Communist Eastern Europe illustrates the transition of jazz from that sweet and wild but politically innocent music, as perceived by young enthusiasts, into "a sharp horn in the sides of the power-hungry men, from Hitler to Brezhnev," as Skvorecky informs his readers in his essay "Red Music," published as a foreword to the English translation of "The Bass Saxophone." While the essay (written in Toronto in 1977) concentrates more on the element of political protest, which was latently and, later, even openly present in jazz in the totalitarian states of both right and left ideologies, "The Bass Saxophone" also brings up instances, such as the one of the "heavenly" singer Milada Pilátová, called Gypsy, who has been chased out of town by young women from the Bata factories in Zlín not only because she becomes a social threat but also because she has "hit too close to the soul, and the ones that don't have any soul can't stand that language, that testimony, that Idea in the cavities where their soul ought to be." Those who know the story of jazz East and West could certainly expand on such an observation endlessly with accounts of sad and tragic lives.

As much as I think I understand Skvorecky's intent and motivation, determined by the time this novella was written, I believe that the blending of the fictional dreamlike adventure of the young musician with the bass saxophone and the more informative essay passages on the history of jazz and the general historical events leading up to the time of the real telling of the story (which must have been very close to the year when it first appeared in Czech, 1967) has diluted rather than intensified the eventual impact of the text. This being said, I also would like to point out that besides the imaginative charm and energy it possesses, "The Bass Saxophone" is an invaluable source of information on the state of jazz in the Third Reich and the Protectorate of Bohemia and Moravia. Grotesque as *Lothar Kinze und sein Unterhaltungsorchester* may seem, it is in its extreme form still a true expression of the reality of its time.

Jazz traveled freely from one metropolis to another in postwar Europe all through the "colorful twenties," and Berlin and other German cities were not excluded from the wave of American cultural influence. On the contrary, jazz thrived there as it did in the whole of Central Europe, and over the years it reached out into the provinces and started competing with more traditional brass bands even in a small town like Josef Skvorecky's Náchod, which is the narrator's Kostelec. The Nazi regime in Hitler's Germany after 1933 found it, of course, quite difficult to accept jazz on ideological principles, although the propagandists did not want to alienate people with an open attack on or an immediate ban of such popular music. The objections of antijazz propaganda conducted by minister Goebbels and carried out by fanatical critics, such as Max Merz and others, were based first on national and racial arguments (it was alien "Nigger-Jew" music). There were also social and cultural arguments (it was not *volkisch* enough, it lacked discipline, it was trivial and libidinous). The ongoing attempts to cleanse and Germanize jazz led eventually to the creation of orchestras like the Lothar Kinze band. The group members came from pure national Aryan stock, but because they were physically handicapped, they were to entertain the soldiers and other meritorious rank and file in the Reich. The orchestra and its performances were a far cry from the authentic music they pretended to play, and in "The Bass Saxophone" they are even worse than the narrator expected. Their mechanical rhythmic style made even famous old jazz numbers into ersatz jazz or swing. Just like the Eintopf dinner, the band was merely something to enjoy before the audience went to the theater. The narrator's reference to "jam session" style passes without a recognition—and it is impossible to guess whether Lothar Kinze's "if you wish" is a manifestation of the band leader's ignorance or tolerance.

In appearance, the *Unterhaltungsorchester* (one cannot resist thinking of it as a parody of the *Deutsche Tanz–und Unterhaltungsorchester*, which was established by the Nazi government and later, after Stalingrad, was moved by Goebbels to Prague) looked like a group of clowns rather than conventional or even unconventional artists; imagery of "some new Hieronymus Bosch," Brueghel, or Toulouse-Lautrec work is being repeatedly evoked. Even the narrator has to comply with the requirement to look like an apparition, which also, for practical reasons of safety, ensues from his tenuous situation. He disguises himself with Groucho Marx moustache and eyebrows and feels, not without reason, like an interloper who smuggles into the performance elements that have been carefully censored—he is the image of a foreign, American-Jewish entertainer, with the inclination to play more genuine, imaginative, and syncopated jazz, while recognizing his own "inferior" national identity. As a matter of fact, this is not the only or first such attempt on the part of the young Czech jazz musician; he has earlier collaborated with German officers who like jazz in an illegal exchange and dissemination of precious sheets of music, and he has enraged the local Nazi boss, Horst Herman Kuehl, by playing a Brunswick record of a Chick Webb recording, starring the black Coleman Hawkins and black Ella Fitzgerald, in the Kostelec cinema to an audience awaiting a German war movie. So while playing with Lothar Kinze a composition originally called "The Bear" but, to take the Russian allusion out of it, re-named properly as "Der Elefant," the narrator of Skvorecky's novella is involved simultaneously in an act of national, political, and cultural conspiracy and in a fantasy of international camaraderie.

This daydreaming comes to a sudden end when the disabled saxophone player appears and resolutely takes back his instrument and his position at the stand. Horst Herman Kuehl identifies the narrator and, enraged again, forces him off stage. A real story, or a vision? The middle-aged narrator maintains, "Dreams really die when they come true, and reality really isn't a dream," and so what remains for safe dreaming is not the future but the idealized past—the time "before the war," as all the members of Lothar Kinze's orchestra, including the leader, nostalgically elicited in their reveries over the friendly dinner. For the young man, "the challenge of the bass saxophone" still rang inside him a quarter century later as "that desperate scream of youth." Besides there were, for him, the ever vital heaven of jazz stars: Adrian Rollini, Spike Jones, Jimmie Lunceford, Django Reinhardt. And there were also the Czech greats, Gustav Vicherek, Honza Ciz, Karel Vlach, and Inka Zemankova. These legendary individuals performed amazing deeds in their own time, which have become embroidered over time into romantic myths and heightened the reputation of jazz. Such mythmaking informs "The Bass Saxophone."

The Engineer of Human Souls:
Skvorecky's Comic Vision

Edward L. Galligan

I would like to praise *The Engineer of Human Souls* for the qualities that might often be seen as defects—for its ramshackle, four-part structure, its odd, rapidly shifting tone, its surfeit of characters, its unglamorous, unassertive hero, and its systematic evasion of clear ideas and firm conclusions. In doing so, I am not playing with paradoxes; I am admiring Josef Skvorecky for being fully faithful to the imperatives of his vision, which is in the great tradition of comic literature. These imperatives are poignantly illustrated by a metaphor found in Jean Renoir's notebook when he was writing his father's biography: the great masters of the best periods "created irregularity within regularity. Saint Mark's Cathedral in Venice: symmetrical as a whole, but not one detail is like another. . . . I propose to found a society. It is to be called 'The Society of Irregulars.' The members would have to know that a circle should never be round." *The Engineer of Human Souls* is a circle most certainly not round, yet drawn with admirable skill and judgment. Like Renoir, Skvorecky embraces imperfection, which is a human inevitability, instead of reaching for perfection, which is a rationalist's dream that ends always in nightmare.

Engineer is the fifth and last of Skvorecky's novels about the life and times of Danny Smiricky. In the earlier ones Danny is portrayed as an emphatically unheroic anti-Nazi (*The Cowards*), as an excessively voluble and therefore inept pursuer of the pretty girls in his small town (*The Swell Season*), as a reluctant non-com in the Czech tank corps (*The Republic of Whores*), and as a man who has finally gotten the hang of going to bed with the girls but who cannot get the hang of passing himself off as a solid citizen in a Communist state (*The Miracle Game*). In *Engineer* he is a middle-aged Czech writer who has had the good luck to wash ashore in 1968 in the free and beautiful city of Toronto, where he can earn a comfortable living teaching American literature in a suburban branch of the university. Since many of the facts of Danny's life bear a strong resemblance to Skvorecky's, one might want to refer to him as the novelist's alter ego, though he does very little for Skvorecky's own ego. It makes better critical sense to look at Danny as a carefully drawn character, a piece of the mirror that Skvorecky has set in the roadway to reflect the reality of his and our times.

Certainly Danny is not a portrait of "an engineer of human souls." That phrase, we are informed on the acknowledgments page, "is held, by many political indoctrinators, to be Stalin's definition of the writer: as an engineer constructs a machine, so must a writer construct the mind of the New Man." Nor can he be an artist, in the powerfully romantic, Joycean sense of the term. He is just a writer of an unpretentious but enduring sort. That is, he is so unimpressed with himself that he does not bother saying much about anything he has written (let alone about his agonies writing it), but he apparently is not capable of not writing. Engineers who would write to Stalin's specifications have come and gone; forgers who would hammer out in the smithy of their souls the uncreated consciences of their races have a nasty tendency to wither and die young. But unable to do his kind of writing in Czechoslovakia, Danny transplants himself to another place where he is free to keep on reflecting life in the roadway.

Danny does have mirrorlike qualities. Abstractions do not quite register on him; persons and things do. He understands Marxist doctrines, of course, to the point of being able to administer sardonic instruction in communist dialectics when he wants to shake up naive students, but the idea of the glory and power of the state has so little real meaning for him that he keeps getting into trouble almost absentmindedly. He neither hates communism nor loves capitalism. Rather, he hates all the rules you had to live by in Czechoslovakia, while loving his freedom to live by impulse in Toronto. He has a great gift for friendship, even with crackpots, and is so loath to enforce rules on others that he cannot bring himself to report students for plagiarizing. Naturally—without trying at all—Danny offends the sensibilities of politically correct thinkers of all sorts just about all of the time. (In this respect I would stress his identity with Skvorecky. I can't think of a single one of Skvorecky's books that won't arouse the ire of the politically correct, apparently unintentionally, but usually before the end of the first chapter. This is a great and enviable gift.)

Linked with his freedom from abstractions and ideologies is Danny's curious passivity; he doesn't so much make his way through life as float through it. He despises the Nazis who established his country as their "Protectorate," but he gets involved in acts of sabotage and resistance only to please a girl whose father had been killed in one of their concentration camps and to help out a friend whose fiery temper has gotten him in dangerous trouble. He also despises the Communists who took over the state while he was a student in the university, but the closest he comes to organized opposition to them is to give shelter for a night or two to a friend wanted by the secret police. When a conversation with one student forces him to think of what might have become of him and of his writing if he had stayed in Czechoslovakia, Danny realizes that fear drove him from that country, "a healthy fear of the gallows, and of its more sophisticated, more subtle, and less bloody derivatives." When a conversation with another student leads to the question of why he settled in Toronto rather than in some more glamorous city, his explanation is that he was offered a job there. This passivity, this willingness to trust in what happens and to leave decisiveness to others, reveals itself even in his sex life. If the woman with whom he has been enjoying periodic bouts of copulation wants them to work their way through the postures described in the *Kama Sutra*, that's fine with Danny. When he falls in love with one of his students, she is the one who seduces him.

Passivity may not be the right word for the quality I am trying to identify; I am not sure English has a single right word for it. But it is a quality Danny shares with most of the heroes of comic literature, one most succinctly defined by a gesture of Don Quixote's: when the knight arrives at the crossroads outside of La Mancha that would determine the course of his and Sancho's grand second sortie, he drops the reins and lets Rocinante decide. Such passivity, so often marking the comic vision, is evidenced, for example, in Huck and Jim choosing to flee from oppression by floating downriver on a raft.

Danny is a writer and a reader of stories, who is much more interested in the lives of the people around him than he is in his private plans and triumphs. Although all good writers are inveterate readers (without exception, so far as I know) most writers as protagonists in novels do relatively little reading unless they are brilliant intellectuals like Stephen Dedalus or romantic questers after knowledge like Eugene Gant. But Danny Smiricky is so much a reader that the seven chapters of *The Engineer of Human Souls* are titled (in order) Poe, Hawthorne, Twain, Crane, Fitzgerald, Conrad, and Lovecraft. The last is H. P. Lovecraft, a founding father of science fiction, who occasionally breaks through the barriers of his own wretched prose to express a haunting vision of human fate. The passive Danny reads to suit himself and to serve his own needs and taste: he relishes Poe's "The Raven" because, as he freely admits, he is sentimental; he does not hesitate to list Lovecraft among the great because Lovecraft has written a few paragraphs that have done great things for him; and he values Hawthorne and Conrad for the clarity with which they expose the evil of the politics of our times. He knows that it is ridiculous to read a denunciation of Stalinism into *Heart of Darkness*, for Conrad was not a clairvoyant; but he also knows that what he found in Conrad's late-nineteenth-century story illuminated the darkness he had to live with in the middle of the twentieth century and that it would be contemptible to deny that personal truth just because he looks silly expressing it in the classroom. Writers read in search of personal truths; critics and teachers do, too, only they tend to be better than Danny at putting a shiny, impersonal gloss on their discussions.

At the same time, the self-negligent Danny is by contemporary standards deficient in both paranoia and self-pity. He has such a great gift for friendship since he realizes that it is people, only people, who give a country beauty and value. Thus the characterizations of his many acquaintances, friends, and lovers, determine the novel's seemingly ramshackle, four-part structure. The random introduction of characters contributes to the apparently ramshackle surface structure of the novel, demanding that the reader participate in creating some order out of this unround comic vision. This looseness also reflects, in a very subtle way, Danny's passivity.

Consequently, the first part has to deal with Danny's life in Kostelec during and right after the war, for that experience has settled his character and given him his sense of stories to tell. The next section deals with his life in the present among all the other Czechs who have come to rest in Toronto. There is no need for Skvorecky to recapitulate the details of Danny's life in the years between Kostelec and Toronto; it is enough to know that it was a lucky life. But the often painful lives of his friends from Kostelec have to be made known; their letters to him over the years are therefore an essential part of the novel. The fourth part that centers on his teaching is obviously necessary, to dramatize Danny's reading and to make real his new life as a Canadian.

A structure like that calls for a large number of secondary characters. The images of all of the people Danny knew in his youth, even the ones who played only a very small part in his life, have a clarity and a depth of focus characteristic of our most deeply held memories. In contrast, the images of his fellow exiles in Toronto are like the cheerful sketches a good caricaturist can throw off. The images of his students lack even that much depth and complexity for the very good reason that he knows them primarily as students and they know him only as a professor. The professor-student relationship has its intensities and its charms but it leaves much unaccounted for.

The best short description of *The Engineer of Human Souls* is the one Skvorecky states as its subtitle: *An Entertainment on the Old Themes of Life, Women, Fate, Dreams, the Working Class, Secret Agents, Love and Death.* If that suggests that it is something of a fairy tale, well and good. But it is a fairy tale for grown-ups, and we need all of those we can get.

Place and Placelessness in *Dvorak in Love*

James Grove

Dvorak in Love, with its emphasis on place, bewilders some readers. They enter it expecting a traditional fictional biography that will imaginatively turn Antonin Dvorak's psychological, familial, and musical life inside out. But they discover that Skvorecky's narrative has become a slippery ride through an impressionistic mosaic with no central point of view, with limited entry into the great man's mind, with a fragmented time scheme, and with a multiplicity of voices often talking about matters only loosely related to Dvorak. This form, even more elusive than the associational narratives of *The Miracle Game* and *The Engineer of Human Souls*, strongly reflects Skvorecky's belief that the essence of a writer is a sensitive uncertainty. It also mirrors the tenuous, fragmented nature of the twentieth century.

These considerations invite the question: Why would Skvorecky use such a modernist narrative to tell the story of Dvorak, a deeply religious, extremely romantic, and quite domesticated genius apparently so much at home in the nineteenth century? One approach to this question is to go back to 1969 when Skvorecky, in the midst of a journey across the United States, stopped in Spillville and contemplated writing "something" about Dvorak. His memory of this small Midwestern community is place-saturated. Its landscape and strong Bohemian flavor made him nostalgic for Czechoslovakia—the beloved, troubled homeland from which he would soon be exiled. At the same time, it caused him to identify with Dvorak's productive summer idyll in this village, which had been a stay against the composer's homesickness for Bohemia.

This memory indicates that the idea of place, right from the beginning, was an important factor in Skvorecky's vision of *Dvorak in Love*. It produces a subtle and profound current within the completed work, one that ties together many of the novel's apparently extraneous stories, makes Skvorecky's Dvorak more than merely quaint, and creates a complex portrait of America in transition. Many characters take journeys in this novel while listening to the wide landscape of Anton's music. They are searching for safety and fulfillment, and all this movement creates an unsettled atmosphere intensely reinforced by Skvorecky's unpredictable narrative.

A major voice in Dvorak in Love is Adele Margulies, a Viennese pianist who has spent years in America, this "outsized continent." The primary consciousness of four chapters, Adele's perspective informs the entire novel, helping Skvorecky keep the problem of place in the foreground. Because she has a persistent desire for the exotic, Adele has drifted into an abiding state of placelessness. She cannot go home again to the Old World, yet finds no permanent, satisfying refuge within America. Adele finds it difficult to enjoy everyday life. Judgmental about things she considers vulgar and often timid in her foreignness, she is increasingly sensitive about her aloneness, vulnerability, and age. Moreover, because she discovers signs of the "relentless advance of biology" everywhere, Adele is continually distinguishing between spirit and matter.

The novel opens as Adele, while traveling to Dvorak's summer home in Bohemia, watches a butterfly hover unsteadily "between the landscape and the sky." Ensconced in her carriage, Adele projects her uncertainty about place onto the butterfly. Despite her fear of nature, she is also attracted to the "brilliance of the profane world in its shadowless splendor." Thus she brushes away a strand of hair veiling the beauty surrounding her. Yet Adele, by eventually associating this dangling shadow of hair with images of human mortality, unwittingly reveals that this unveiling stems as much from her fear of corruption as from any acceptance of nature. Such ambivalence also rests behind Adele's response to Vysoka, Dvorak's village, which she considers backward. Always the outsider, Adele feels exposed like "a manikin in a shop window." Yet she wants to mix, as her African American lover, Will Cook, does. She wants to be like Dvorak, at home in his garden, his local pub, his church, his music studio.

> There was an unreality to it all. Amid the aroma of dumplings and the throaty gurgling of the incontinent pigeons, little Aloisia's running nose . . . amid all this were born melodies that perhaps only Schubert could emulate, music from heaven. She glanced at this man blessed with the gift of song, dejectedly examining the sinking foam in his tankard. . . .
>
> Then she understood. . . . The Pope washing the smelly feet of twelve filthy old men, in memory of Christ's act of service. Heaven touching pigeon dung.

What Adele sees in the composer—with appreciation and dismay—is a reconciliation of the place tension that so troubles her. Later, in New York City, Adele again recognizes this when she compares Dvorak to the composer Anton Bruckner. Adele remembers how she found Bruckner revolting, yet fascinating, as he told her vulgar, "magnificent" stories about holding Schubert's skull and wanting to kiss the remains of Beethoven. Implicitly comparing herself to the composers, Adele recognizes that Bruckner's stories, like Dvorak's life, contain a passionate, earthy, transcendent acceptance of life, death, and place. This receptiveness infuses Dvorak's flutes, vibrating with the rhythms of Vysoka, as well as Bruckner's "angelic" organ music, grounded in the "incense of the country church."

Through Adele's Manichaean conflicts, Skvorecky objectifies the nineteenth-century romantic/naturalistic tension over environment. Played out throughout *Dvorak in Love*, this conflict is especially evident when Adele travels to Vysoka in 1895 to lure the master back to America. Adele's deterministic vision ties the "weather-beaten" train station to one image of transience or death after another. As Dvorak voraciously eats a sausage, Adele sees him as part of the overriding biological drama which also forces her to watch a fly "become tangled at last in a freshly spun spiderweb where it began to struggle for its life." Here, Dvorak is the victorious gorger in the battle for survival, but soon he will be gorged by death. She perceives this future in his rheumy eyes and in his fear that he cannot write music anymore.

Yet Adele, despite her pessimism, cannot resist wondering where the miracle of this man's music comes from. She keeps asking this question because music is the only thing she trusts. It can temporarily make places integrated or transcendent, romantically meaningful for her. In Vysoka it releases her by putting "the mundane world to flight and [driving] her thoughts into the cheerful abstraction of sounds," by helping her imagine, as she closes her eyes in the carriage, that she is dancing a slow waltz on the dusty road, by carrying her nostalgically back to the Viennese street dances of her youth when she was not placeless.

Dvorak suggests to Adele that his talent largely comes from being open to his environment, no matter where he is. In the railroad station, to her statement, "Your whole world is in [your music]," the composer responds, "I've enjoyed everything I've done. That may be the root of it." Still, Dvorak realizes that time is running out. Only in Vysoka can he have the security to compose his final works; thus he cannot return to America, despite its attractions. Suddenly, Adele realizes that Dvorak, like her, exists "between the landscape and the sky." He, too, needs safety. Even with his great talent, even with his strong religious and romantic beliefs, he is not immune from the fear of becoming placeless. This is something she can understand, and this ties Dvorak to the many other place-worried characters in this novel.

The America that Dvorak must finally resist is a culture moving quickly. As Skvorecky writes, the 1890s "was an extremely interesting decade, the decade of transition between two lifestyles, the decade of the big inventions that changed life so much, the decade of the great Columbian Exhibition, the time when the blacks first tried to find a voice of their own among the many voices of the continent." It was an era of intense movement, opportunity, exploitation, disillusionment, and excitement—a wild time punctuating an expansive century. The 1890s were worthy of Dvorak's refrain "Only in America." Dvorak's perspective, however, is only a fragment of Skvorecky's panoramic treatment of America. The novel's realistic attention to place becomes symbolic as Skvorecky confronts the country through many "inside" and "outside" voices, while following many journeys across America.

This panorama begins with New York City, whose crudity, ruthlessness, and glamour represented the best and worst about the country for many nineteenth-century observers. Skvorecky catches some of the city's flux through Francis Thurber, a wealthy businessman and husband of Dvorak's patroness. As he gazes out his office window, Francis watches a "panto-mime" where one of his workers whips a horse until getting reprimanded by some upper-class folk. Apart from the buzz of the street, yet feeling implicated in this nasty little affair, Thurber remains uneasy while reading a letter from his wife and watching a ship from Hamburg enter the harbor—one probably carrying more immigrants. He recalls how his wife, who "is an American first and last," sometimes talks with her father in Danish and becomes suddenly "exotic and irrevocably part of Europe." Bemused, lonely, and uncertain, Francis concludes, "America is—divided personalities. Partly from these shores, and partly from God knows where."

With its impressionistic narrator, who has a Jamesian appreciation and ambivalence for Old World-New World tensions, this episode signals Skvorecky's intent to create a complex pluralistic portrait of America. Indeed there are "divided personalities" everywhere in *Dvorak in Love,* and they point to the uncertainties and confusions embedded within the American Dream.

Take the Thurbers. Their class and wealth make them "insiders." Yet they feel like "outsiders" because of Francis's conflicts with the monopolies and Jeannette's battles with the music establishment. The "inside" status allows them to remain secure as upper-class Americans, while still believing they have social, moral, economic, and cultural responsibilities to America. The Thurbers do not experience Adele's abiding placelessness, regardless of what their country does to them. At the same time, despite their class consciousness, the Thurbers' avant-garde attitudes help them to appreciate the divided, uncertain American sense of place. For one thing, Thurber sees that America—despite its swagger and success—still suffers from an inferiority complex, causing it to have a stunted, dissociated national culture. He is not surprised, then, that Americans swoon over Dvorak.

Jeannette, in her romanticism and patriotism, wants to transcend racial and sectional divisions by encouraging and subsidizing African American musicians to attend her conservatory. She also recruits Dvorak to argue for her Whitmanesque goal of recognizing and nourishing America's diverse voices, so they might come together—without losing their individual integrity—to create a national music. Jeannette strives for a synthesis grounded in an immersion, at once appreciative and reconciling, within all kinds of music. Like Adele, she sees Dvorak, the master who uses folk music within his nationalistic compositions, as the embodiment of her dream.

Thurber pictures his wife as a heroine idealistically trying to catch a "phantom" in a cultural wilderness where the public, while neglecting and abusing its own musicians, will enthusiastically accept the authority of

Dvorak when he demands that American music find a base in its native soil. Thurber's feelings are supported by Skvorecky's bittersweet portrayal of the obstacles facing the pioneers of American music: heroic, romantic, and often placeless figures like Urelli Corelli Hill, Anton Philip Heinrich, and Theodore Thomas, who perform in one difficult environment after another, continually trying to further "the sacred cause of music," while seeking a creative relationship with "this wild continent."

Their stories also show a country alienated from much of its own music and consequently diminished in its sense of place. For example, the neglected immigrant composer Anton Philip Heinrich, an "incomplete genius struggling to be born," travels all over bearing witness to America. His music, so rooted in place, includes an eccentric, grandiose symphony about Yellowstone and other complicated, obscure passages "meant to conjure up Comanches hunting buffalo." According to one of the more interesting secondary voices in *Dvorak in Love*, a little tuba player who is very sure of his place and whose voice is a comic counterpoint to these sadder stories, the forgotten Heinrich was "unquestioningly American, something old Borax [Dvorak] could never be." Having played for almost everyone, the tuba player celebrates the time he made his instrument sound "like the thunder of the Rockies" for Heinrich's symphony. And there is also Theodore Thomas, another immigrant who knows America inside out, yet who has just lost his position in New York City. Trained in Europe, as a young man he wandered America, from saloon to saloon, playing his violin for small change. Much later, as part of Jeannette Thurber's ill-fated opera company, he journeyed across the country again. Yet he realizes that his groundbreaking role in American music will not be appreciated by an "ungrateful country" that finds Dvorak irresistible. He can only steel himself for still another journey—this time to Chicago for a new position as conductor—and depend on his faith that America, with all its flaws, "always gives you another chance—it's not like Europe."

With his passion for jazz and awareness of Dvorak's interest in the Negro spiritual, Skvorecky also takes pains to develop the precarious position of the African American musicians in such a racially insecure culture. Specifically, Harry Burleigh, Sissieretta Jones, Will Cook, and Maurice Strathotte endure the "double consciousness" that W. E. B. DuBois describes. On the one hand, they try to gain entry into the music establishment, which demands that they abide by white European standards. Their efforts lead to painful memories of journeying from the South to the North or to Europe for difficult auditions where they felt exposed and placeless. Yet, as Sissieretta knows, nothing ultimately ensures their being accepted: "she would never be more than an exotic curiosity singing arias in the intervals between Black Samba gutter songs. She had never been cast in a real opera." Prejudice is the irrational, arbitrary trump card often barring them from "the game." On the other hand, they have their African American culture—the life stories and songs filled with pain, accommodation, joy, and pride that only the blacks *know*. This music, so rooted in their history's disrupted sense of place, represents a potential "home" where they can find and celebrate their own voice; where they can sing themselves into history as subjects, not objects; where they can create their own sacred spots and anthems. This is what Dvorak is calling for, and their breakthrough finally happens in the twentieth century, but only after Strathotte, for instance, has struggled for years to have "anyone . . . take [his] Plantation Dances seriously."

For these musicians, as for Adele, music is a recurrent, albeit temporary stay against placelessness—an indefinable, transcendent force that can paradoxically connect people to the concrete realities of this world. For example, Thomas remembers an incident when he found some hope within the "musical wilderness" of America: "Here I am, standing in a one-horse town in Nebraska, and a tattered old man tells me he heard my orchestra twenty years ago, and the experience stayed with him for the rest of his life. I've been waving the baton for a quarter century, and sometimes I wonder whether it's all in vain. But that old codger from Nebraska persuaded me it's worth it after all." This faith in music explains Dvorak's importance for so many others. Saturating himself with impressions no matter where he finds himself and then using his genius to turn these impressions into song, Dvorak often persuades that "it's worth it after all." This gift is what Burleigh passionately affirms when he recalls how the haunting sound of the French horn in the *New World Symphony*—born out of the melodies of the great spirituals—miraculously carried him *home* to the "voice of my granddaddy." It gave expression to the loneliness and nostalgia so deep within his own divided consciousness.

However, Skvorecky, with his quicksilver touch in this novel, keeps twisting the reader by periodically having characters wonder about the depth and authenticity of Dvorak's realization of America. Specifically, Thurber retrospectively admires the energy that made Dvorak open to the city's cabaret life, to New York's Lower East Side, and to the nation's music. Yet he also believes that the great man was finally a European "who, through no fault of his own, didn't understand the principles on which this country is based." Dvorak was too old when he came over and too culturally determined to have a complex appreciation for his new milieu. Other characters support Thurber as they describe the composer's language difficulties, ignorance of American history (notably in his conversations about slavery), limited travel in the United States, and reliance upon superficial sources, like *The Song of Hiawatha*, Buffalo Bill's Wild West Show, and Stephen Foster, for his "folk" music. Their reports even give a little credence to the petty music critic James Huneker, who judges the Symphony No. 5 in E Minor: *From the New World* as shallow, since it depends on naive impressions of American folk idioms. The tuba player reinforces this opinion when he questions Dvorak's attempt to incorporate Indian rhythms into his music.

Skvorecky never completely buries this skepticism. However, he heavily tips the scales toward the more positive image of a Dvorak who manages to appreciate and affect America, despite and because of his foreignness. He listens raptly to the city and nature. He enjoys Sokol halls, minstrel shows, cabarets, parades, and railroad stations. He is an enthusiastic audience for stories about the early American musicians, the Czech immigrants, and the slave experience. This energy is behind Burleigh's admiration of Dvorak's filling himself with Negro melodies: caring "nothing for pigment, he heard only music, understood it, heard the cry emerging from it." Still, Burleigh understands Sissieretta's dismissal of Dvorak's admiration for Stephen Foster: the Czech only appreciates Foster's "soaring and lyrical" melodies—not the buried slave "words, in that painful dialect." Therefore it will not be Dvorak but the "black, earthbound saxophone [that will] slaughter Foster's maudlin, sentimental lie."

The Thurbers, like Burleigh and Sissieretta, see Dvorak—regardless of his limitations—as connecting, rather than dividing American culture. The couple makes this point by tying his music to place. Francis realizes that there has been an improbable synthesis of highbrow/lowbrow culture when he hears the *New World Symphony* in the unlikely setting of Coney Island. Jeannette's recognition is much more passionate. Fifty years after Dvorak's stay in America, his great symphony haunts her. Her sense of place having been undermined by her own physical decay and by the alien sounds of the modern world, Jeannette repeatedly listens to it, the music leading her memory and imagination back to the 1890s. It takes her back to Dvorak's stay in New York City and back to the Catskill housewarming when the composer spontaneously collapsed all place and social distinctions by playing second fiddle with "a rabble of mountain fiddlers." It takes her into the mystery of his music: the "paradox of saliva, moist breath and trembling reeds [became] immaterial sweetness, a harmony of wood pervaded by the call of the forest, the ocean." Finally, it takes her back to that triumphant opening night when she first heard the symphony evoke the beauty, breadth, and diversity of the American continent. His music, as it does for Adele, makes Jeannette feel less homeless.

Skvorecky writes that he experienced "the flavor of myth" when he visited the "Dvorak places" in New York City. Just as intensely, Skvorecky "felt" the presence of Dvorak in Spillville, the village transformed by the composer's stay during the summer of 1893. Skvorecky visited Spillville and later wrote about it because Dvorak had given the village this quality. Thus in Dvorak in Love, when one of the early pioneers of Spillville comically tells about the composer's visit, he acknowledges that the town tries not to besmirch Dvorak's reputation. It has become too tied to Spillville's common identity.

Dvorak comes to this Bohemian community because he needs a rest from the city and from feeling like a foreigner. Huneker, sounding much like Adele about Vysoka, cannot understand why Dvorak would journey half-way across America to this "odd little town . . . in the middle of nowhere." He does not understand that Spillville is ideal since its geography and culture—so mindful of Bohemia's—give Dvorak the security to work and relax. With no real language difficulty, Dvorak is more at home here. He participates in the church, gets deeply involved in the heavy saloon life, and even becomes a primary player in an apocryphal court case about prohibiting beer in Spillville. Furthermore, as Dvorak roams away from the town, taking notes about bird sounds, walking, and fishing, he embodies the Emersonian ideal of the artist.

This openness makes his secretary, Joseph Kovarik, remark that Dvorak profits from *everything*. For example, after Dvorak accidentally disturbs the heiress Rosemary Vanderbilt's naked "beautiful phantom's pilgrimage" on the Turkey River and after he escapes a beating for this comic intrusion, the composer recollects and saves the incident's landscape (its moonlight, its sounds, the surface of the river) in a song that becomes the germ for his opera *Rusalka*. Skvorecky again associates this creative energy to Dvorak's romantic religious identification with nature—something not so available in the city, something the awed Kovarik sees firsthand: "The master . . . then sank to his knees and turned his face to the heavens, to his God, radiant above the countryside. The red beads slipped through his fingers, as bright in the sunlight as the berries of a mountain ash."

On the one hand, Skvorecky wants us to remember that Dvorak's journey to America—with its security and comfort, with its freedom of movement between the New and Old Worlds—has been fundamentally different from the Czech immigrants' precarious and usually irrevocable journeys into uncertainty. Dvorak, honored in his native land and devoted to the Czech landscape, does not want such a break. Yet Skvorecky shows how Dvorak's stay in America helps him empathize with the immigrants' struggles to assimilate the spirit of a place that has no past for them. Moreover, through their stories and through the nightmarish account of how Dvorak's daughter Otylia tries to elope, Skvorecky creates a New World filled with possibility, hardship, freedom, and disillusionment.

There is, for instance, Franta Valenta's journey away from the economic imprisonment of owning "two acres of swampy land" in Bohemia and toward the dream of becoming a "real farmer" with a hundred acres in America. As Valenta crosses the Atlantic Ocean to New Orleans and then makes the long ride up the Mississippi River, Skvorecky portrays him as a pilgrim searching for refuge in bewildering and endangering places. Still, his story ends happily. Franta becomes the prosperous *farmer-settler*, who realizes the American Dream for himself and his family. He would thus agree with Miss Rosie Novak, another Czech immigrant, who reacts to the "miracles" of the 1893 World's Fair by exclaiming, "I guess that's America. Anything is possible here."

In letters home Dvorak talked about the homeyness and beauty of Spillville. But he also wrote about the emptiness, wildness, and fragility he felt there. Skvorecky projects this sense of alienation and malaise into the novel's dramatic oral structure—most notably through the old settler's storytelling in "Corpus Delecti." In this chapter the narrator humorously affirms Spillville's history, romance, vitality, and his own strong sense of place. At the same time, he intentionally reveals the mean, sometimes tragic streak of marginality and desperation within the village. Therefore, besides celebrating the distinctive marks the settlers had made on the landscape (the eight saloons, the Church of St. Wenceslas and its famous clock, the farms, the cemetery), he tells about Spillville's horrors and disorder. The village is sarcastically called "Swillville" because of its alcoholism. A young woman is buried alive. A baby dies of the delirium tremens because of its mother's drinking. Disease is common and often fatal. It seems as if the town has barely been able to control a panic of the spirit emanating from being too exposed within this New World garden, whose natural riches and intimidating scale demand so much inner strength.

Although Dvorak hears about all sides of Spillville, Skvorecky never has him directly face its darkness. And only rarely does Dvorak react to the harsh stories he hears. In making this decision, Skvorecky allows Dvorak's pastoral interlude in Spillville to remain quite placid and unspoiled. He also gives up the chance to take the reader deeply into Dvorak's mind. This silence suggests that Skvorecky is not interested only in the experiences of Dvorak but also in a more general meditation about how human beings survive in an increasingly rootless world.

Skvorecky also does not have Dvorak learn about his daughter's attempt to marry Kovarik (an incident with no factual basis). As the couple attempts to get married in a neighboring Iowa village, which has gone totally to seed, Otylia suffers intensely because the church, the place's signature of sacred space, is a desolate hovel manned by a drunken minister. Having imagined a marriage in the pastoral beauty of a country church, Otylia suddenly finds her soul lost in a "sanctuary [which] resembled a pillaged warehouse." Through this trauma, which permanently scars her, Skvorecky intensely objectifies the misgivings that the historical Dvorak expressed in one letter: "It is very strange here. Few people and a great deal of empty space. . . . there are only endless acres of field and meadow and that is all you see. You don't meet a soul. . . . And so it is very 'wild' here and sometimes very sad—sad to despair." However, Skvorecky never allows Dvorak to face what the unprotected Otylia experiences. As a result, he returns to Vysoka blithely praising America. In contrast, his daughter is so haunted that almost everything looks unsafe or dead, even back in Bohemia. Seeking no more adventures, Otylia only wants marriage as a permanent refuge.

For a work titled Scherzo capriccioso in its Czech edition, *Dvorak in Love* is filled with a great deal of sadness, illness, death, and placelessness. These qualities are even stronger in Dvorak in Love than in Scherzo capriccioso because Skvorecky has restructured the chapter order of the English edition, so that it ends with the narrative of the elderly, lonely, frail Sissieretta. Besides being the novel's final riff on how racism can threaten a person's sense of place and identity, her story also shows how the effects of illness and time can inevitably restrict, change, and stunt the capacity of human beings to respond fully to their environments. As Sissieretta remains confined to her house, admitting that "it's getting darker all the time" and wondering about her life's meaning, Skvorecky invites the reader to turn back to the other place-haunted and often place-deprived characters in Dvorak in Love. The time-obsessed Adele remains so apart because she fears the change inherent in place. The Countess Josephine Kounic, Dvorak's great love, has a confining, terminal illness that makes her memories and spyglass "her only connection with the village, the countryside and her family during the final months of her life." The ninety-five-year-old Jeannette Thurber questions the worth of her life as age increasingly limits her sense of place. Otylia carries an estranging fatalism and despair back from America. And Count Kounic, as he follows Dvorak's coffin, remembers the dead Countess and knows that the places in Prague where he and his wife walked have been irrevocably emptied by her dying.

Most important, Dvorak is part of this pattern, too. Much of the novel, in fact, is an elegy to him—all the memories acting as constant reminders that this vital man, who always resisted placelessness, died less than ten years after leaving America. Consequently, the reminiscences provide a frame for the episode in the Czech train station when Dvorak decides not to return to America because he can take no more chances when it comes to finding a clean, well-lighted place. This decision to remain home highlights, once again, the pervasive nostalgic strain in *Dvorak in Love*, especially since it is linked to his grief for the recently deceased Countess. His love for her, along with his longing for Bohemia, is what spurs the pastoralism in the Cello Concerto in B Minor, a piece throbbing with "the very embodiment of longing." Composed in America, revised in Bohemia, the concerto is intensely dualistic, as are so many things in this novel. Even though Dvorak says that he has wanted to keep it purely Czech, to keep the sounds of New York City out of the composition, it echoes with both "the alien distances of America and the Master's desperate love for the countryside of his childhood." Yet, as Dvorak's acolyte, Hanousek Wihan, stresses, the concerto still works, for it achieves a profound synthesis between the New and the Old Worlds, therefore fulfilling the demands of the composer's memory and music.

By making Dvorak so nostalgic, Skvorecky, the émigré artist, indirectly raises the issues of whether the beauty of one's homeland is replaceable and whether an artist's talent is inevitably diminished by the distance of exile. Skvorecky, who has stressed in his essays that the artist can thrive in a new world, is much more ambivalent in this novel: Dvorak's artistry prospers *because* of New York City and Spillville, yet his identity remains essentially tied to Bohemia. He cannot conceive of ever leaving his homeland for good; he would lose himself, especially now that he is older.

As much as anything else, it is this ambivalence about place that rests at the heart of *Dvorak in Love*. It is represented through a fragmented mosaic that appropriately tries to keep the reader always a bit displaced. It thematically ties together most of the characters who hover around the great composer. It gives the portrait of Dvorak increasing depth by continuously impinging on his nineteenth-century sensibility. It links the novel's comic, romantic, pastoral, pathetic, and tragic elements. And it is what finally makes *Dvorak in Love* such a fulfilling realization of that vague "something" that Skvorecky started contemplating during his first visit to Spillville, not long before he became an émigré, not long before he began living in that problematic space which he once identified as being "between two worlds."

American Themes in *The Bride of Texas*

Helena Kosek

Josef Skvorecky's canon is characterized by a spiritual bond with American culture which, since his youth, has played a major part in his professional and artistic development. His personal fate granted him an experience of the greatest importance for a writer, namely life on two continents and complete familiarity with two cultures. The basic feature of his novels is precisely his ability to let various perspectives confront one another, thus creating the entertaining, realistic surface of his work. From *The Cowards* to *The Bride of Texas*, this surface has become increasingly transparent, thus revealing more and more of the depths below. Each single realistic episode has become part of a multileveled mosaic that expresses the complexities of reality and perceives life like a Schopenhauerian tragedy where individual details have the character of farces. This is certainly evident in Skvorecky's recent novel, *The Bride of Texas*, which is more historical and more dominated by Americans than any of his other fiction. Yet *Bride* is, in the end, a natural continuation of some abiding features of Skvorecky's artistic development.

One of Skvorecky's first completed and published stories, "The Babylonian Event" (1946), is about the meeting of a Czech girl with a soldier from the United States Army. The possibility of their mutual verbal contact is restricted to a few words in English and German. Their communication reminds us of some episodes from The Bride of Texas. The short story is interesting because it reveals Skvorecky's inherently perfect ear for spoken language. Important parts of the story are the dialogue passages in which language is revealed as a source of misunderstanding rather than communication. In fact, the characters' communications are mostly nonverbal. Unlike the reader, neither the girl nor the soldier has the faintest idea about the world of the other, and their imaginings are resolutely dismantled as entirely wrong. Also Skvorecky ironically undermines the stereotyped biases about Americans, for the soldier is an intellectual interested in cultural artifacts, while the girl tries to move their encounter in a direction that—according to all stereotypes—should please her partner:

The stairs were steep. They walked behind each other. The American watched the girl's legs. Europe is full of beautiful things, he thought. Beautiful ones and destroyed ones. He looked at the girl's slim calves. Such legs, the steeple of a cathedral, a secession café, the face of a cat, a flying sea gull with its little legs pressing to its body under the arch of a medieval bridge, a hunter's bloodhound concentrated on the black point of its nose, running along the track of a wounded fox. Europe. And fair hair that glistens with the gold of valueless human curls. He remembered his wife's hair.

And within him suddenly the images of these two different female fates merged, the fates of all those people whom he had met during the last two years, in England, in France, in occupied Germany, the fates of all those people in this terrible unique world, fates welded together by this silent terrible country. It seemed to him that he was still hearing the noise of moving tanks, and the weight of the battle almost smothered his throat when they arrived on the gallery of the tower that was surrounded by the blood-red Western sky, enflamed, as it were, by the endless conflagration of the war.

In Skvorecky's first novel, *The Cowards*, with its often-noted spiritual and artistic affinity to such famous American works as Ernest Hemingway's *A Farewell to Arms* and J. D. Salinger's *The Catcher in the Rye*, dialogue is again an important tool for the examination of problematic communication. Skvorecky's distinctly autobiographical novel reflects the author's abiding love for jazz and attraction to American culture. In fact, while writing *The Cowards*, Skvorecky was studying English, completing his doctorate in 1951 with a dissertation on Thomas Paine.

Sam Solecki convincingly argues that the strong orientation of *The Cowards* toward America was one of the reasons the political powers reacted so strongly against the book as well as its author:

In the debate which has its roots in the nineteenth century and continues today in Skvorecky's and Kundera's essays over whether Czechoslovakia is an East or a West European country and whether it should look East or West for its cultural models, The Cowards turns emphatically West. Danny's predisposition or bias is indicated when he is shown often perceiving and judging in words and images drawn from American literature and movies. These references and allusions, together with the occasionally Hemingwayesque style and the numerous titles of jazz numbers, are among the constitutive elements of Skvorecky's style and in themselves embody and express both Danny's and Skvorecky's essential attitudes and values.[1]

Already in The Cowards there occurs an obvious confrontation of both levels. In the mind of the Czech reader the programmed and provocative nonheroic stance of Danny Smiricky, the novel's first-person narrator, is bound to clash with the ideologically supported myths about the rebellion against the Nazis and the liberation by the Russian Army. As Milan Kundera succinctly states, Skvorecky at the time committed a deadly sin when he wrote from an apolitical perspective about taboo political themes. The counterpoint of this comic perspective is the history of the Second World War and the author's protest against a time that dehumanizes the individual by changing him into a symbol.

Central to the protest is Danny's devotion to jazz, which anticipates the music's central importance in the novella "The Bass Saxophone," about which Graham Greene wrote: "To my mind Josef Skvorecky is one of the finest living writers. His two short novels *The Bass Saxophone* and *The Legend of Emoke* I put in the same rank as James Joyce's *The Dead* and the very best of James's shorter novels."[2] For the narrator of "The Bass Saxophone," jazz also provides the opportunity to escape the oppressing realities of the Second World War, reflecting Skvorecky's fear of pomposity through the novella's lyrical declaration of love for jazz specifically when confronted by a reality that could have emerged from a Hieronymus Bosch picture. Obviously, it is not by accident that the Czech theme of *The Cowards* is presented in a Hemingwayesque style while the tribute to jazz is written in a Central European, expressionist and existentialist tone:

but there is a memento—an intimate, truthful moment God knows where, God knows when, and because of it I shall always be on the move with Lothar Kinze's orchestra, a sad musician on the mournful routes of Europe's periphery, surrounded by storm clouds; and the somber bass saxophone player, the adrian rollini, will time and again remind me of dream, truth, incomprehensibility: the memento of the bass saxophone.[3]

One can therefore claim that even before his departure from Czechoslovakia in 1968, American culture was a predominant part of Skvorecky's spiritual world and was integrated into his professional world as a writer. During the 1950s and 1960s, especially when he was not allowed to publish, Skvorecky spent much time translating and writing about American literature. Indeed, between 1959 and 1969 his numerous academic publications included translations and studies of Ray Bradbury, Henry James, Ernest Hemingway, William Faulkner, Sinclair Lewis, Dashiell Hammett, Raymond Chandler, and William Styron. In the sixties he edited Lewis's selected writings as well as Hemingway's collected works. Igor Hájek draws attention to this valuable aspect of Skvorecky's career: "It was here that Skvorecky earned a repute when in his multiple role of editor, critic, essayist and translator he almost singlehandedly rehabilitated modern American literature, until then represented mostly by Howard Fast."[4] Skvorecky himself has stated that during his stay in Czechoslovakia he was occupied mostly with American literature. In contrast, after moving to Canada, he turned to Czech literature; for instance, his first work published there is a history of the Czech film during the sixties.[5] At the same time, in his regular programs for the Voice of America, he closely followed and continued to introduce contemporary American literature to the Czech reader.

In Canada, during the seventies, beginning with *The Miracle Game*, Skvorecky began to develop a personal style that characterizes all his later novels. Skvorecky himself characterized it in his *Samozerbuvh* as the separation of various thematic topics into small episodes, which he then merged into one whole. This resulted in an almost surrealistic composition. In *The Miracle Game* and *The Engineer of Human Souls* this form expresses, through the eyes of the narrator, the chaos of the modern world. In *Dvorak in Love* the composer's stay in North America and the secret of his genius are illuminated through the viewpoint of the various narrators, who, though close to Dvorak, often contradict each other. The author deliberately stresses the fact that each testimony is fragmentary and partial: the fleeting light of truth can be perceived only at the points where the varied perspectives intersect—especially those tied to Dvorak's music. This more fragmented form, however, still relies heavily on the interplay among the author's direct voice, dialogue, and narration marking his earlier works. And, again, his language is a vehicle for expressing the difficulties of communication between people from various linguistic areas.

The author thus places an extraordinarily demanding task not only on the reader but on the translator. He and Bohumil Hrabal belong to those contemporary Czech prose writers who are considered by many as untranslatable. Yet Skvorecky has found in Paul Wilson a translator who performs this difficult task admirably, even if some levels of speech naturally remain inaccessible to the English-speaking reader. This was probably the reason why some Canadian critics considered *The Engineer of Human Souls* excessively long.

From this novel onward, the confrontation of various narrative perspectives also becomes a confrontation between the Czech or Central European perspective and that of the United States or Canada. The author is obviously aware of the demands that such a method makes on the reader. Therefore he seeks particular points of contact with the reader's associative abilities: in *The Engineer of Human Souls* he dedicates each chapter to an American author (Conrad being the exception) whose works thus form a context for the North American reader and act as counterweight to the Czech perspective of Professor Smiricky in his discussions with his students. In *Dvorak in Love* Skvorecky achieves a variety of comic effects by presenting American reality as seen through Czech eyes and vice versa. And in *The Bride of Texas* Skvorecky counts on the American readers' knowledge of history. He counterpoints the tragic events of the American Civil War against the kaleidoscope of minute, often comical details and always entertaining individualized anecdotal episodes.

As Skvorecky portrays Czech immigrants participating in the Civil War, he also confronts Czech history by having characters repeatedly reminisce and tell tales that scoop certain events from the flow of time: life in Austria-Hungary, the beginnings of Bach's absolutism, the hard life of Czech cottagers. The narrator even leads the reader to the current century and the creation of the Czechoslovak Republic. To make the fragmented structure even more complex, the war, with its historical and political turning points, is described from two perspectives: from below by the Czech volunteers, particularly and most expressively those of platoon commander Kapsa and

Jan Amos Schweik (in America Shake), and from above by the generals after platoon commander Kapsa joins the staff of General Sherman. The view from above is also sustained in four individual chapters, the Writer's Intermezzos. This writer, a close friend of General Ambrose Burnside, closely follows and comments upon events occurring in the background of military and political life.

The novel is also challenging because Skvorecky portrays the simultaneous awareness of immigrants whose past in Europe is shared in the new reality of America by only a handful of their fellow Czechs. For Cyril, Sergeant Kapsa, Ursula, Shake, and others, the past emerges gradually through evocations, the memories of the old world that they have carried into their new lives. For instance, their memories of the little hearts and doves of Moravian folklore are suddenly Americanized when connected with the image of a bison—an association symbolizing the mixture of cultural influences on the immigrants. Such influences invariably lend color and humor to the narrative.

These passages, however, almost inevitably have their tragic counterpoint. Among the best parts of the book is the fourth chapter where scenes about the founding of the Lincoln Slavonic Rifles are interspersed with realistic scenes describing the battle at Bentonville. This is also why the only completely fictional character among the volunteers is called Jan Amos Schweik/Shake. The war is frequently commented on by gossip at the campfire, and Schweik is a good story teller. Like *The Good Soldier Švejk*, *The Bride of Texas* is a novel where the tragic details of war have the character of a farce. But here the similarity ends: *Švejk* is a novel about the absurdity of war; *The Bride of Texas* tries artistically to come to terms with an important chapter in American history.

Obviously, it is the author's conscious or unconscious aim to represent American themes in a form inspired by Czech and Central European literature that seeks to capture a flash of the truth about life at a point where two opposite poles intersect. For instance, the associations of the name Jan Amos Schweik/Shake bear witness to this, for it is a composite of two well-known very different Czech cultural figures. Jan Amos Komenský, better known as Comenius, is probably the most famous Czech exile of all time, whose contribution to world culture is familiar to all generations of Czech readers. On the other hand, Hašek's Švejk—despite various popular misleading interpretations—remains an enigmatic figure: the reader knows nothing about his past or his psyche. His stories do not tell anything about him personally but explore the encounter of an individual with war. In contrast the reader learns more about Skvorecky's creation, Jan Amos Schweik/Shake: specifically, that he left the seminary where he was studying to become a priest, and that the experience of the horrors of war has shaken his belief in God. Moreover, Skvorecky gradually undercuts Schweik's image as merely a folksy storyteller, since his stories, together with those of the other Czech volunteers, give the war a human dimension. The English translation of the name *Schweik* into *Shake*—again comprehensible to international readership—suggests the shook up, surrealistic kaleidoscope of narrative structure that Skvorecky uses to express reality as an incomprehensible multilevel mixture of opposite viewpoints.

Besides being a novel about the absurdity of war, The Bride of Texas is also a love story. The novel, in fact, begins during the last year of the Civil War with the wedding of a Moravian-American girl, Lida Toupelikova, to an American officer, Baxter Warren II. Skvorecky has borrowed the core of Lida's experiences from a story by the Czech correspondent Josef Bunata, as she becomes in America "wife Linda, formerly de Ribordeaux, born Toupelik from Lhota, Moravia, Austria, Europe."

In Skvorecky's hands Linda's story raises the question of whether Skvorecky—again consciously or unconsciously—may have used it in order to draw attention to another perspective. *Gone with the Wind* has sometimes been considered a novel about American history; actually it is a soap opera love story which, with its celebration of the Confederate cause, is the very antipode of Skvorecky's perception. By borrowing part of his plot (the love story) from Buňata's undeniably kitschy model and integrating it into an organic whole, Skvorecky creates remarkable subtexts in *The Bride of Texas*. For example, Linda's happy destiny finds its counterpoint in the fate of Dinah—a slave girl and mistress of Mr. de Ribordeaux—who disappears without a trace in the chaos of the war. For Linda, Cyril, and the majority of Czech immigrants, America is the land of freedom, where the present secretly harbors the possibility of a promising future. Dinah's fate, on the other hand, is inescapably tragic. Its poetic subtext harkens back to Skvorecky's earlier novella "Emöke." The *Bride*'s postscript, a list of the secondary literature he used in the novel, bears witness that Skvorecky studied a great number of sources. The majority of the characters are based on historical models, which possibly explains why the reader sometimes has the impression that less devotion to these models would have resulted in a better fiction. Whenever he reports on historical facts, his style tends to get disproportionately wordy and overloaded. Luckily there are only a few of these instances (a notable one occurs when the daughter and later the granddaughter read to Kapsa accounts of the battles in which he had taken part). In contrast, whenever his power of imagination has free play, Skvorecky's genius for spontaneous storytelling allows him to bring alive the world of America in the last century. The reader, then, admires Skvorecky's ability to breathe life into a situation through minute detail, scraps of dialogue, sharp climactic sketches, and comically exaggerated caricatures.

Skvorecky sees "modern man's turning away from abstraction, from purely verbal solutions, from pretended absolute knowledge and terms, towards concrete facts."[6] Thus he leaves it up to the reader to search for the deeper sense of these facts. As in *Dvorak in Love*, the events of *The Bride of Texas* are merely fragments of a deeper, more general theme. *Dvorak* was a lyrical tribute to genius and to the beauty of an art that penetrates beyond the narrow borders of states. It celebrates how Czech culture belongs to the Western world. *The Bride of Texas* is a tribute to freedom and democracy, a tribute to America: to all those unknown little people who were driven from their homeland by evil economic or political forces; to those who had enough strength to begin again in the New World where they found a better future. In the process it is a tribute to the openness of America with its mixture of various cultural, national, and linguistic traditions.

Consequently, the war of the South against the North is, to Skvorecky, a struggle for the process of democracy. The defeat of the Union would have been, according to him, a defeat of the nineteenth century, for it probably would also have been decisive in the development of Europe. One of the novel's characters puts it this way:

If the war had turned out differently, the old country wouldn't be the American republic it had turned out to be—a dream that had never crossed his mind on that slow sail across the Atlantic, with the wily Fircut, to where a war awaited him and then a long life. Would the expeditionary forces of some Northern States of America have fought in the war that happened much later in Europe? If they had, would the Confederate States of America have sent proud descendants of the victors of '65 to bolster the other side, the Austro-Hungarian monarchy? Even in the new century, officers battling on the side of the imperial armies would have been accompanied by black servants. If his general had lost.[7]

The author himself adds in his postscript to the Czeck edition of the novel:

Despite the fact that it was an army of civilians and therefore around the campfires there blossomed self-depreciating and often more than crude black humor, despite the fact that American ex-servicemen, in contrast with European veterans, did not boast with serious expressions about heroic deeds but rather with an insidious smile about their cowardice, I cannot but give them my sincere admiration. Of course I like America but I do not think I exaggerate.[8]

Skvorecky's profound familiarity with Czech as well as American literature, with culture as well as history has been enriched since 1968 by his experience of life on two continents and has been the inspirational source and the spiritual background of his writings. His talent for capturing a slice of reality with small, realistic details and for entertaining the reader with successions of comic episodes, reveals his aversion toward abstractions and ideological generalizations. Skvorecky counts on his audience's associative abilities, life experiences, and knowledge of history to help them find the key for understanding this complex novel's subtexts. It is not surprising, then, that after the novels inspired by his own experience, he has now turned to themes relating to values that have always been a part of his spiritual world—paying tribute to freedom and to the American democracy which provides it with living space. It is also logical that Skvorecky does this by means of characters who are not romantically heroic. *The Bride of Texas* is the result of the symbiosis of American and Central European literary traditions in Skvorecky's work.

NOTES

[1] Sam Solecki, *Prague Blues: The Fiction of Josef Skvorecky* (Toronto: ECW Press, 1990), 45.

[2] Graham Greene, "Greeting to the Laureate," *World Literature Today*, Autumn 1980, 524. .

[3] Josef Skvorecky, *The Bass Saxophone* (Hopewell, NJ: Ecco, 1994), 209.

[4] Igor Hájek, "Editor, Translator, Critic," *World Literture Today*, Autumn 1980, 574.

[5] Josef Skvorecky, *All the Bright Young Men and Women: A Personal History of the Czech Cinema*, trans. Michael Schonberg (Toronto: Perter Martin, 1971).

[6] Josef Skvorecky, *The Bride of Texas*, trans. Kaca Polackova Henley (New York: Knopf, 1996), 243.

[7] *The Bride of Texas*, 283-84.

[8] *Neve´sta z Tezasu* (Toronto: Sixty-Eight Publishers, 1992), 616.

Variations on American Themes:
The Bride of Texas

Maria Nemcova Banerjee

First loves don't just fade away. They usually outlive the significance of the initial object of desire by turning desire into an end in itself. Nostalgia, that passion of memory, proves most powerful when it attaches to an experience of adolescence, as in the case of Josef Skvorecky's infatuation with America. He was sixteen, just like Danny Smiricky in *The Cowards* (1958), playing tenor saxophone in a jazz band camouflaged as a regular dance orchestra. In Kostelec/Náchod and everywhere else in Nazi-occupied Bohemia, jazz had been outlawed as a racially tainted, debased form of music. But for Danny and his friends, it is the sweet and reckless voice of American freedom, so loose and intimately casual, at hand and still alluring with an endless erotic prospect. Adolescent love in its desperate intensity often mimics some arcane flirtation with death. But Danny's jazz playing was star-crossed by history, which makes the danger real.

The Danny Smiricky persona, entangling a boy's sexual desire with jazz and the fantastic adventure of American freedom, accompanies Skvorecky's literary career from his brilliant debut in *The Cowards* through other fictions, notably *The Miracle Game* (1972) and *The Swell Season* (1975). It reappears one last time in the ambitious, partly retrospective *The Engineer of Human Souls* (1977), where the narrator is a middle-aged Czech novelist in exile, making his living as a professor of American literature at the University of Toronto.

Danny's fictional existence hangs on the device of the first-person narrative, originally cast in the form of a diary that records a voice caught in the quick of adolescent subjectivity. I remember my first reading of *The Cowards* shortly after the Czech text had been published in Prague and the stunning effect of Danny's voice on me. His speech felt intensely alive and unrehearsed, and yet I knew that no living Czech could have spoken like that, surely not in Náchod in the last days of the war. It had a throwaway, sexy precision of phrasing, as in jazz, improvising a distinctly American illusion of beauty.

"You spend your life saying the same things over and over again in different ways," says Skvorecky, borrowing the words of his friend Milos Forman for the epigraph to *The Swell Season*. This admission applies to the spell America has cast on Skvorecky's fictional world. The magic stuff of Danny's inexperience turns into an object of nostalgia for the aging novelist in exile, whose imagination mixes memory with desire as it cuts back and forth between accumulating patinas of time—America never losing its intrinsic significance for Skvorecky. His passionate engagement with American culture has survived the test of sustained exposure to its realities and grown stronger with years of studying and teaching it. What emerges is a mythopoetic conception of an America identified with the unfinished agenda of human freedom, a value conceived as a quasi-spiritual need to express the potential of the individual self somewhere beyond the given here and now.

As a regular contributor to the Czech section of the Voice of America, Skvorecky reviewed the American cultural scene with scholarly competence and a sharp eye for provocative issues. In October 1989 he went on the air with a gloss on the old Negro spiritual "Oh Freedom!," a song that originated in 1863, apparently in response to Lincoln's Emancipation Proclamation. With the urgency of pent-up hope, just a month short of the magic moment when the velvet curtain would open on a new Prague, Skvorecky reflected on the various interpretations of the concept of freedom. He pointed out that in the Hegelian formula, prevailing in Marxist thought, freedom is defined as a necessity understood in the grasp of human consciousness. The sublime paradoxicality of identifying the oppressive experience of nonfreedom with its opposite offers the possibility of a mind at play, delighting in its capacity to negate a body mired in the contingencies of material existence. Such mystical cunning once bedeviled the radical Belinsky into a brief reconciliation with the reality of Nicholaevite Russia, a lapse of common sense for which he would apologize. In more heroic terms the paradox of freedom hexed out of a perceived necessity provides the spine for the contemplative regimen that brought an emperor, Marcus Aurelius, to the same school bench with the slave, Epictetus, in the age of a declining empire. Skvorecky, broadcasting to the Czechs over a collapsed Berlin Wall, rejects the Hegelian definition of freedom as minimalistic, holding instead to the American notion that all human beings, not just those who can think philosophically, aspire to live freely. He concludes that freedom is the only human necessity.

In 1969, after a disastrous turn in Czech history, Skvorecky traveled across the United States. This would be his last American trip as a Czech citizen. When he returned, he was a writer in exile, an immigrant ready to settle down in North America, leaving behind, among other things, an interrupted series of newspaper feuilletons. This imaginative reporting on America in the throes of the Vietnam War would wait until 1980 to see publication as a book he called a "tall tale" about America. In Czech the title *Velká povídka o Americe* figures as an original coinage, a deliberately literal translation from English, suggesting something with the magnitude of myth which may, however, be nothing more than a tall tale or a barefaced lie.

In these feuilletons, as he crosses the continent with his wife in an old

Pontiac, the Czech novelist and reader of Mark Twain picks up on all the larger-than-life manifestations of American popular culture playing itself out in a year of bared souls and bodies. Skvorecky responds with visceral sympathy, from the occupation of Willard Straight Hall by the black radicals of Cornell, through Mormon land, to the battle for People's Park in Berkeley. At the same time, his distinctly Czech humor, a reflex of his people's stubborn determination not to be taken in, cannot resist the easy targets of American consumerism in the age of excess when moral rhetoric and material wastefulness run equally high. But unlike so many European observers, he is rarely judgmental. Of course, the cruel violence of American life in the shadow of Vietnam does not escape him. Yet he refuses to adjudicate the loud quarrel within the conscience of the young counterculture: between those who spell America with a *k* and those who hope to rouse its better angels by carrying flowers into the angry streets. Because he looks at the American scene through a lens filtered through the indelible image of Russian tanks in Prague, he cannot share the young Americans' desperate disillusionment with their country, which he calls "The great child of history." Rather his celebratory impulse finds release in delighting at the prodigious inventiveness of American verbal humor. The serious implications of what he is witnessing, that thrashing of moral imperatives inside the crucible of constitutional rights suddenly grown derisory, would have to wait for much later to be duly considered by him.

Specifically, the problematics of American freedom form the ideational core of *The Bride of Texas*. Written between 1984 and 1991, it represents seven years of creative labor backed by extensive research. It is the story of Czech immigrants in America experiencing the complex process of acculturation through the ordeal of the Civil War. The action unfolds exclusively on American soil, with selective incidents from the old country relegated to flashbacks or occasional storytelling.

The historical axis of the novel runs through the return leg of Sherman's March to the Sea, moving north from the conquered Savannah through the Carolinas to Bentonville, where the Northern army countered Johnston's attack but, refusing to engage in a major battle, pushed farther north to join Grant against Lee in Virginia. We are on the Union side with the Czech contingent of the Twenty-Sixth Wisconsin Regiment for seven weeks of a strenuous campaign. Skvorecky's eloquent description of the smell of the burning turpentine woods in North Carolina reminds the reader of the human cost and the excruciatingly delayed promise of final victory.

The Bride of Texas consists of five long chapters of war action anchored in third-person narrative, alternating with four intermezzos narrated by a woman. In the "male" chapters the blood and bravado of the seemingly endless combat is relieved by an equally continuous flow of storytelling around campfires, where comic invention gives chase to the pathos of war.

The capillaries of myriad plot lines, tangling retrospect with prospect in a narrative manner that commingles fact with fable, deliver the personal histories of a dozen or so Czech and Moravian newcomers into the epic stream of the war.

The first-person narrative may be Skvorecky's natural element, but his uncanny ability to create the illusion of overheard speech triumphs in all forms of *skaz*. He explains in his postscript that he had no way of knowing how his Czech soldiers actually spoke. In the nineteenth century the distinction between spoken and written Czech was a rigid linguistic convention. People wrote down conversations not as they heard them, but as they thought they should have been spoken. Thus in the absence of reliable models Skvorecky is free to improvise a lived-in, individual Czech or Moravian idiom for each of his characters, an illusion of a real speech breathing through the flow of verbal situations.

The process of acculturation to America is one that involves both loss and gain. In linguistic terms this can amount to such hybrid idioms as the contemporary American-Czech-speak Skvorecky has recorded with his comic pitch, thus provoking ire among his fellow émigrés. In this novel the young men who confabulate by campfires sometimes have to plumb their memories for the missing Czech word or substitute an Americanism when nothing else fits. The effect is more poignant than comic, reminding us that the stories are now merging with the mythical land in which countless newcomers are dying.

Among all the storytellers, the virtuoso voice belongs to Jan Amos Shake, the only one of the Czech Union soldiers who is not based on a documented historical figure. The man's real family name remains in doubt, but in Chicago Marenka Kakus calls him Mr. Schweik, in an anachronistic giveaway that decodes the personage as the paradoxical composite of the historical ambivalence of the Czech national character. Like Comenius, the seventeenth-century philosopher whose baptismal names he bears, Shake has heard the call of a religious vocation and then left his native country to escape persecution. He admits to being a half-baked, defrocked priest who absconded from the seminary because of a love affair with the beautiful daughter of a Prague rabbi. But since he is also a master of the comic lie and a bona fide rogue, we cannot swear to anything he says about his past. On one point he stands quite firm. He may have entered the battle for the freedom of black slaves wearing a metal chest plate under his uniform, but he is not a deserter nor a subversive. Like Skvorecky, this experimental American has a personal investment in large ideas as well as strong convictions about the issues at stake in this war.

In spite of the massive research for the novel, which took him from the private archives of the Czechs in Chicago to those of the U.S. Military History Institute near Gettysburg, Skvorecky denies that he is writing history. He insists on being a fiction writer poaching on the preserves charted out by professional historians. Thus he takes liberties with his sources. He has gathered all his Czech Union soldiers into the Twenty-Sixth Wisconsin Regiment, whereas in reality they were scattered among several units. But he vouches for the authenticity of several details that may strike the reader as fantastic. As in the novel, Breta, a black Union soldier, did speak some Czech, and some Chicago Czech immigrants did indeed petition the Austrian Consulate for the restoration of their Austrian passports out of fear of being drafted. Skvorecky makes effective use of this last incident as part of a satire on the Czech national characteristic to cop out of history, the flip side of its abiding skepticism about governments. This trait comes alive in a vignette showing how the good new citizens, who volunteered in droves to parade in red zouave pants under the banner of the Lincoln Slavonic Rifles, are instantly deflated by the first bugle call. The few Czechs who stand their ground fight under the command of the Hungarian Slovak, Geza Michaloczi, equipped through the bounty of the Bohemian Jew, Pan Ohrenzug.

Skvorecky's approach to history proceeds from the same mind-set as Tolstoy's, who used family memoirs and the reminiscences of ordinary people to correct the optical illusions of leaders and historians viewing war through binoculars. Yet he too understands military strategy and excels at reconstructing the topography, not just the sounds and smells of a battlefield. So he places an observer close to Sherman's command. He is Sergeant Kapsa, a professional soldier who had deserted from the Austrian army when a love affair took a tragic turn.

Skvorecky's American novel is thus rooted in a gesture of piety. His great uncle had fought for the Union, but his name is missing from the archives, obliterated by translation, from Skvorecky to Earwigan or perhaps by distortion to Square. But unlike Tolstoy, who resurrected his parents as central characters in *War and Peace*, Skvorecky leaves his elusive uncle to a postscript. Instead Skvorecky resurrects and emphasizes a forgotten Czech-American writer by using his fictions as a source for the romance at the heart of *The Bride of Texas*. Josef Buňata (1846-1934), editor and journalist, recorded the Czech experience in both journalism and fiction, while supplementing his meager income by rolling cigars. A free thinker and utopian socialist, he eventually converted to the values of American democracy during the New Deal. Skvorecky's postscript reveals a lively sympathy for this confrere, whose idealistic effort went to nought when his audience melted away in the proverbial American pot. By recalling a lowbrow storyteller like Buňata, Skvorecky once more shows his fondness for popular genres.

The conflicting claims of high and low literature are also a personal dilemma for the woman who tells her own story in the first person within this larger story of the men at war. She is Lorraine Tracy, a fiery New England abolitionist married to a professor who holds out Thackerey as the norm of novelistic respectability. Driven under cover, Lorraine writes her successful novels using the pseudonym of Laura Lee. They are romances based on the timeworn formula of love's triumph: a race to the altar by an intrepid heroine through a Victorian obstacle course. Lorraine, a disciple of Margaret Fuller, reveals her incipient feminism by making her heroines always more clever than the inevitably handsome men whom they are pursuing. This is Lorraine's literary signature.

Although Skvorecky is anything but politically correct, he has given some thought to the questions raised by feminist criticism. In reviewing Leslie Fiedler's *What Was Literature?* for the Voice of America, he used gender as a key to reconsider Poe's paradoxical division of literature into the popular strain, whose authors are destined to oblivion even as their works continue to be read, and the elite strain, which warrants immortal renown to the authors while dooming their works to the dust of library shelves. Skvorecky points out that in Poe's time, best-sellers were typically written by women. But he does not follow through with the feminist argument about the need to overthrow a literary canon that elevates the creativity of white males while marginalizing the achievements of women. Like Fiedler, Skvorecky chases a different hare in rejecting the narrow criteria of elitist criticism. He argues that the appeal of such eternal best-sellers stems from their tapping emotionally charged myths, whether the authors are men like Twain and Hašek or women like Harriet Beecher Stowe and Margaret Mitchell or just anonymous male/female voices like those who first sang the spiritual "Oh, Freedom!" It is nevertheless significant that Skvorecky has left it to a woman, born and bred in the bone of New England, to articulate the intellectual content of the mythopoetic vision of American freedom that he has made his own.

Lorraine's life adventure begins in Liberty, Rhode Island, with an incident that her fictional formula keeps reversing. She is courted by a handsome young officer named Ambrose Burnside and almost succumbs to the persuasion of his inarticulate love, only to change her mind in extremis, by fleeing from the altar where he patiently awaits her vows. The humiliated suitor goes on to become a Union general while she herself marries a professor, moves to Ohio to keep house, brings up her children, and writes novels. In a twist that lends a Czech tonality to the voice of this American bluestocking, Lorraine has a distinctly maternal foible for all the men in her life. As a respectable matron and mistress of a cultivated Midwestern parlor, she welcomes her rejected suitor back into her life, assuming the role of Burnside's confidante and staunch defender.

It is interesting that Skvorecky placed Burnside, the spurned lover destined to become a failed general, at the core of a novel about a fateful war born in the shame of an American conscience enslaved by the doublespeak of its constitutionally enshrined freedoms. Burnside's name is immortalized because of his remarkable facial hair, while history has stressed how he compiled a record of ignominy as the commander of the Army of the Potomac at Fredericksburg and during the Mud March. Nevertheless, he was a brave soldier. He began well at Bull Run, which made Lincoln select him as a replacement for McClellan. But his bad judgment was proverbial, leading him to commit a political faux pas in the arrest of Clement Vallandigham, the Copperhead Democrat who ran for governor of Ohio in 1863 on a virulently antiwar platform.

Skvorecky presents the Vallandigham affair, which embarrassed Lincoln and became the most notorious civil liberties case of the war, from the partisan perspective of Lorraine, who sees her friend Burnside, now military commander of Ohio, as a hero and Vallandigham as a demagogue manipulating free speech for personal ambition. In this episode both sides of the Civil War claim to fight under the banner of freedom, with the rebels claiming exclusive ownership of the Jeffersonian ideal. Consequently, Lorraine faces the problem of the legal limits of dissent, for she sees Vallandigham as appealing to constitutional principles on behalf of a cause that denies the benefits of such principles to others. This problem, of course, accompanies American democracy from its inception. Tellingly, Skvorecky weighs in on Lorraine's side in his postscript. He offers the key to this episode by defining it in terms of the classical agon that pitted Antigone, the defender of unwritten moral laws, against Creon, who adhered to the letter of the law in an act of spiritual treason. Burnside, like Antigone, has acted in the name of his reverence for the dead. And Lincoln eloquently recognizes the weight of this motive when he commutes Vallandigham's death sentence into banishment.

Lorraine's single literary flop in a lucrative publishing career is her serious novel based on the life of her black maid, Jasmine. Her *Carolina Bride* mixes abolitionist outrage with romance by leading her black heroine on the underground trail of freedom, from the tribulations of plantation life to the promised land in the North. There she finds happiness by marrying her good-for-nothing but handsome lover, the former house slave Hasdrubal.

There are two brides from Texas in Skvorecky's plot. Both step out of short stories by Buňata where love's heartbreak is healed by reunion. However, Skvorecky devises his own endings. Lida Toupelikova, the daughter of a landless Moravian family that emigrates to Texas, has lost love and innocence in the old country but recoups by twice marrying money in America. The first throw of the dice nets her the young master of de Ribordeaux plantation, who ends as a drunk and a suicide. Next, switching to the winning side of the war, she weds a Union officer, heir to a rising California family. Lida's success story, which takes advantage of the opportunities her adopted land offers for second chances, underlines the materialistic strain in the American pursuit of happiness. Her brother, Cyril, who falls in love with the beautiful house slave Dinah, who is Ribordeaux's mistress, exemplifies the more idealistic aspects of the quest. The two couples with their interlocking fortunes are the stuff the American dream is made of, a rough fabric woven in the woof and web of greed and renewable innocence.

The novel's final scene brings the two narrative streams of the novel together by staging an encounter between Lorraine and some of the Czech soldiers who have survived the war. It is set in a Chicago restaurant run by Jasmine and Hasdrubal, where the Czech veterans are holding their commemorative dinner. The famous writer, for her part, is celebrating her private reunion with Jasmine, whom she has finally located after a long and complicated search. Lorraine socializes with the Czech immigrants and their ladies, some of whom are her devoted readers. As evidenced by their attire and the tenor of the exchanges, these Czechs have done well for themselves in Chicago and on the farm. Sergeant Kapsa, now a family man happily married to the widow of a fallen comrade, achieves a moment of supreme satisfaction when General Sherman, cracking into a smile of recognition, extends his hand and greets him by his Czech name, Kapsa, not the Germanized Tasche, under which he served in Austria.

Cyril Toupelik, a veteran grown rich from his invention of a press that extracts oil out of cotton seed, is in the room with the other celebrants. But his happiness is yet incomplete, as he is still looking for Dinah, who disappeared somewhere down the river from the now-ruined de Ribordeaux plantation where they had secret trysts and where he swore to marry her one day. It is a measure of Skvorecky's success as a storyteller that he engages his reader's emotions in Cyril's project to recover his bartered bride. Still, as the novel ends, that unfulfilled happy ending seems to be at hand, beyond the text's confines, already a prospect on the ever-changing human map of America.

A *Josef Skvorecky Checklist*

Robert L. McLaughlin

Fiction

Zbabělci. Prague: Československý spisovatel, 1958; *The Cowards*. Trans. Jeanne Nemcova. New York: Grove, 1970.

Legenda Emöke. Prague: Československý spisovatel, 1963; "Emöke." *The Bass Saxophone*. Toronto: Anson-Cartwright, 1977; New York: Knopf, 1977; Hopewell, NJ: Ecco, 1994.

"Bassaxofon." *Bablónsky příběh*. Prague: Svobodné Slovo-Melantrich, Václavské námčskí, 1967. "The Bass Saxophone." *The Bass Saxophone*. Toronto: Anson-Cartwright, 1977; New York: Knopf, 1977; Hopewell, NJ: Ecco, 1994.

Smutek poručíka Borůvky. 1966. *The Mournful Demeanor of Lieutenant Boruvka*. Trans. Rosemary Kavan, Kaca Polackova, and George Theiner. London: Gollancz, 1973; New York: Norton, 1987.

LVICE. Prague: Československý spisovatel, 1969; *Miss Silver's Past*. Trans. Peter Kussi. New York: Grove, 1974.

Tankový prapor. Toronto: Sixty-Eight Publishers, 1971; *The Republic of Whores*. Trans. Paul Wilson. Hopewell, NJ: Ecco, 1993.

Mirákl. Toronto: Sixty-Eight Publishers, 1972. *The Miracle Game*. Trans. Paul Wilson. New York: Knopf, 1990; New York: Norton, 1992.

Hříchy pro pátera Knoxe. 1973. *Sins for Father Knox*. Trans. Kaca Polackova Henley. New York: Norton, 1988.

Konec poručíka Borůvky. 1975. *The End of Lieutenant Boruvka*. Trans. Paul Wilson. New York: Norton, 1990.

Prima sezona. 1975. *The Swell Season*. Trans. Paul Wilson. New York: Ecco, 1986.

Příběh inženýra lidských duší. Toronto: Sixty-Eight Publishers, 1977. *The Engineer of Human Souls*. Trans. Paul Wilson. New York: Knopf, 1984.

Scherzo capriccioso. Toronto: Sixty-Eight Publishers, 1983. *Dvorak in Love*. Trans. Paul Wilson. New York: Knopf, 1986.

Návrat poručíka Borůvky. 1991. *The Return of Lieutenant Boruvka*. Trans. Paul Wilson. New York: Norton, 1991.

Nevěsta z Texasu. Toronto: Sixty-Eight Publishers, 1992. *The Bride of Texas*. Trans. Kaca Polackova Henly. New York: Knopf, 1996.

Podvídky tenorsaxofonisty. *The Tenor Saxophonist's Story*. Trans. Caleb Crain, Kaca Polackova Henley, and Peter Kussi. Hopewell, NJ: Ecco, 1996.

Nonfiction

All the Bright Young Men and Women: A Personal History of the Czech Cinema. Trans. Michael Schonberg. Toronto: Peter Martin, 1971.

Jiri Menzel and the History of the Closely Watched Trains. Boulder: East European Monographs, 1982.

Talkin' Moscow Blues. Ed. Sam Solecki. Toronto: Lester & Orpen Dennys, 1988; New York: Ecco, 1990.

Headed for the Blues: A Memoir. Trans. Kaca Polackova Henly. Hopewell, NJ: Ecco, 1996.

The Culture of Everyday Venality:
or
a Life in the Book Industry

Margaret Wehr

Here is the rap on independent/non-profit/alternative literary presses like McPherson, Semiotext(e) Autonomia, Feminist Press, Coffee House, Dalkey Archive, Sun and Moon, Permeable Press, Asylum Arts and many others:

* they're ineptly run by visionary but incompetent people living in former doll factories in Brooklyn or quaint Ruskinesque cottages in Oregon;
  * they have no money for quality production, promotion, or royalties;
  * they owe printers a lot of money;
  * you can't find their books anywhere.

For those who speculate beyond the ready (and not entirely inaccurate) assumption that these publishers are simply terminal fools, the material cause of all of the above becomes quickly clear. These presses are what they are because they have no money (i.e., are "undercapitalized," i.e., are not capitalists).

Why are they "undercapitalized"? Often it's because these presses began with nothing. The only "original accumulation" these people have ever had is the impressive shelves of books which they have read and have continued reading in dead earnest since high school. So it follows that these presses are undercapitalized because these publishers are literary people and have no business skills, experience, or instincts. They don't know how to manipulate their resources so that on one bright day, lo and behold, they could have that mythic creature, a "cash reserve." But this is all well understood: non-profit literary publishers are idealistic and poor and the only reason they're in this game is that they don't like what they see commercial presses doing to their much beloved books.

There is, however, another reason for the financial distress of non-profit and independent literary presses, one that is less often understood even by the people running these presses. The third reason I would offer for the inadequacies listed above is that **these presses are not able to function adequately because they are day in and day out screwed by the routine and hardly-worth-mentioning venality and psychopathology of everyday American business practices.**

I would like to bring to your attention the composite business experiences of a single (made-up) publisher whose particulars I have pieced together from anecdotes and documents that have been supplied to me in conversations with the publishers of the above listed (and several other) real-life presses. The names have been changed even when the individuals involved were far from innocent.

The name of this composite press is the Matinée Press. It is located in Oregon, near Portland. It publishes high-quality fiction and poetry of very independent, if not particularly avant-garde, aesthetics. As its publisher likes to say, with a disarming simplicity, "I want to publish the books that I like." It was founded in 1978 by Thom Nagy, a Ph.D. in American lit who didn't much like being a professor and who only went to graduate school in the first place because he wanted to take more workshops in writing in the local MFA mill. He went on to write a dissertation on the work of Paul Metcalf, which dissertation was promptly published by Bowling Green University Press in a quantity of 1,000 copies—772 of which were eventually sold to Daedalus on remainder, 72 of which sold-through, 700 of which were pulped and turned into corrugated insulators for too-hot coffee cups at Starbucks. Thom Nagy's one abiding literary conviction was that good and unusual writers should be published, good and unusual books that are out-of-print should be brought back into print, and both of the preceding should be kept in print for as long as the press could manage to survive in his roomy basement or whatever other unoccupied space he could find with an outlet friendly to his desk-top publishing equipment. Not bad convictions these, as convictions go.

The first and most obvious flaw in Thom Nagy's grand plan was a) he had no money, and b) he knew nothing of the book publishing business. Actually b) was a fortunate thing because if he had known even one of the many truths he would come to learn about the book business, he would have stopped with a shudder and never begun the now highly respected Matinée Press.

But he got lucky early. He published a funny sort of postmodern detective novel called *All the Doors Were Lo(c/o)ked*—a Derridean thriller playing on the theme of the absent and the present and incidentally exposing the involvement of the LAPD in the cocaine business (that's the "c/oked" part of the title)—which, through a mostly unbelievable series of benign influences (remember when John Leonard was editor of the *New York Times Book Review?*), took off. With the modest profits from this book and the attention his astute editorial judgments were now justly receiving, Thom Nagy was able to expand the professional base of his operation. He got on decent terms with a short-run printer, found a really top-notch designer at the local art college, and—oh! *bonne chance!*—signed a contract with a national distributor. What's more, this distribution company, Froggy Native Boy Quality Book Distribution in New York City, was run by none other than the famous Ethan Walters, the man who had published so many of the great scandalous European (especially French!) writers of the fifties during the heyday of Olympia, Evergreen, Grove, et al. Now Thom Nagy was working with a legend! He was working with the very publisher of his favorite books in graduate school! Didn't this conceivably mean, his large but innocent mind worked, that he too was conceivably the stuff of legend? My God, the name of Walters's company was taken from Molly Bloom's soliloquy! Talk about being in the right hands!

It is here that our plot thickens. For now young Thom Nagy and his precious love-child, Matinée Press, have joined forces with the (entirely mysterious) business practices of The Book Industry.

In brief, leading up to 1996 (the point at which our thickened plot became a veritable ragout), Matinée endured the following business obscenities:

* After four modestly successful years, Froggy Native Boy fell six months behind in its payments to Matinée. Thom Nagy's creditors were screaming bloody murder. Nagy considered taking out a personal loan to cover the mess. He sought another distributor and found one. He left F.N.B. while being owed $15,000, of which he saw, in the course of the next ten years, maybe one penny on the dollar. Worse yet, Thom Nagy kept hearing strange reports of his best backlist titles turning up in bookstores in England and Europe. Had he been given a strictly accurate closing inventory report by Ethan Walters? Or had the blackguard stolen not only his money but his books as well?

* The second distributor was little better. It was Damned Right! press of Sacramento, California, another small publisher hoping to join common force with other like-purposed publishers precisely to avoid the kind of experiences they all seemed to be having with pirates like Froggy Native Boy. Unhappily, in spite of Damned Right!'s best intentions, they were unable to succeed where Froggy Native Boy had failed because—but how could anyone have suspected this?—bookstores don't pay distributors that can't threaten them. They will pay Random House because Random House can threaten to withhold the titles from all of its many presses (without which blockbusters the shelves might appear a tad bare) but they will not pay little Damned Right! distribution because . . . who gives a darn if a few small press books aren't on the shelves? Most shocking, as Dan Paisly, Damned Right!'s guiding genius, told Thom Nagy, most bookstores claimed that they were doing them both a favor to stock their books at all and that if they were going to insist on being paid, well, the entire relationship would have to be reexamined. Business philanthropy went only so far, you know.

* Reluctantly, Thom Nagy had to look again. This time a little deeper in debt. Add another $10,000 to Froggy Native Boy's $15,000 payments in arrears. Thom Nagy made a brave move. He not only changed distributors,

he hired a professional business manager, Harold S. Westman, former president of the prestigious Universal Publishers Group, someone who really knew this insidious game (for indeed Thom Nagy was beginning to suspect that this was an insidious game) from the inside. So he took a big chunk of a rare grant and started paying out a salary (new uncharted terrain: BUSINESS OVERHEAD). His new distributor was Smalle and Smalle, run by Maryanne Smalle and her chiropractor husband. To listen to Westman, it seemed like a good deal. She had lots of sales reps, good relations with the chains, and what was clearly a very determined disposition. Only a few things made Thom Nagy nervous. The catalog had things in it like the *Bridal Gown Creative Bridal Guide Annual*. And Hand Jive, publishers of not-so-vaguely seamy cartoon books. And Great Day in the Morning Press which appeared, if Thom Nagy understood, to be devoted to books about breakfast cereals. But he was assured by his heady and confident new business manager that Maryanne Smalle was a very shrewd, hard-nosed and capable business woman and he was in good hands.

Okey-doke, said poor Thom.

Well, in the course of a very usual four-year period of moderate success, even the "hard-nosed" Smalle fell behind, one month at a time, and Thom Nagy began once again to suspect that he was going to get screwed. To make matters worse, Harold S. Westman took a sudden powder, claiming that the years of publishing stress had taken a toll on him and he was heading out for his cabin (for he had a cabin) in Idaho. With more than a little trepidation, Thom Nagy began looking into the funny notebooks in which Westman always seemed to have his nose. The notebooks with the lines running north to south, some of them red lines, and the rest a blizzard of numbers. What could they be about?

It took awhile but it didn't really take a long while, because Thom Nagy was finally a bright guy. He concluded that, quite on his own, Westman had dug yet another tidy $20,000 dollar hole for Matinée Press. The infrequent checks from Smalle and Smalle had gone not to pay printers (whom Thom Nagy could practically hear breathing very hard right outside his not-very-substantial door) but to pay the part-time salary of Westman's little crew of mostly unneeded assistants (one of whom was apparently a semi-alcoholic near-street derelict who spared Thom Nagy the unpleasantness of firing him by abandoning his car at a local intersection and running off, literally, for the hills from which he was finally dragged all disheveled by police, counselors, and family). This same semi-alcoholic young man had also misplaced several checks from Smalle. Westman had of course continued to receive his own salary until the last untidy dollar was gone. Finally, Thom Nagy discovered in the back of one of the notebooks in Westman's pencilled scrawl a list of curious IOUs to authors from whom Westman had essentially misappropriated monies intended for royalty and foreign rights payments. Between the money paid to semi-alcoholic and otherwise useless employees and the money filched from authors to float the nonetheless sinking ship of Westman, Thom Nagy found himself another (should he say self-inflicted?) $20,000 in debt.

Who in the world, he wondered, would be dumb enough to print another of his books?

Fortunately, at about this time Distinguished University Press, long an admirer of Nagy's skillful and caring editorial vision, came along and offered to help. They could take over not only distribution but also marketing and promotion. They were nice people. Nothing like the aggressive and punishing Maryanne Smalle. Thom took out a big loan (part of which was secured by his little red Honda Civic) to float the press during the transition, held his nose, said his prayers, and jumped.

It was at this point that Thom Nagy met another player in this tale of the psychopathology of everyday American business practice. It was called "a distributor's contract." He had signed one, he dimly remembered, way back when with the bearlike figure of Harold Westman looming over him, chuckling, lighting one of his ubiquitous pipes, and bearing the brave mien of a man who knew what he was about. But what was in the contract, well, Thom Nagy couldn't say for sure. But Maryanne Smalle could. Apparently, even though she was six months in arrears in her own payments to Matinée, she was still well within her rights in creating a reserve against returns from bookstores up to 25 percent of the previous years sales (never mind that that was 25 percent of money over half of which she had never paid to Matinée to begin with). Thom Nagy was what we used to call flummoxed. Still, things began to become clear to him. Big things. Things about the nature of an entire so-called "industry." He realized for the first time the gigantic stupidity of basing an entire multibillion dollar industry on what was essentially "consignment" terms. Local honey producers might leave their locally made honey at the supermarket on consignment, but an entire national industry? He realized the farcical, laughable dopiness of imagining that the comical crew of incompetents—that Distinguished University Press flung to the far corners of the continent and referred to as "Sales Reps"—actually knew anything about any book that ventured beyond indiscretions concerning Dennis Rodman's disinclination for cunnilingus. Thom Nagy could train his pet cockatiel to do a better job.

Closer to home, Thom Nagy wondered how it was possible that he could be said to owe Smalle and Smalle 25 percent of total monies, most of which Smalle still owed him. It seemed metaphysical to him. Sort of like what he remembered of Kantian antinomies. But Smalle seemed to know exactly which came first, the chicken or the egg; what came first were Thom Nagy's eggs, all (or both) of them. Ms. Smalle was always capable of reasoning through Thom Nagy's objections, in her brusque and efficient way: "That is what the contract allows and that was what I am going to do."

"But don't worry," she cajoled, "you'll get it all back in one year providing that there are not large returns."

In short, Smalle and Smalle kept the previous six months sales as a debt to Matinée and then proceeded to legitimately (which is to say, contractually) keep the next three months of sales as a reserve against returns. Only one other thing you should note here: nothing in the brilliant contract devised by Harold Westman required Smalle and Smalle to keep this so-called reserve anywhere other than in its own quite active in-and-out checking account. For, indeed, poor Thom Nagy wouldn't know an escrow account from a rock dove.

For a while it appeared that Distinguished University Press would succeed so wildly where Smalle and Smalle had failed that new revenues would keep him afloat and important into the next century. But then, and this brings us up to the present, on one sad day in the summer of 1996 he received his sales report from Distinguished U. There was bad news. Returns had been heavy. Thom Nagy sighed. Well, it was nobody's fault. We got the books in stores and they just didn't sell through. He looked at the lengthy returns pages. And it began to dawn on him. Page after page with the unmistakable imprimatur of the enormous bookselling marvel, coast-to-coast, a thousand stores, the Behemoth and Nimrod Co. Then he looked at the ISBN numbers for the books returned. What were these numbers? He didn't recognize them. Were they even his books? He looked through his catalogs. At last he found them. Books sold in 1993! Books sold in 1992! Books sold in 1982! It was as if Behemoth and Nimrod were in fact simply an enormous and very constipated digestive system that had with an imponderable energy one day found its autonomic system and with a wild convulsion that began on the west and east coasts simultaneously rolled thousands and thousands of books that Thom Nagy had imagined sold for years back to the publisher. There was one book returned by the hundreds that Smalle and Smalle had only sold five hundred of in the first place. Thom Nagy had to wonder: Had anyone ever actually bought even just one copy?

Nagy was unhappy. He put his sad little publisher's head in his sad little editor's hands. Then, as you see in movies, like Jimmy Stewart realizing something really bad, it came to him. These thousands of returns had gone to the wrong distributor! They should have gone to Smalle and Smalle, who—after all, dear God!—had the theoretical reserve. Now he was going to have to pay once to print the book, twice to protect against the book's return, and thrice to accept the return itself.

Believe me, Thom Nagy's phone started getting a workout. He called Smalle. Would she accept the returns? No way. Too complicated. Would only cause more headaches. Would she then at least pay him what she owed the press? Sorry, we don't have a dime. Smalle and Smalle had just received its own returns from Behemoth and Nimrod one hundred times the size of Matinée's little sum. Distinguished University Press, could you please ask B&N to consider redirecting its accounting to Smalle and Smalle? Sorry, not worth the effort. B&N is probably not really aware that it even carries your titles. Best not to call too much attention to the fact. It could affect future sales.

Oh but there were other fantasies. The independent book stores of America would rally to his cause. Why, he'd be the first publisher to refuse to sell to Behemoth and Nimrod. He'd sue Smalle and Smalle. Reviewers would support him. They'd help him tell the truth! And he'd place an article in the *Nation* exposing the whole sad mess. In fact, he immediately picked up his last issue of *Nation* and, lo and behold!, it was devoted to the corporatization of America. Damn it, he had allies after all! But then he turned to the back of the issue.

And there it was.

The future. A sadder but wiser future, to be sure. For the entire back page of the anti-corporate issue of *Nation* was an enormous paid ad (oh paid it was with money Thom Nagy was sure had filtered to the bookselling giant from some of his own *stolen* money (yes, *stolen* was the word he used now; he was getting a little paranoid (not to mention pathologically obsessed!))) bought by "America's Bookstore," Behemoth and Nimrod.

Which, he wondered, would be more important to *Nation*: his little virtuous tirade or Behemoth and Nimrod's $$ for full-page ads?

His little house of cards crumbled. Whom was he kidding? *Nation* wasn't going to print his exposé. And if he wasn't going to do business with Behemoth and Nimrod, he might as well get out of publishing altogether. The chains were over 50 percent of his sales. And the independents? he checked it out. Only one of the so-called major independents in the whole of these United States had ordered more than two copies of any book in his spring list. The independent bookstores were out to save one thing: their own asses.

But wait a minute. One last hope. Reviewers. The people who had written about and loved his books, supported his quixotic endeavors for years, they'd rally to his cause. *The Village Voice* could organize a benefit! But once again, reality checked in. In fact, the great independent *Voice* hadn't run a full review of one of his books since the earliest days of the press (days which could only now seem to him wickedly blessed). And, to make matters much worse, he was having a peculiar kind of trouble with reviewers of late. It seemed that many literary reviewers also fancied that they were writers. No less than five important reviewers had submitted books to Thom in the last two years. They had all been rejected. This had put a not-so-curious damper on their collective enthusiasms. In fact, Thom suspected that he'd been blacklisted at some places. For example, *Hava! Java!*, a new glossy big city weekly, had stopped running reviews of Matinée's books when in the past he'd practically been able to wallpaper his office with the glad tidings.

The culprit here, L. A. Salieri, had actually written to Thom about it:

Dear Thom:

Even though I think doing an interview with you for *Hava!Java!* is a great idea (it's terrible the things that have happened to you in the book business!), I am temporarily declining the possibility. For the reason that Matinée has not made any decision on publishing my manuscript. I will be changing my mind on doing the interview if the above situation is dealt with.

In fact, Thom had written a very (very!) generous note of rejection to the semiliterate Salieri. Guess he wanted Thom to try again. Even now, though, the sentence fragments and other instances of creeping idiocy made Thom a little ill. This was who carried his cause to the public. A perfect, self-deluded, and probably crazy dolt.

From which many awesomely accumulated truths, Thom Nagy could conclude but one thing which became the one great, grand inevitable Truth of his career in the Book Industry: **the only entity that really has to live by its contracts, the only entity that is really expected to pay its debts, and the only entity that will certainly have to pay interest on its outstanding debts is absolutely the smallest entity in the system. Namely: precious Matinée Press.**

The wild expansiveness of this insight literally floored Thom Nagy. He pitched backwards and might have received a nasty blow to the head were it not for the fact that he fell right on top of a pile of submissions, hundreds of them, sent in just the last two weeks and not yet removed from their spongy mailers. On this cushion, the extraordinary naïveté of the world's writers, he could always depend.

Book Reviews

Paul Metcalf. *Collected Works, Volume One: 1956–1976.* Coffee House Press, 1996. 591 pp. $35.00.

There is a type of American genius whose genius consists largely in its uncanny ability to express the American Genus. If this type were French, we'd call it a *bricoleur*: a person who, lacking the "right" tool, takes whatever is at hand and makes it work. In this sense William Carlos Williams didn't write poems because there is no "poetry" in his poems. Charles Ives didn't write symphonies because there is no "symphony" in his symphonies. As Hugh Kenner put it, poets like Williams are makers of a "homemade world." The reader wants to ask of this "pure product," "Where did you find this stuff, this bric-a-brac? How and why did you cobble it together? And why in the world do you think it's a poem/symphony/novel?" The response of this Type is most appropriately, as Williams himself put it in *Kora in Hell*, "I'll do what I want when I want and it will be good if the authentic spirit of change is upon it."

Paul Metcalf, working within this very eccentric "American grain," is one of these seekers of the "authentic spirit."

This is the first of three volumes collecting Metcalf's work to be published by Coffee House in the next two years. The jewel in this first volume is the short novel *Genoa*. It is the densely layered story of Mike Mills, an M.D. working on an assembly line at a GM plant, who is not so much obsessed by as possessed by reveries and meditations about Herman Melville, Christopher Columbus, and his brother, Carl Mills, an executed murderer.

Mills is a character who is only superficially a part of his present moment. He has a job. His home is in the middle of the suburbs (although it itself is a nineteenth-century farmhouse). His children are being raised by the television set. Dinner comes out of the Frigidaire. In other words, he lives in a world of asphalt over history. But Mills himself is rooted through the present into the monstrous reality of the past. The old stone hearth and chimney in his mislocated home seem to radiate this past up through the house into the attic study where Mills reads and writes while the rest of twentieth-century America negotiates its present with "talking cereal boxes."

Genoa is, in 1996, certainly even less "what the age demands" than it was when first published in 1965. But for those who still can imagine that language hardwires us to our own dense past, Metcalf has much to offer.

It is a book like this that makes it clear why a press like Coffee House— and independent, nonprofit publishing in general—is so critical to our collective future. [Curtis White]

Marie Redonnet. *Nevermore*. Trans. Jordon Stump. Univ. of Nebraska Press, 1996. 123 pp. $32.00; paper: $12.00.

Marie Redonnet has created a genre unto itself: let's call it the Redonnet. The Redonnet is a work of prose fiction of novella length (roughly one hundred pages) and narrated in that blank style common to the modernist tradition that has its source in Kafka (her dedication to Danilo Kiš is most apt at this point). Yet her prose is also cinematic in that it reads like a story treatment, i.e., a synopsislike encapsulation of the shooting script to come. What's more, in her newly translated work *Nevermore* she achieves a weird hybrid of cultural mythologies, almost as if the overheated melodramas of film noir at its most baroque was used as a vehicle for political and metaphysical allegory. Threading through this high- and lowbrow stew are several stock figures—one character in search of his past (notebook in hand, a New Novelesque homage), another fleeing hers, a third attempting to repair an ancient injustice. Then there are circus freaks a nightclub singer (at the "Eden Palace," no less), mad preachers, evil plutocrats who have meetings aboard yachts named *Moby Dick* and *Salve Regina*, a documentary filmmaker, a volcanic eruption. . . . If you can imagine Orson Welles's *Touch of Evil* as remade by a David Lynch with a social message, you will have a sense of the weird morphing of familiar subjects and thematic ambitions. The cast of *Nevermore* is technically North American, but the weight of their lived past is palpably not of our hemisphere, evoking post-World War II dictatorships and detention camps in a south of the border setting (a volcano lurks in the background). In her deliberately crafted oppositions of the secular and sacred, the personal and the public, the corrupted powerful and the corrupted victims of power, she evokes our contemporary morass. Yet the author eschews solutions. Redonnet's characters and their stories carry the charge of metaphors, but ones unanchored from their referents, a shorthand for meanings that stubbornly resist a fuller transcription. *Nevermore* becomes both the name of a new nightclub and the title for a book that may never be written. As our detective and would-be writer meditates: "What makes his book so difficult to write is that it is a book of memories written in the absence of memories." What begins as detective fiction ends as fairy tale. Which is a way of saying that Marie Redonnet has perfected the art of postmodernist fabulation. [Dominic Di Bernardi]

D. N. Stuefloten. *Mexico Trilogy*. FC2, 1996. 298 pp. Paper: $12.95.

D. N. Stuefloten is at once a chronicler of the grotesque and a minute detailer of our world. In these three novels, *Maya*, *Ethiopian Exhibition*, and *Queen of Las Vegas*, Stuefloten creates imagined landscapes characterized by his "despair . . . and passion." His range is often encyclopedic, as in *Maya* when he provides a detailed catalogue of the natural and geological world. His places are always grounded in these particulars and so vibrate with clarity.

In *Maya* three actors are abandoned on a film set, which could be a battlefield, which could be in Mexico or Vietnam, which could be on Santa Monica Boulevard. Stuefloten is determined for precision and all three novels reveal a persistent impulse to describe and redescribe. Stuefloten's dialogue is arched and punctuated by the same staccato rhythms employed in his narrative prose. But Stuefloten shows a tinge of disbelief in language's ability to achieve any accuracy, for we are often told that we will be given more details later. Later never comes.

It is appropriate that all three novels are peopled with actors and directors constantly perceived through the camera's viewfinder, a tool as inadequate as language. Language becomes the peephole into Steufloten's manufactured worlds. And it is language that both creates and destroys them.

Dichotomies are important to Stuefloten: despair/passion, creation/destruction (the actors in *Maya* are peppered with bombs as they work), and, inevitably, appearance/reality ("This is movieland. Nothing is real."). In *Ethiopian Exhibition* an African city poses as Puerto Vallarta and convinces tourists to believe the charade. The Las Vegas in *Queen of Las Vegas* is of papier-mâché. Osgood Fetters, one of the actors in *Maya*, returns in *Queen of Las Vegas* as a script writer saying, "It's no good, you see, trying to impose a particular order on your material. The order—the story—has to grow out of its material." And so too there is form and content. The content of *Mexico Trilogy* is often alarmingly grotesque and its form a lyric beauty. The two are inseparable. Language cannot particularize the world, it seems, yet may entertain its visitors. [Thomas Lecky]

––––––––––

William S. Burroughs. *My Education: A Book of Dreams.* Picador, 1996. 193 pp. £6.99.

My Education assembles descriptions of Burroughs's dreams sometimes dating as far back as the 1970s. It is a volume that contains some of the raw material used in his novels, but Burroughs also includes brief commentaries on the status of dreams. On the one hand, he rejects the Freudian view of there being a clear continuity between the waking and dreaming life of the individual; on the other, he rejects the dismissive view of dreams as "neural housecleaning." Defending the importance of dreams amounts to defending the importance of his own fiction for Burroughs, and their apparent randomness and unpredictability carry anarchic value for him in disrupting the orderliness of contemporary life. Burroughs reflects ironically on Kerouac's romantic confidence that dreams could give access to psychic depth and tends instead to go for paranoid evocations of forces or meanings just out of the observer's reach. One fragment describes himself asleep under a drape and being visited by a black dog symbolic of death. Many of the pieces gathered here are haunted by death, but in this instance Burroughs cannot pin down the identity of the other (dead?) human presence in the dream. In another example Burroughs figures himself as disoriented in a subway station while a man "with very pale gray eyes" sitting at a nearby table suggests: "Mr Burroughs, why don't you call 6410?" The reader is denied any space to wonder how the speaker knows Burroughs's name and is led to infer that the number might signify a room in the hotel mentioned at the end of the fragment. Typically these dreams imply larger autobiographical or cultural narratives that are never made clear. Instead the reader is given glimpses of Burroughs's friends and associates, his reading of novelists like Conrad, and, of course, snapshot views of gay sexual experiences (usually summarized very tersely as "making it"). The sheer number of references in these dreams to other fiction implies a self-consciousness to the volume. Although its title suggests learning and apprentice-work, *My Education* is really a retrospective on Burroughs's own output, with many interesting comments on, for instance, his method of abruptly shifting context so that no individual version of the real can ever quite gell. In one piece the description of a pension is informed by a confidence that it is situated in Tangier but the dreamer is shocked to discover that the outside view belies this assumption. And this process is constantly being repeated in the dreams as in Burroughs's fiction. Place and person shift abruptly with surreal consequences, and Burroughs repeatedly designates these experiences as taking place in the "Land of the Dead." For all these reasons, *My Education* makes a surprisingly accessible companion to Burroughs's published fiction. [David Seed]

William H. Gass. *Finding a Form.* Knopf, 1996. 354 pp. $26.00.

Gass is a writer who has always believed in public discourse, that the act of the critic and scholar is to engage as wide an audience as possible in matters of serious intent (that is, that these things *matter* or at least have consequences for the body politic) and that, therefore, the form of the discourse must itself be engaging, resonate, enlivening, and at times, vituperative. The present collection hits the mark in every way, though one may mourn that there are not more critics who see their function as this, as opposed to the academic specialist who, if he speaks to anyone more than himself, speaks only to other specialists in deadening prose. One might especially wish that other novelists might so speak more often, though of course one knows that many of them have little critical ability and can speak, quite poorly and unintelligently, only about themselves. Gass is this rare figure whose critical abilities go hand-in-hand with his fictional ones.

Appropriately enough, this volume opens with a biting attack on award giving, starting with the Pulitzer for fiction, which has a remarkable history of recognizing the bad and the forgettable, and moving on to many others that champion the mediocre and fashionable in the name of literary quality. This essay is followed by one given to the subject of the use of the present tense in fiction, a practice Gass generally abhors but one which is perfectly suited to readers raised on television and those writers who have their fingers on the pulse of their generation (the minimalists, of course, come in for the most severe tongue lashings here).

In another essay, one that begins with rather painful descriptions of his childhood and therefore partial explanation for his having become a writer rather than a car salesman or a contented businessman, Gass lays down his aesthetic, which has always been his aesthetic, old-fashioned (Aristotle, Aquinas, Gilson) and therefore radical for our times: "I believe that the artist's fundamental loyalty must be to form, and his energy employed in the activity of making. . . . The poet, every artist, is a maker whose aim is to make something supremely worthwhile, to make something inherently valuable in itself." All of this is opposed to such perennially acclaimed aims as understanding the world, understanding ourselves or those near and dear to us, reflecting or mirroring one thing or another, making the world a better place, societal improvement, the betterment of one group or another (women, blacks, gays, the aristocracy, whatever), or the ever-favorite replication of *reality* in a kind of condensed version that makes reality even more real.

Other chapters are given to Wittgenstein, Nietzsche, Robert Walser, Gass's beloved Spanish (well, at least one, Juan Goytisolo) and Latin Americans (Fuentes, Lezama Lema, Cabrera Infante, Cortázar, Vargas Llosa, though one glaring omission here is Fernando del Paso, an omission I am sure Mr. Gass will rectify in any future edition), Danilo Kiš, Ford Madox Ford, and of course Gertrude Stein roams the pages freely. And there is, towards the end, a particularly interesting chapter entitled "The Music of Prose." The temptation here, which I will resist, is to quote endlessly from Gass. Better just to go read the book, but rather than reading it cover to cover, one should more profitably read a chapter a day—there is too much in each of them to move swiftly on. Or one may be better advised to stop and reread the works he has reference to (I do not remember my Walser the way that Gass remembers his).

The book is an utter pleasure and is itself a working demonstration of the author's recurring theme: the celebration of language and the power of prose to create and re-create the world. I will not bother to say that it should be the winner of one of those prizes that Gass scorns, nor do I think he need worry about this happening; his politics, aesthetics, and intelligence are wrong for the committees. [John O'Brien]

John Barth. *On with the Story.* Little, Brown, 1996. 257 pp. $23.95.

Although *On with the Story* is John Barth's first collection of short stories since *Lost in the Funhouse* (1968), readers of his recent novels will find themselves in familiar territory. Barth once again puts fiction under a microscope to show us how it works, to remind us of its fundamental elements, and to push these elements as far as they will go. He insists that stories are not absolute in any sense, underscoring his point by beginning the book with a story entitled "The End: An Introduction" and concluding the book with continuations of the eleven stories that precede the conclusion, in reverse order.

This inconclusive conclusion is just one of the many dazzling ways in which Barth knits together this collection of stories. Another is the series of interchapters depicting a vacationing husband and wife who exchange stories in bed. In this aspect, the book resembles a Barth novel like *The Tidewater Tales* or *The Last Voyage of Somebody the Sailor* in which storytelling becomes a kind of serious game, as it once was for Barth's favorite literary predecessor, Scheherazade in *The Thousand and One Nights.*

This is not to say that there is nothing new in this collection. Barth has in fact discovered any number of new ways to illustrate his ideas about the nature of fiction. In the manner of Italo Calvino, he relies on physics to explain the motivations or actions of characters. (Laws of physics run rampant throughout the book; the first epigraph is a Heisenberg equation, and the book's final chapter has one character inscribing Schrödinger's wave-function equation across the buttocks of his naked lover). At one point, Barth cleverly puts *On with the Story* into the hands of his characters, one of whom has torn out a page from it to use as a bookmark in another book. Perspectives shift, worlds are brought into a new focus, objects or characters resurface, and the reader can only shake his head in admiration.

This *is* to say that even though the novel has been Barth's genre of preference, this collection proves that he is still a master of the short story. Not only does he issue graceful pronouncements about the state of fiction, he also manages to tell good stories. Especially admirable in this respect are "On with the Story," " 'Waves,' by Amien Richard," and "Ever After." The characters are thoroughly developed and easily recognizable, the plots are engaging, and one can almost feel the warm sand under one's feet or taste the dry Chablis that the author describes so lovingly. There is a cheerful, honest texture to these stories for all of their intellectual play that makes them enjoyable while still stimulating. *On with the Story* could just as easily be a beach book as a classroom text. Barth wouldn't have it any other way. [D. Quentin Miller]

Peter Parker, ed., Frank Kermode, consulting ed. *A Reader's Guide to Twentieth Century Writers*. Oxford Univ. Press, 1996. 825 pp. $35.00.

This kind of guide never particularly succeeds, omitting writers who should be included, including ones who shouldn't, giving simplistic overviews of the works, entries never long enough and yet—given what is usually said—also thankfully short. This guide provides us with all of these problems and more (including a binding so cheap that it broke the first time I opened the book). The Brits are usually the worst at such creations, and the team of Parker and Kermode do not fail to live up to this reputation. So, some examples of the omissions: on the British side, though B. S. Johnson is at last included (for years the British did not want to lay claim to one of their most interesting writers, no doubt because he did not tell stories), Alan Burns and Aidan Higgins are not. On the American side, Neil Simon is included, as well as such luminaries as Erica Jong, Anne Rice, and Chaim Potok, but Gilbert Sorrentino, Paul Metcalf (whose complete works are now being published by Coffee House Press), William Eastlake, Edward Dahlberg, and Rikki Ducornet are not (the method for inclusion with the Americans was apparently arrived at by virtue of the publisher—large commercial house is good, but small publisher is bad, unless one has achieved a certain notoriety, such as Charles Bukowski). Among the Canadians, Douglas Glover, the most interesting of contemporary Canadian novelists, is excluded. Rather than excusing himself for the obvious omissions and strange inclusions, Parker defends his choices on the basis of having his volume represent authors who have an appeal to the general reader (William Gaddis and John Barth are included—no comment necessary), and says that "a very few writers have had to be excluded (none of them of great significance)." I love editors whose stupidity rises to the level of allowing them to make such statements. One final note: Harry Mathews is included, which is strange in view of those who are not, but the key to his inclusion may lie in the fact that the critic, in a very short entry, twice mentions that Mathews came from wealth and must himself be wealthy. True or not, would that Parker have explained that some writers achieved inclusion on the basis of economic background—if he had, the volume might make more sense or might even be more interesting. Oxford should consider a future volume entitled "Wealthy Writers of the Twentieth Century." [John O'Brien]

W. G. Sebald. *The Emigrants*. Trans. Michael Hulse. New Directions, 1996. 237pp. $23.00.

This novel, which is surely one of the best novels to appear since World War II, cannot be reviewed briefly. I will try, nevertheless, to emphasize a few details that demand more significant explorations. The novel consists of four parts. Each is an eccentric extended portrait of a person: Dr. Henry Selwyn, Paul Breyter, Ambros Adelwarth, and Max Ferber. The narrator tries to discover their pasts; he hopes to confront the reasons for their dramatic acts of re-creation and self-destruction. He tries to find a pattern linking "the emigrants" because he uncannily knows that he is related to them. Thus the novel becomes a search for *kinship*—literally and symbolically. It is a detective story about origins and endings, about the nature of history and memory. The narrator recognizes that his search is somehow doomed to incompletion.

The novel is filled with photographs: stills of childhood activities and, perhaps, more profoundly, with ones of cemeteries, enigmatic loads, journals, and hotels. The photographs are the remnants of the past. They must be studied as closely as the words of the narrator. Therefore, the novel, in part, is an "album" of what the relationship is between word and image. This is an occult text, one which defies clear, closed meaning and genre. It is autobiography, biography (of four characters), travelogue, meditation on the meaning of the Holocaust, Germany, past and present, self and other, word and world. It uses a four-part structure as does a symphony or *Pale Fire* and demonstrates that the four parts, usually closed, may be "violations," not the perfection of closure.

Perhaps the last words of the text express the "final solution" or the mystery of any solution. The narrator sees three women at a window: "Who the young women are I do not know. The light falls on them from the window in the background, so that I cannot make out their eyes clearly but I sense that all three are looking across at me." The vision is a long passage. The narrator cannot understand the relationship of this deception and one elsewhere. He does sense that these women are *possibly* the three fates: "None, Decume, and Morta, the daughters of night, with spindle, scissors and thread." The text is a mysterious interpretation of noninterpretation. [Irving Malin]

Paul Auster. *Why Write?* Burning Deck, 1996. 58 pp. $20.00; paper: $10.00.

This volume collects seven essays by Paul Auster, all having to do, more or less, with writing. The most important is the title piece, reprinted from the *New Yorker*, in which Auster answers the question of why he writes with five vignettes—some autobiographical, all apparently true—illustrating stranger-than-fiction coincidences. The message seems to be that, even in a chaotic world governed by nothing but chance, unexpected connections, *meaningful* connections, occur; writing helps to find the connections and to create the meaning. The other pieces range from "Word Box," a photo essay, to my favorite, "A Prayer for Salman Rushdie." This is a short but rewarding collection from one of our best writers. [Robert L. McLaughlin]

Alexander Theroux. *The Secondary Colors: Three Essays*. Henry Holt, 1996. 312 pp. $19.95.

I'm unsure whether my not having read Mr. Theroux before this collection of essays places me at an advantage or disadvantage; I can only guess that an appreciation of his work must be an acquired taste. In this follow-up to his similar *The Primary Colors*, Mr. Theroux expostulates at length—great length—upon the colors orange, purple, and green. The three sections of the book are more catalogs than essays, which is not necessarily a criticism; their "measureless intensity and wayward poetic enchantment" (see book jacket) are often compelling, and certain passages are inarguably breathtaking. Still, Mr. Theroux's persistently condescending tone and, in places, fierce mean-spiritedness make this "feast for the senses" suitable for nibbling only, a few pages at a time. Reading this book is not unlike listening to a post-dinner party boor: while part of you is enthralled by his unbounded erudition, another part is ready to bolt to your feet, throw your cocktail in his face, and hate yourself for ever falling in with any group of people so ready to tolerate his company.

Theroux's rhetorical approach—purportedly in the tradition of Montaigne and Plutarch—is simple; for each of the three colors he assembles a mélange of associations, connotations, and facts historical and otherwise that are in any way (*any* way) related to that color. It's a conceit that demands example: "A subjective list of things that seem orange to me are: the human knee, owls, fan lights, the word Dixie, Winnie the Pooh, laughter, old classrooms, the poems of Eugene Field, face-to-face coitus, the whole concept of bread, patently futile stupidity—like the dumb giants of storybook fame—cashmere, Bix Beiderbecke's cornet wailing on 'Riverboat Shuffle' . . ." and so on, for another half page or so. Endless lists of pure desiderata, sometimes set in striking juxtaposition. Of purple: "Cordovan leather, severe shock, oyster shells, gasoline, varicose veins, clay mud banks, the Liebestod of Wagner's Tristan and Isolde, and the sun shining through a person's paper-thin ears." Such passages engage all our senses and subtlest proclivities; put simply, they delight.

But go back to that first example. To that "patently futile stupidity" part. It's when you start taking in thicker sheaves of the text (again, inadvisable) that you start to notice the atmosphere of condescension thickening. The book's steady accretion of insults and self-aggrandizement are less the stuff of "satire and strong opinion" (again, refer to the book jacket) than just plain nastiness. Certain fifties' TV celebrities are "woefully dopey," a pronouncement swiftly followed by Theroux's list of "bad writers" (Rod McKuen, Maya Angelou, and Ayn Rand). Is it unintended irony when, in this same paragraph, we are told that purple is the color of ostentation? I'm not sure which I found more tedious: Mr. Theroux's Tourettish name-dropping or his ceaseless reminders following translated passages from Greek and Latin: "my translation." And I could never quite figure out why he finds the Brady Bunch vapid, yet holds the Simpsons in near veneration.

I've never found myself reading so aggressively in my life, every minute factual error (orange is *not* the color of Disney's Goofy, but Pluto!) made me want to take the author by the throat and sneer, "Yeah, well you're wrong, Mr. Smarty Pants!" Really, each time I put the book down, I felt like I wanted to go out and pummel somebody.

But perhaps the above says more about me than Mr. Theroux. As mentioned, there are in this book passages of brilliant, even sublime prose. And I'm sure there are many readers who won't blink an eye at Mr. Theroux's sarcasm passing for irony. I'd just like to know who they are. [Joseph Allen O'Rear]

Editor's Note: The official position of the Review of Contemporary Fiction *is that sarcasm is one of the great underused, as well as undervalued, rhetorical methods and its use need not be a failed attempt at irony. In fact, our official position is that irony is oftentimes a failed attempt at sarcasm.*

———

David Albahari. *Words Are Something Else.* Trans. Ellen Elias-Bursac. Ed. Tomislav Longinovic. Foreword by Charles Simic. Northwestern Univ. Press, 1996. 215 pp. Paper: $15.95.

In these twenty-seven stories David Albahari reveals his preoccupation with family, self, and the nature of writing. These are not uncommon concerns but are somewhat unusual in a contemporary Serbian writer. Eschewing a strict political agenda, Albahari instead treads on more local terrain, though not without building the Central European political and cultural worlds into the subtext.

This edition presents the stories chronologically, allowing us to see the changes in Albahari's focus from family—and particularly paternal—relations to the self and the indeterminacy of language. All are terse, taut pieces; most are narratives and the early stories may even seem a bit old-fashioned to some. This might be a cultural matter. Nevertheless, the stories are carefully controlled and details are handled deftly, both by Albahari and his translator Ellen Elias-Bursac.

I prefer the later stories where Albahari explores language, often humorously, as at the opening to "My Wife Has Light Eyes:" 'This will be a simple story,' I think, 'And it will have no compound sentences.' 'Don't be silly,' says my wife. 'That sentence is already pretty compound.' " There is a seriousness, though, as in "An Attempt at Describing the Death of Ruben Rubenovic, Former Textiles Salesman," in which the title alone betrays a writer's anxieties: "The lines that follow, pages I cannot yet predict, events, sounds, things that happen, a place: all of this is just an attempt. The words I'll use, the sentences I'll string together, the questions, the statements: all of it is unreliable"

"Sometimes the legend comes before the person, other times after,"

Albahari writes in "Mute Song," the volume's final story. The legend—and I interpret this as meaning both cultural lore we inherit and the cipher with which we attempt to interpret—is language. The lore and the cipher—Albahari's language—probe mothers, fathers, wives, children, cultures—and the self at their center. [Thomas Lecky]

Rosalyn Drexler. *Art Does (Not!) Exist.* FC2, 1996. 187 pp. $19.95.

Julia Maraini, the first-person narrator of Rosalyn Drexler's latest novel, *Art Does (Not!) Exist,* begins her story with these words: "This book will help me decide which project to present for an NEA Fellowship in Visual Arts-Based Performance, Video, and new genres." We understand very quickly that Julia Maraini is a video artist, or less exaltedly, we understand that Julia Maraini's response to anything in her life, urine streaming down her basement apartment windows, an acquaintance confessing to sodomizing cows, human skeletons between her refrigerator and stove, is to film it, to record it on video tape. Not much enters Maraini's life that doesn't find its way onto tape or into images. Even Julia Maraini's husband, the genetic scientist Josef Konrad, from whom she is recently separated, finds himself on the "Geraldo Show" exposing his step-father's cruelty to him as a child and ultimately—as the *live* audience watches passively transfixed—stabbing him to death.

What is at work in a novel whose primary project is the literary depiction (ekphrasis) of lives and deaths placed on video? Certainly one task we assume as readers is to help curate Julia Maraini's oeuvre ourselves: Which video project *should* she send to the NEA in application for a fellowship? Another task we meet as readers, not extricable perhaps from the first, is to think about the possibility that none of this is art, not even the book we're reading; that all of it is art; that we no longer have a clue about what art is; or more profoundly what its office (interest?) is within our irretrievably contemporary lives.

An arena of insights within the novel centers around the idea of revision or corrections, errata, if you will. We are not unaware as we read the text of *Art Does (Not!) Exist* that it is riddled with errors. A character's name fluctuates between Ann and Jane, and words are misspelled or variously spelled. Certainly as I read I wondered if FC2 was bereft of copy editors, and then it dawned on me that perhaps the fact that I was "catching" these errors, that I was annoyed and reacting and wondering What the hell! was a point the novel was happy to make. That when I exclaimed across the bed to my husband, "You'd think they could at least get Jayne Anne Phillips's name spelled correctly," I was still in the land of the perceiving, the reacting, though within that land just barely, and as copy editor. There are marked contrasts in the novel between the all-accepting reactions of people viewing videotapes or television and the reaction we have as we read the imperfect—intentionally imperfect, I hope—text of this novel. I suppose that we—on some level—remain critical, active, energized, bemused.

The novel ends wonderfully, satirically with a list of editing mistakes, "Corrections," made in an absurdly gushing article from the *New York Times* "Arts & Leisure" section on the now famous Julia Maraini, "the preeminent artist of her time: 1994 to 1995 and one-half." When the article claims that Maraini's work "appropriates without apogee, the entire history of art," it is a beautiful example—error or no error—of an entirely substanceless response to art, Maraini's or anyone's. I wonder if part of Drexler's meditation doesn't finally suggest an America without self-reflexive abilities, without much of a capacity for acute perception. Even reader as copy editor is better than the complete and utter lack of critical response artists receive today in the United States. I suppose Drexler is suggesting that in order for art to exist there must also be a context in which it is actively examined, even if just typographically?

On my darkest days I'm not sure I really believe the above, but I certainly appreciate from where the sentiment is coming, and though I've probably been lugubrious in my reception of this novel thus far, I must quickly say that there is great smart fun here, and much of it eddies around the literary representations of Julia Maraini's various videos. Both in and outside these videos there is an entertaining and motley crew of characters, and the remove we enjoy by reading about these videos and their subjects instead of viewing them the way the medium intends they be viewed is hysterically amusing, enlightening, even sobering. But this is not a sober book and when I had to put it down, I was anxious to return, to take up the very funny—read satirical—story of Julia Maraini's apotheosis as an artist in today's America. As a scholar said to me in complete wonder a few years ago, "I didn't know anyone wrote a novel of ideas anymore." Here ya go, darlin' and it's a dandy. [Michelle Latiolais]

Cyrus Colter. *The Beach Umbrella and Other Stories.* TriQuarterly Books and Northwestern Univ. Press, 1996. 225 pp. Paper: $14.95.

This volume brings together two collections of Colter stories, and it is a delight to see them back in print. Rather than re-reviewing them, I want only to draw attention to two of the stories that, to my mind, are two of the most remarkable stories ever written and rank along with anything by Chekhov. The first is the title story, "The Beach Umbrella," which records a man's visit to a beach in the waning days of summer, hoping there (together with his new beach umbrella) to make contact with others on the beach who seem always to have a wonderful time. The effort miserably fails, the sky is overcast, no contact is made, and the character readies himelf to return to his normal life, utterly defeated. The second story is called "Moot," about an old man and his dog, the only creature with whom the man has any kind of relationship, and even this one does not work very well. Both die, and the story ends with workers showing up to clean out the junk (the man's lifelong possessions) to make room for the next tenant. Both of these stories are composed in a completely dead-pan, matter-of-fact, numbing prose, a prose that piles one mundane fact upon the next, moving character and reader toward an ending that terminates any possibility for hope or change. They are brutal stories that lodge themselves in one's emotional network, so that the perception of the world is pemanently altered.

To the naive, the stories will seem "old-fashioned," but fashion has nothing (or should have nothing) to do with art, and it is the art of these stories that makes them so penetrating and disturbing. This is a very powerful book that no one should ignore. [John O'Brien]

John Banville. *Athena*. Vintage, 1996. 232 pp. Paper: $12.00.

John Banville has always been interested in perceptions of reality. His wonderful historical novels—dealing with Kepler, Copernicus, Newton—are attempts not only to create the scientists' minds but to demonstrate that scientific discovery arises from psychological origins. Cosmology and psychology are married. In this brilliant novel—surely one of the most fascinating texts written in the last few years—he offers a cunning, ghostly work—an odd exploration of the narrator's reality. The narrator, who chooses to call himself "Morrow," writes a "letter"—this novel—to Athena, who has disappeared. He cannot address her properly; he calls her "you" and then proceeds to refer to "her." The shifting tenses characterize his mental wanderings, and so does his use of oxymorons, puns, anagrams. Thus we must read this text with great care—the care we give to *The Sacred Fount*. And indeed the narrator's style and interest in vampires and ghosts and occult phenomena demonstrate that he resembles James's narrator in that puzzling masterpiece.

We do not know how to interpret Morrow's perceptions. Is he mad? Is there an Athena? Why does he call her A? These questions are never answered because his world is one of hesitation, unease (disease?). It is "muddled"—to use one of his words—and it may be a dream or hallucination of enormous proportions. Morrow is a critic of painting. And he offers detailed descriptions of seventeenth-century paintings. The paintings may not exist, may function as his *own* projections. He sees in *Pygmalion and Galatea*, painted in 1649, the "violence" of "sudden passion." He sees "ambiguous sexuality" in this "phantasmal" and "death-drunk work"—to use his words—details that correspond to his own life. Several questions come to mind. Do the paintings exist? Are they copies of original works? Although Banville offers a truly shocking revelation of Athena on the last page, he leaves open the possibility that the revelation, the "evidence" of Athena is psychotic. Here is merely one sentence that conveys the duplicity of Morrow—deliberate or undeliberate—and the duplicity of Banville: "I say *her*, but of course I know it was not her, not really."

The turns and counterturns of Morrow's words undermine any *stable* interpretation. The text is, perhaps, an "interpretation of interpretation," a dream-work of the highest order. It is our *Turn of the Screw,* a transgressive work which puzzles and amazes us. [Irving Malin]

Shakar, Alex. *City in Love: The New York Metamorphoses.* FC2, 1996. 164 pp. $19.95; paper: $11.95.

Imagine for a moment the New York City of the last ten or so years of contemporary fiction—that dark, cynical landscape of Easton and Janowitz, where violence is mitigated only by irony, hopelessness by resignation. Now imagine a giant hand reaching down to a corner of the city and pinching in its fingers an edge of this sheen of despair: slowly it peels back the gritty film, exposing below the surface a city shivering not with angst and moral inertia, but with imagination and vision and heartbreaking hope. Suddenly the vision of the city given us by the yuppiehacks of the eighties and early nineties seems jaded and false; a new city emerges, mythic and grand and unsentimentally beautiful.

This newly unmasked city is the setting of the six stories in Alex Shakar's *City in Love: The New York Metamorphoses,* winner of the 1996 FC2/Illinois State University National Fiction Award. In these stories (which find their inspiration in the *Metamophoses of Ovid*), Shakar's eminently memorable characters perceive the landscape of fin-de-siècle New York City through lenses of mythic imagination. The opening piece, "The Sky Inside," tells the story of a museum guard who attempts immortality by literally inscribing himself upon the city; told in multiple voices, its forty pages accelerate toward a climax more visceral and evocative than many novels achieve. In "Waxman's Sun" Danny Waxman's search for his lost father below the subway tunnels of Manhattan is both tender and heart racing, sad and redemptive; based on the story of Icarus, Shakar's version transmutates into a wholly surprising, original myth. All of the characters in the collection are recognizably human, yet striving to be more than human; what a refreshing contrast to the de riguer solipsism of contemporary fiction's urban dwellers!

And these stories are technically innovative in the best way; that is, Shakar's structural "experimentation" is always at the service of, indeed, dictated by the thematics of his story at hand. The last story in the collection, "City in Love," is remarkable for both the sophistication and absolute necessity of its startling narrative technique: based on the story of Narcissus, the threads of a secondary story, "the voice in your ear," are woven into the primary story by way of an intricate authorial "game" that would make Georges Perec clap his hands wildly. Still, Shakar's often profound literary inventions never overshadow the emotional intensity of his fundamentally romantic fictions—the reader feels not detached admiration, but engaged marvel at the resilience of the characters and the ways they find not merely to survive in the city but *live*, even, sometimes, after dying. [Joseph Allen O'Rear]

Samuel R. Delany. *Dhalgren*. Wesleyan Univ. Press, 1996. 801 pp. Paper: $17.95.

Nothing would be easier than to declare Delany's 1975 magnum opus a literary masterpiece that far excels the limitations of the science fiction genre. Nothing would be easier, but then nothing would be more denigrating to Delany's work and his critical intentions. Delany has always stressed his love for the uniqueness of science fiction, and he has provided some of the most illuminating studies into how the genre requires an audience to read in a different manner. Yet, while Delany has defended the distinctiveness of science fiction, his own works have pushed the genre beyond its usual boundaries. This is especially true for *Dhalgren*.

Dhalgren is a novel of space exploration that investigates the inner space of time and memory. Like one of Italo Calvino's invisible cities, Delany's Bellona is a surreal metropolis where the lines between the imagination and the concrete have been erased. The protagonist wanders this postapocalyptic city and, having forgotten his name, becomes known only as the Kid. He is enmeshed in a realm where the space-time matrix has become unglued, where places move and time becomes random. The Kid is immersed in a psychotropic zone where the city's remarkable control on personality dramatically affects his writing. Composing in a found journal, the Kid can never quite remember whether the writing in his journal is his own or a previous owner's. Perhaps the most fascinating feature of Delany's novel is the Kid's journal, which serves as the final chapter. Crossed out passages remain. Columns of text emerge in the middle of other passages. Texts written at different times stand next to each other. With this journal the reader witnesses the effect of the spatial and temporal dislocations of the city on the Kid's consciousness.

Delany's fiction fascinates us with the intersections of race, gender, class, sexuality, textuality, and consciousness. *Dhalgren* is a sexy, sexist, and sexual book that challenges how we read and how we perceive the world and its inhabitants. This hallucinatory book contains elements of what we might usually think of as science fiction—the appearance of two moons, a sun five-hundred-times too large—but the setting is also urban realism. *Dhalgren* shares with such controversial genre-bending books as J. G. Ballard's *Crash* (1973) and Joanna Russ's *The Female Man* (1975) the quality of challenging the boundaries between the marvelous and the realistic, showing us the greatest of what science fiction can offer. [David Ian Paddy]

————

Annie Ernaux. *Exteriors.* Trans. Tanya Leslie. Seven Stories Press, 1996. 95 pp. $16.00.

It has always seemed to me that a great deal of "description" and "details" in novels are done a disservice by being made to serve the "story." That is, an opening paragraph in a typical novel exists for the sake of setting up character and story, its language subservient to these, and its function finally reduced to that of background music and decoration; in other words, the point is to get past these things, to get to the story, for which these serve as introduction. In *Exteriors* Annie Ernaux foregrounds these materials, composing a book made up of short sections whose purpose is to isolate these details in and for themselves: phrases overheard in a grocery store, graffiti scribbled on a wall, a train passenger clipping his nails, what's playing on the Sunday morning radio. More often than not, such registrations are made without comment and even more often without reminder that the person registering is a novelist—this is not a romantic attempt at showing how a writer sees the world. Instead, Ernaux gives the world its due; the details, the overheard phrases, a brief scene from a train's window—here they are, in themselves. Taken in a certain direction, these could have turned into prose poems, but I think Ernaux purposely stays clear of that form, as much as she does the diary form despite a 1985-92 frame for the book. Instead, she presents and recognizes the everyday, the mundane, the trivial, all of which undergo a strange transformation when so isolated. This is a remarkable piece of writing, and one of the first new books to be published by Seven Stories Press. [John O'Brien]

————

Nelson Algren. *Nonconformity: Writing on Writing.* New York: Seven Stories Press, 1996. 130 pp. $16.00.

To understand Nelson Algren's *Nonconformity,* the reader should first make his way through David Simon's afterword which documents his struggle with what "was clearly a major find. Algren's only book-length work of nonfiction, a work from the period of his first writing." But then he adds that "the essay was unpublishable as it stood: a mess of impossibly long quotes by others interrupted its flow; Algren's own words often read too much like a notebook, too little like an essay." Unfortunately, in its published form it still reads too much like a notebook, too little like an essay. To add to the confusion, there is the question of how much of the nine brief sections is Algren's and how much comes from his favorite sources: Fitzgerald,

Twain, Faulkner, Mr. Dooley, Henry Adams, Adlai Stevenson, Chekhov, Conrad, Rimbaud, Dostoyevsky, de Beauvoir, Kafka, Whitman, to name only the more important sources. After subtracting the afterword, the historical note, the appendix, the notes, and the many long quotations throughout the nine short sections, there are less than thirty-five pages of Algren's credo, "a text about the responsibilities writers carry with them, about the unendingness, as it were, of the writer's art" (editor's afterword). Simon sees the real subject as the "debt owed by writers to the lives they write about." However, Algren's subject matter is too often "quite banal—himself, other writers, the writing art, the responsibility of the intellectual, the dangers of conformity for those who create." I write this knowing that Algren is one of my favorite writers. He and Studs Terkel are to Chicago what Henry Mayhew and Dickens were to London. Like Dickens before him, Algren wrote passionately of the dank underbelly of the city he saw as being perpetually "on the make." I wouldn't trade "A Bottle of Milk for Mother" and the novel based on it, *Never Come Morning*, or *The Man with the Golden Arm* for all of Algren's nonfiction. Having said that, what there is of Algren in this critical mélange is worth noting and preserving, for it is, apparently, all we have of Algren's thinking about the state of literature. [Jack Byrne]

Guy Davenport. *The Cardiff Team*. New Directions, 1996. 192 pp. $22.95.

Not a lot happens in most of the stories in Guy Davenport's *The Cardiff Team*. Instead of focusing on plot, Davenport focuses on moments that beautifully evoke innocence, experience, desire, or fulfillment. The stories can stand alone, but, read together, they overlap in characters and incident and interact thematically. The characters long for connection with others in societies that encourage alienation. From George Santayana seeking to connect with a British army officer, to Robinson Crusoe desperately striving to return to the deserted island he sought to escape, to Swedish boys at summer camp trying to accommodate their feelings of love, Davenport's characters attempt to form make-shift teams, to become ad hoc families, to find a meaningful home. Indeed, the form of the book is a model of such connections. Davenport incorporates other texts, from poems to *Scientific American* articles, and characters from fiction and history. More complexly, the various stories bleed into one another, as characters from one story appear in or are discussed in others and whole episodes jump from story to story. The result is that as we read we're treated to tiny revelations when we make connections and that we're asked intellectually to create the bonds that the characters seek emotionally. This connects to a second shared theme: Davenport's characters seem over and over to act out the conflict between the intellectual and the physical. Many of the main characters live in their minds and are contrasted with the men and boys around them who, while intellectually mundane, live in their bodies and with nature.

These themes come together and are supposed to be resolved in the long, troubling title story. Set in contemporary Paris, the story presents a twelve-year-old boy, Walt, as a synthesis of the intellectual and the physical: he is an acclaimed genius who is remarkably in touch with his own and others' bodies, with the smells and the sights of nature. He is also the center of an odd *ménage à cinq* made up of Walt, his mother, her lover and Walt's tutor, Marc, Walt's friend Bee, who appears to the world dressed as a boy named Sam, and Cyril, an unhappily repressed rich boy who learns the joy of sex. Walt's polymorphous perversity breaks down societal codes and replaces them with a structure in which the characters relate happily, guiltlessly, and selflessly. Marc tells Cyril, "Polycrates burnt the gymnasiums of Samos because he knew that every friendship forged in them were two revolutionaries. Our real families are our friends." Unfortunately, this conclusion is problematic. A family based on sex between adults and children seems far from idyllic, and the constant talk of erections, masturbation, and so on is more tedious than revolutionary. Despite this reservation (and considering the story's length, it's a major one), the other stories in *The Cardiff Team* have much to recommend them: they are beautiful, intelligent, and thought-provoking. [Robert L. McLaughlin]

———

Jalal Toufic. *Over-Sensitivity*. Sun & Moon, 1996. 312 pp. Paper: $ 13.95.

A question which naturally arises with a consideration of this book is how to classify it. My first thought was that it belonged to the domain of film studies since film is so obviously a central concern to Toufic. Indeed, the range of films he deals with is impressive. (Among his favorite directors are Hitchcock, Passolini, Resnais/Robbes-Grillet, Deren, Lynch, Herzog, Tarkovsky, Buñuel, Solas, Godard, Wenders, Kurasawa, Parasher, and Ray.) Yet Toufic's work is not content to stay within these boundaries. He shifts (seamlessly) to consider painting (Van Gogh, Magritte, and Bacon), photography (Sherrie Levine and Man Ray), psychology (particularly schizophrenia and madness), and political events such as the Civil War in Lebanon and the Gulf War.

Toufic's book defies strict generic classification as well. He has in fact created here a new kind of book. The lack of distinct chapter headings (in contrast to the fragmented epigramatic style of his earlier book, *Distracted*) makes for densely packed prose, placing unusual demands on readers. (Where does one stop for a break, for a breath?) The abundant, copious notes function uniquely, more as extensions of points, so integral to the text that the reader is apt to keep two bookmarks—one in the text and one in the notes—and flip frequently back and forth from text to note. (References to his two previous works, *Distracted* and *(Vampires): An Essay on the Undead in Film* are common, noting overlapping arguments.) Portions of the book (notably toward the beginning) take the form of letters, written to particular people at particular times from particular places. At times autobiographical references erupt in the text.

Perhaps the best means of understanding Toufic's project is to attend closely to the book's title—*Over-Sensitivity*. The hyphen is critical. Toufic offers here an extended meditation on what he terms the "over" mode. The concept (which he spends the entire book demonstrating) resists simplification. This over mode, however, might be understood as any situation in life, in film, in literature, in photography where one thing is going on at the same time as something else, or where an interiority and an exteriority contend with one another, or where media and world intermingle, where one part moves and another is immobilized, where two channels play simultaneously. He thus is particularly interested in voice-overs, dance films with distinct "immobilizations," film allusions, and various other sorts of disjunctive juxtapositioning. Toufic's discussion subtly and logically slides in the end to a discussion of works of art demonstrating "radical closure," seemingly hermetically sealed, seemingly cut off from the world. "In the case of radical closure," he writes in the book's last line, "there is an enigmatic direct influence of the artwork on the world." [Allen Hibbard]

Siri Hustvedt. *The Enchantment of Lily Dahl*. Holt, 1996. 275pp. $23.00.

Although I did not review Siri Hustvedt's first novel, *The Blindfold*, I admired it. It is, like this one, a ghostly philosophical attempt to understand the intricate foldings of dream and reality. This second novel confirms her "spooky" talent. She deliberately sets her characters in a small town—a kind of Winesburg—which seems to be an ordered world in which common routines or rituals take place. But the town, Webster, is an "alternate threshold"—to use her phrase—a place of enchantment.

Lily Dahl, a waitress at the Ideal Cafe—notice the name—soon discovers that there are secrets. She is unsettled by the the oddity of Martin, a young man whose stuttering suggests private knowledge. She keeps listening to old Mabel, who is writing a work about her experiences. She is fascinated by *A Midsummer Night's Dream*, a play in which she has a part. Lily is, in effect, confronted by the foldings of private and public performance.

Although Lily is, at first, an "observer," she seems to become another "grotesque," a secret sharer. And she makes one wonder about her own perceptions, her "invisible world." Does she know her reasons for spying on these people? can her epistemology be trusted? has she created her own dream? Thus the novel becomes an ambiguous web—a hide-and-seek performance. Although Hustvedt's language is apparently clear, it seems to embody a duplicitous quality. Dahl is like doll; enchantment becomes dangerous. At one point Martin says about his doll—yes he has made a likeness of Lily—"the word becoming flesh, Lily—the in-between moment." And as I slowly begin to reread the text, the statements take on new meaning. If "Dahl" and "doll" are mirrored puns, perhaps the entire novel is about the relation between word and world, the (re)incarnation of word as flesh—reality.

This novel, then, becomes a reflection of its themes; it is an "enchantment" about the "angers of enchantment," a "performance about performance." It folds into itself and it becomes the "medium"—the "in-between," the "alternate threshold." [Irving Malin]

Sapphire. *Push*. Knopf, 1996. 157 pp. $20.00.

For the first sixteen years of her life, Claireece Precious Jones (but "only motherfuckers I hate call me Claireece") wants one thing from her mother: the older Ms. Jones, housebound and enormously overweight, should say to her lover—who is both Precious's father and the father of the girl's two children—"Can't you see Precious is a beautiful chile like white chile in magazines or on toilet paper wrappers. . . . Git off Precious, fool!" In *Push*, the first novel by performance poet Sapphire, Precious never gets her wish. Instead, Mama forces the girl to binge, beats her until she delivers her first baby prematurely (a girl called Little Mongo, for Mongoloid), and finally drives her out of the house when she learns Precious is pregnant for the second time.

Precious is, of course, a name dripping with irony, given to her by the same woman who has perpetrated these crimes. Ironic, too, is the picture of the white child on the toilet paper wrapper: Precious's vocabulary of images is so impoverished that in her mind the summa of beauty and love is attached to something to be used, in the most degrading way, and discarded. This novel chronicles Precious's struggle to haul herself out of the discard pile. Along the way, two people tell her to push: one is a paramedic coaching her through Little Mongo's birth, the other a teacher at the alternative school to which Precious is rerouted during her second pregnancy. But no amount of effort will save her; when eventually Mama resurfaces, it is to announce that Precious's father just died of AIDS. Naturally, the girl and her newborn son are infected; thus even as she tries to better herself—to rescue herself—Precious is doomed, just like the product that bears the white child's image. "We is a nation of raped children," she has learned; and even "the black man in America today" (her father) "is the product of rape."

Incest, rape, Harlem, AIDS: Sapphire's material is sensationalist and horrific—not necessarily bad qualities—but she puts it all to such didactic use that we never fully enter Precious's world. We never, for example, see her mother as more than a one-dimensional monolith; and even in the collection of Precious's poems that concludes the volume, we barely find out what life is like away from the incest bed or the classroom. In fact, *Push* hardly ever gets out of school; most of the action takes place there, as we watch Precious's emergence into literacy, her poetry and personal narrative part of a class project. And it is apparent that the reader is to be taught as well: We learn not only that life in the ghetto is desperate but also that incest is damaging and fat girls are sensitive about their weight. These are all valuable lessons, certainly, but lessons that Sapphire might have presumed people interested in this novel would already have learned. Perhaps the book would have been more effective if its author had concentrated more on plot than on message—on showing us Precious's world instead of pushing to be sure we think the right away about it. [Susann Cokal]

Louise Neri, ed. *Silence Please! Stories after the Works of Juan Muñoz.* Scalo, 1996. 175 pp. $27.50.

Published by a Swiss press in cooperation with an Irish art museum and printed in Germany, this collection of eleven stories by American, English, Irish, Portuguese, and Spanish writers takes as its starting point the work of a Spanish sculptor, Juan Muñoz. The exhibit of his work at the Irish Museum of Modern Art provided an occasion for these stories; without it they would never have been written, they would not exist and we would be poorer without this cumulative gift of word and image.

Through dialogue, self-conscious colloquialism, existential internal monologue, letter, libretto, tape-recorded message, radio broadcast, etc., writers such as Dave Hickey, Patrick McCabe, Lynne Tillman, and Marina Warner have crafted short fictions that sometimes directly and other times obliquely take off from and/or return to a visual work by Muñoz. Words do pleasing and odd things herein and it is a pleasure to read a story and then return to the photograph of the particular art work from which it sprung to see the nature of the relation. For example, in Luc Sante's "Tabula Rasa" an occupant of a hotel room that seems to be sealed off in a no-time and no-place begins to draw as his only solace. The picture he draws: that which precedes the story of his entrapment. Such interweaving of image and story is especially ingenious and delightful in Quico Rivas's "The Story of Estraperlo."

I found myself liking narratively complete stories, such as the aforementioned one by Rivas or Vik Muniz's "Pygmalion Mâché," more than the ones that were fragmented, such as John Berger's "Will It Be a Likeness?" His story sounds to me to be the one in the collection that is closest to art criticism, and therefore it is the story least in the spirit of the activity which was to move away from "the closed-off, stillborn nature of much art criticism" and into a more imaginative world, a world such as Muñoz's and such as that depicted (echoed?) in most of the stories that his world has evoked. [Dennis Barone]

Michael Brodsky. *Southernmost and Other Stories*. Four Walls Eight Windows, 1996. 341 pp. Paper: $14.95.

Wallace Stevens writes in his *Adagia*, "The final belief is to believe in a fiction, which you know to be a fiction, there being nothing else. The exquisite truth is to know that it is a fiction and that you believe in it willingly." Michael Brodsky's new collection of stories contemplates this willingness. The novella "Southernmost" proposes the fictional meeting of Stevens and Hart Crane in Key West, the southernmost of the title. But it is also the figurative southernmost of the imagination, where both Stevens and Crane rigorously pushed themselves, that Brodsky is after.

For Brodsky, Stevens and Crane reflect two poles: Stevens the corporate man, whose willingness to dive into fictions Brodsky's narrator often sees as a tendency for rationalization, and Crane the recalcitrant bohemian, whose intractable imagination destined him to his final plunge. The raw impulse of desire, suggests Brodsky, led Crane to language—"the language of their own transformation." The narrator who recounts this meeting admires Crane's insistence on the transformative power of poetry to affect the world and sees Stevens as an obese pretender. Thus is Stevens Crane's arch rival.

What is most disturbing about this statement is the perceived gulf between these two poets, both of whom, in my mind, were after similar imaginative ends. The narrator comments that "[Crane's] life—any life— was too brief to encompass meaning." It is unfortunate that Stevens—who also lived a life—cannot in some way correspond to Crane, if only because he espoused that great willingness for fictions.

Southernmost serves as the groundwork for the later stories. In "Bagatelle" the fragility of narrative is encountered in the inability to unravel the mystery behind an assassination. We are told in "The Assessed," "And that vengefully vigilant and elliptical telling will necessarily resist—parry—almost apotropaically—all paraphrase." It is the very telling itself that is mired in fragility. Our lives, our languages, are lost in a maelstrom of Babel. And yet Brodsky is a writer, an immensely talented writer, and our willingness to believe aside, his words somehow become the imaginary line connecting the poles. And that, in the end, is the correspondence: the line written in words between Stevens, Crane, and the author of their fiction. [Thomas Lecky]

Andrew Holleran. *The Beauty of Men*. Morrow, 1996. 272 pp. $24.00.

A sign of the extent to which Andrew Holleran's first novel, *Dancer from the Dance*, has achieved the status of one of the great works of recent American literature is the number of critics from Bruce Bawer to David Leavitt to Dennis Cooper who have gone out of their way to denounce it as dangerous. As the Yeats-inspired title suggests, *Dancer from the Dance* is about whether an eroticized aesthetics of life is the means to personal fulfillment or self-erasure. Holleran's awareness of both the corrosiveness and the allure of such an eroticized aesthetic is what has made the book so compelling and controversial. His counter to the eroticized aesthetics of the New York gay scene has been the homely domesticity of small-town Florida. However, in *The Beauty of Men*, his long-awaited third novel, Holleran recognizes that the homely domesticity of Florida is no more enlarging or less destructive than the gay eroticized aesthetic he had left in New York. A devotion to beauty or a devotion to family ends up destroying the devotee, yet distancing oneself from either beauty or loved ones results in an equally empty egoism. Caught between his mother, paralyzed in a nursing home, and his obsession with Becker, a gay father, Mr. Lark—the protagonist of *The Beauty of Men*—prepares himself for what the narrator of *Nights in Aruba*, Holleran's second novel, unconvincingly asserts that he must do: live his own life. At the end of the novel, Mr. Lark is taking his first step to discover what he wants, to engage as well as be engaged.

The Beauty of Men begins in a cold, hard, rather documentary manner that reflects Lark's attempt to distance himself from the AIDS pandemic that has killed so many of his friends, the paralysis that has whittled his mother's life down to a nub, and the suburban isolation that reduces community to Peeping-Tommery. But the limitations of this style are far too clear, and slowly the prose achieves the sinuosity that is the hallmark of Holleran's voice, a style that marks both his emotional rapport with and intellectual distance from his subjects. The result is that *The Beauty of Men* is his most moving and disturbing gay novel, replacing *Dancer from the Dance*'s exploration of the convulsions of youth with the reconstitution of middle age. [David Bergman]

Hanif Kureishi. *The Black Album*. Scribner, 1995. 276 pp. $22.00; paper: $11.00.

The Black Album is the second novel written by this hip, energetic, and talented English writer who is the author of the screenplays for *My Beautiful Laundrette* and *Sammy and Rosie Get Laid*. The third-person narration centers on Shahid, a college student in West London in 1989 who comes from an affluent, nonpracticing Muslim family in Kent. Kureishi, who recently co-edited *The Faber Book of Pop*, packs his novel with references to current theater, art, music, literature, and events, including *The Godfather*, Toni Morrison, Lorca's *The House of Bernarda Alba*, *Scarface*, Prince (whose obscure album gives the book its title), *A Clockwork Orange*, and an assortment of music videos. One current event central to the story is the controversy surrounding Salman Rushdie's *The Satanic Verses*.

We first see Shahid in the hallway of his student flat as he meets the enigmatic Riaz Al-Hussain, a prophetlike community activist, writer, and leader of a group of Islamic college students. Riaz and his followers quickly enlist Shahid's help with their political projects, including the protection of an Indian family being harassed on a housing estate. Shahid is specially selected to wash Riaz's laundry (which is quickly stolen), and to transcribe Riaz's religious poetry. In an event that parallels both the story in *The Satanic Verses* and the controversy surrounding it, Shahid creatively transcribes Riaz's poetry, and trouble ensues.

Shahid has come to the college to study with a young instructor named Deedee Osgood, whose sign above her desk reads "All limitations are prisons." Shortly after Shahid becomes Deedee's student, they sleep together, but Shahid is determined to keep this half of his life concealed from Riaz and his followers, who would condemn Shahid's time spent with Deedee making love, dancing, and experimenting with drugs. Shahid's life gets even more complicated when his older brother, Chili—into cars, money, drugs, and sex—seeks help from Shahid when his own life spirals out of control.

Shahid is a person adrift, easily led in one direction and then another. Although the novel addresses with wit and humor many pressing issues such as racism, the conflict between art and religion, and the plight of immigrants, it is unable to fuse the action of Shahid's story and the ideas Kureishi wishes to examine. In spite of this fault, *The Black Album* is packed with energy, is full of humor, and makes for a lively, entertaining read. [Michael Reder]

Eric Darton. *Free City.* Norton, 1996. 176 pp. $18.00.

If Hawthorne, Poe, and Kafka had collaborated, *Free City* may have resulted. Written in the form of a daybook, forty entries in all, by a man whom we know only as L. (we do not know this until quite a ways in, and, in fact, the book is a dictation by L.), *Free City* records the near overthrow of a politically free German town (this may be a contradiction in terms, but let this pass, the Germans known better for their atrocities than their freedoms) by a Machiavellian figure, Roberto, also known as Rodolpho, who has fled to Germany from Italy. Initially R.'s benefactor and protector, L. leads the way to preventing R.'s ambitions. Inventor, scientist, essayist, chemist, surgeon, and planner of kingdoms, L., with the help of the multilingual F. (a duck) and A., orchard-caretaker and budding dentist (L., despite his amorous acrobatics with A., does not know her age but guesses that she must be older than he because of her "occasional use of archaic verb forms"), thwarts R.'s plans by creating a flawed Air Galleon (airplane, of sorts) from which R. hopes to be able to destroy the Free City. L., now blind, flees, along with his cohorts, to Italy where he will be a professor at the University of Siena. When all of this takes place is difficult to determine, though we are told that, at some point during these forty days, a French philosopher and mathematician named Descartes has recently died (that date would be 1650). Written in a style that is utterly invented, authentic, and arched, and transpiring in an atmosphere of eeriness that would make Lovecraft envious, *Free City* introduces a very interesting first novelist. [John O'Brien]

———

Tobias Wolff. *The Night in Question.* Knopf, 1996. 206 pp. $23.00.

"Last night was a series of misunderstandings. I just want to . . . straighten everything out," asserts a character in one of the fifteen short stories in Tobias Wolff's new collection, *The Night in Question*, thus providing something of an emblem for this assemblage of contemporary tales concerned with how people manage their way through the inconsequential if not prosaic situations that ultimately constitute the history of our moral conduct.

His first book of fiction in over a decade, Wolff presents a collection of masterly rendered stories in meticulously honed form, elegant and exacting small works, subtly measured and perfect in tone. Neither cautionary nor didactic, these stories chart the path of life events which begin innocuously but unravel into complexity, extremity, and import. In "Chain" a father rescues his small daughter from a vicious dog only to have his actions begin a vengeful chain of events that spins out of control and eventually ends in senseless tragedy when he reluctantly complies to punish the dog's owners. In "Mortals" a journalist neglects to confirm the reports of a death and is fired for writing the obituary of a man who, it turns out, is still alive. A woman's brief nap in a stuffy car in "Lady's Dream" reveals the moment in her youth when she made the decision to marry her husband despite their disparate personalities and histories, despite her other options. In "Powder" an almost divorced father—"rumpled, kind, bankrupt of honor, flushed with certainty"—turns an almost-bungled vacation into something special by treating his skeptical and disappointed son to a magical (and illicit) Christmas Eve drive through snowed-in Pacific Northwest roads. Wolff demonstrates the tenuousness of our instinct for self-preservation in "Sanity," in which a teenage girl, her father hospitalized after a breakdown, marshals whatever means she can to lure her stepmother to stay with her, and again in "Casualty," in which a smart-mouthed soldier in Vietnam is killed just six weeks before he is supposed to return home.

Wolff's stories are discriminating, resonant, compassionate, wry, lyric, and humorous tales about people trying to do the best they can, about how they sometimes succeed, and about how they sometimes don't. [Jeanne Claire van Ryzin]

Sven Birkerts. *Tolstoy's Dictaphone: Technology and the Muse.* Graywolf, 1996. 262 pp. Paper: $16.00.

Tolstoy's Dictaphone represents nineteen writers' thoughts on the Internet, computers, typewriters, and telephones. These are essays about culture and its relationship to technology; to speak as broadly as possible, these are essays about being creative Homo sapiens at a time that may not honor the attempt. Included here are new essays by past *RCF* contributors Sven Birkerts, Jonathan Franzen, and Paul West. Essays by Gerald Howard and Carole Maso originally appeared in the "Future of Fiction" issue (Spring 1996).

Most of these essays present more than an argument for or against the encroaching technology. The better essays eschew the "for or against" line of thinking entirely, blur the obvious either/or reaction implicit in such a debate and rhetorically bushwhack a more difficult, third road. Each of the essays provides an argument about how reading, writing, and the business of meaning has changed or how the writers suppose it will change in the future, but what distinguishes the third-roaders from their shriller cousins is that they freely (and wisely) apply techniques of memoir, research, and observation, and cite historical precedents and examples; in the end they achieve much more than the complaints of cranks.

A great and unexpected highlight in this collection is finding out that writers are only slightly less superstitious than star relief pitchers but probably bigger fetishists when it comes to their tools. There is Wulf Rehder's "gold-and-black fountain pen," Daniel Mark Epstein's "oak desk with an arabesque book rail," and Paul West's DeVille 470s. Albert Goldbarth reveals he wrote his essay with "a Bic Pen in a one-dollar spiral-bound notebook." Everyone who uses a typewriter mentions the brand name, all loyal to their Royals. Franzen and Askold Melnyczuk talk about their first typewriters with the sort of hushed tones and adjective-studded prose most people reserve for first loves, and Paul West, by the way, writes in the nude.

Being unfortunately unable to discuss any of these essays at length, I'll choose Birkerts's own for some inspection. His essay, not surprisingly, continues in much the same vein as the sharper and more critical chapters of his 1994 book, *The Gutenberg Elegies.* In that book, an earlier collection called *American Energies,* and more recent reviews, Birkerts has called for a fiction responsive to and aware of the culture around it, a fiction that arrests the culture or at the very least does not hide from it. It has always seemed strangely incompatible for Birkerts to ask certain things of fiction that imply that the work and its author must be embroiled in the muck of the culture at the same time that Birkerts himself opts out of the disagreeable elements of that culture.

One can begin to see the steep price of turning off and going unplugged, of saying "Refuse it" as Birkerts does at the conclusion of *Gutenberg.* When Birkerts tries to describe how the experience of reading from a screen is different from reading a book, he can't. Or rather he can't without reaching for the following awful metaphor: "To which I can only reply that outwardly nothing about our fiscal processes changed when we went off the gold standard (nobody but tourists ever saw the vaults at Fort Knox), but that an untethered dollar feels different, spends differently, than one secured by its minim of bullion." I wanted to believe this was ill-considered, but I found the same metaphor posed in nearly the same context in *Gutenberg*. Someone needs to take Birkerts aside and kindly explain to him that invoking the gold standard has next to no rhetorical force, and even then only with an audience of Steve Forbes, Lyndon LaRouche, and certain segments of the militia community is Birkerts likely to curry favor.

Ironically (or maybe sadly), the decision to refuse any and all encounters with the new technology has stolen from Birkerts any chance of anecdotal argument and will eventually lessen the impact and authority of his writing on the subject itself. The reader of this anthology need only compare Birkerts's essay with contributions by Robert Pinsky or Alice Fulton, whose essay on screens relies on the sort of metaphors (of computers, screens, and information) that Birkerts will not access and therefore cannot know.

Tolstoy's Dictaphone is the first in a projected series of book-length forums from Graywolf Press. The idea is to gather a good, thoughtful bunch of writers and to have those writers address topics other than their own writing. Not very remarkable sounding, but when you consider that an entire generation of minimalist writers has grown up, gotten old, and received tenure while only rarely giving themselves to the task of writing an essay (excepting the occasional book review, of course), you can see how exceptional a book like this is. This is a shame. Writers should write more than only fiction or poetry. If the new writers (and readers) set out to create the sort of fiction Birkerts describes as fiction critical of its culture, then they should not miss the opportunity offered by these Graywolf Forums to show how the metaphorical worlds of their fiction or poetry refer to, bump and brush up against, mock, mourn, or mimic the modern world, our world. [Paul L. Maliszewski]

Julian Fox. *Woody: Movies from Manhattan.* Overlook Press, 1996. 285 pp. $26.95.

I very much wanted to like this book because the work of Woody Allen is due serious, critical treatment, but Fox's study is, finally, disappointing. With no thesis that I could detect, the book proceeds from movie to movie, providing sometimes interesting (read: gossipy) background information (where certain scenes were shot, which actors were considered for roles but later dropped, reactions of actors to a kind of controlled chaos of Allen's methods, Allen's original conceptions that frequently got changed radically, sometimes during the filming itself or in the editing room). Fox attempts to play the role of fan/enthusiast and critic/scholar, a role he does not balance very well. Though several people and sources are quoted, Fox does not use footnotes and sometimes does not even attribute the quotation to anyone; we almost never know when he is drawing upon previously published materials and when his quotations or observations are derived from interviews he conducted. Perhaps most bothersome is that there is no *theory* to his approach, and therefore no guidelines that he draws upon—why invoke biographical details? why not? why mention where certain scenes were filmed but omit many other significant ones? why tell us what the actors thought? Anything and everything seems to be open for inclusion or exclusion.

Oh, well. The book is worth reading if only because of various background materials that Fox does provide (I had thought that the philosopher-psychologist who commits suicide in *Crimes and Misdemeanors* was based on Bruno Bettelheim, but Fox gives some evidence that it was Primo Levi). Still, Woody Allen, America's greatest narrative master of the last thirty years, needs his Boswell, or better, his Kenner. [John O'Brien]

Reginald Gibbons and Susan Hahn, eds. *TriQuarterly New Writers*. Northwestern Univ. Press, 1996. 198 pp. Paper: $14.95.

Equally divided between fiction and poetry, the contributions in this collection are marked as much by their quality as they are by the editors' conscious attempt to assemble a diverse set of experiences. However diverse these experiences, the visions offered by these writers are most decidedly personal. Terri Brown-Davidson's sexual and sensory poetry, which is often tinged with the macabre or features love interests juxtaposed against the discomfiting presence of such third parties as babies or puppets. Page Dougherty Delano writes about the life of a union organizer in the coal industry and about adolescent struggles with the body and identity. Loretta Collins uses the ordinary things of life—shoes, soup, photographs—to illuminate more general human experiences of death, violation, abandonment and misogyny.

Fiction writers Yolanda Barnes, Eileen Cherry, and Cassandra Smith investigate family relationships wherein conflicts arise because characters have been too close, too intimate. Barnes examines the critical moments when people with long histories come together after years of separation. As she alternates between past and present, she builds small dramas of the mind, where victories are pyrrhic and empty. Cherry offers stories about growing up in Alabama and the senseless conflicts between women as they struggle for power and status. Cassandra Smith's fiction is surprisingly rich and reminds us of the density and power of language as she tracks three generations of the lies mothers and daughters tell each other. (Indeed, however diverse the lives of these ten writers, most share the care and attention to language born of their years spent pursuing M.F.A.s and Ph.D.s.)

Poet Dean Shavit and fiction writer Tammi Bob explore their Jewish heritages and the continuing need for coming to terms with the atrocities of the Second World War. Dean Shavit writes about family, his grandparents, their lives, and the touching act of his grandmother preparing his grandfather for burial. Tammi Bob's stories address the effects of World War II, immigration, and nationality on a young Jewish girl who lives in the United States. Bob is concerned with how these issues come to bear on her heroine's interactions with young men, especially her family's responses. Also set against a rich backdrop of the mid-twentieth century, Steve Fay's poem "The Milkweed Parables" is a quiet stunner.

William Loizeaux is, perhaps, the exception to the largely personal explorations of his fellow contributors. Loizeaux is more interested in the private spaces individuals need to nurture and sustain relationships. The respect, love, and relationships that such privacies foster, however, are not without their own problems.

The editors showcase these ten writers with multiple offerings from each. In most cases, this is not nearly enough. We await collections from each to see how their themes develop, to discover how they come to terms with their personal and family histories. [Rick Henry]

Bruce Wagner. *I'm Losing You*. Villard, 1996. 327pp. $23.00.

Wagner uses lines from Salvatore Quasimodo as an epigraph: "Each alone on the heart of the earth / impaled upon a ray of sun: / and suddenly it's evening." His Hollywood—which is, of course, a metaphor of America—is a "killing field." The battle lines are drawn between generations, conglomerates the A and non-A lists, the body and mind; on every page there is the possibility of forced entry, rape, impalement. Although he gives us hosts and parasites, victims and victimizers, he recognizes that the positions, roles, and identities change rapidly. Thus he is less interested in individuals than in crowds, shadows, ghosts—he captures the transitions of power, the swift successes and failures.

Every page vibrates with allusions to pain, hiding, linguistic twists; his language is devious, jittery, double-edged. On one page the "Dead Animal Guy"—as he calls himself in one incarnation—says: "If our critters found a nice little niche to make his quantum leap to the Great Unknown, there's not a 'heck' of a lot I can do short of taking a few bites out of your wall— which I don't think would thrill either one of us." The problem is located in the struggling locations, the "niche" versus the "leap," the "bite" which rips a hole out of the house to *save* the house from the "critter" (always referred to as "Fluffy"). The "heck" seems to fight the "Great Unknown." The oddity of the speech is the conjunction of different modalities of diction: "heck" and "Great Unknown," "hole" and "niche." The body, for example, is invaded by the HIV-positive "critter"; the film is a rewrite of a rewrite; the self is transformed by chance—a writer becomes an agent; a psychiatrist is a patient. The entire text is shifting; it is a word-quake. Where is stability? How does one gain peace?

And the ironies proliferate like viruses. Wagner's text refuses to rest in the comfortable niche, "the Hollywood novel." It fights genre infection; it battles for supremacy of *The Day of the Locust, The Last Tycoon,* and the movie scripts of these novels. Therefore, it is possible to view Wagner's brutle text as another battle ground, another power play. [Irving Malin]

Jean Hegland. *Into the Forest.* Calyx, 1996. 208 pp. Cloth: $25.95; paper: $13.95.

Into the Forest is a frighteningly believable dsytopian novel narrated by a young woman who has lost nearly everything in life that she values and so has to construct a new belief system in order to survive in her much-altered world. Like Margaret Atwood's *The Handmaid's Tale,* Hegland's novel is set in a near future, when gas becomes scarce, communications break down, electricity fails, and various diseases sweep the United States. Seventeen-year-old Penelope is the narrator, a bright young woman whose major goal in life is to attend Harvard University. However, when her parents die and the northern California town she lives near runs out of food, she and her older sister Eva must learn to fend for themselves as the infrastructure of the United States disintegrates.

Penelope's journal writing becomes a record of the transformation of her life. She remembers happier times and these memories at first are interspersed with her attempts to live in a seemingly unstable world. She voraciously reads the encyclopedia and studies French so that when schools re-open she'll be able to attend, but she slowly learns that what is more important are practical life lessons like how to grow and store food, how to conserve what clothing and tools she and her sister have, how to cure illness with herbs, and how to live in the forest where they are effectively marooned. She comes to realize that book knowledge is not enough to help one survive rape, giving birth, or serious illness.

The language of the novel changes as Penelope's values change. She starts out loving her books, her sister's dancing, and each artifact that speaks of her parents. Their home is in the beginning a refuge, from the terrible things taking place across the country, from wild animals and desperate men. By the end, however, the forest is where their life must be, because it can provide food and shelter, as it did for the Native Americans who once lived in this area. It is truly the only place where they can plan a future.

Into the Forest is a novel full of despair and hope, written by a true storyteller who evokes nothing but admiration for her indomitable heroine and her sister. [Sally E. Parry]

H. Porter Abbott. *Beckett Writing Beckett*. Cornell Univ. Press, 1996. 216 pp. $32.50.

With the all too pseudoscientific emphasis on pre-text—drafts, notes, and so on—indicative of the recent shift in criticism to the study of literary origins, Abbott's interest in and utterly convincing demonstration of the posttextual dimension of Beckett's work or, more accurately, the Beckett text as an on-going activity, a continuous rewriting of previous efforts, is most welcome. In their preface to *Drafts* (a 1996 issue of *Yale French Studies*), Michel Contat, Denis Hollier, and Jacques Neefs cite genetic criticism as the "last wave in a triple assault against the autonomous complacency of the work of art"; "Sociocriticism and new historicism," they explain, "opened the work to fields that are contemporaneous yet heterogeneous; reception theory opened it to a future mapped out by the act of reading; now, genetic criticism opens the work to what preceded it." In his study of Beckett, however, Abbott breaks newer and far more substantial ground than that favored by the geneticists in arguing that a fictive corpus may—through the exploration not of what preceded, but of what followed—open onto a terrain both distinct from the historical and narrative associations of autobiographic writing and delineated by the textual topography of what he terms autographical action.

Indeed, autographical action is the thesis that subtends the diverse subjects treated in the book, subjects that extend from the postnarrativity of Beckett's art (the result, precisely, of the undoing of the generative illusion) and its advancement of the utopian literary tradition (the undoing of the myth of Beckett's apoliticism) to the "agony of perceivedness," the self-conscious awareness of audience and reader characteristic of all Beckett's work. The reading of Beckett Abbott proposes is antithetical to any notion of writing as a retrieval (real or fictive) of the past, privileging, rather, the active mode and temporal immediacy that the actuality of writing implies. Hence, his concepts of "narratricide," of the "trope of onwardness," and of a "continually self-reconstructing oeuvre" provide the basis not only for a powerful and exceedingly rich analysis of the texts in question but access to a more fully integrated view of a life work—recontextualized by Abbott as a life project to which the writer was consciously committed—than could be offered by practitioners of any of the temporally grounded critical approaches cited by Contat, et al: above. It is thus in a genuinely hermeneutic perspective that the originality of Abbott's endeavor may be said to reside. And if this book constitutes a major contribution to Beckett studies, it does as much for autobiography in its invaluable demystification of the complex relations maintained by Beckett to his life, the world, and his literary oeuvre. [Lois Oppenheim]

Johnny Payne. *Chalk Lake*. Limited Editions Press, 1996. 165 pp. $18.95.

Set in Kentucky, Johnny Payne's novel *Chalk Lake* is as interesting for the way it thinks about place and the effect of place on people's lives as it is for its plot and characters. Indeed, the strongest thing about this book is the locale's ability to become significant while remaining largely in the background.

The main character of the book, Serena, returns to Kentucky both to be with her dying father and to try to regain control over her life. While there, she comes into contact with drifting and struggling friends, gets involved in co-owning a farm as part of trying to keep a dream alive, and concocts a scheme to get pregnant. Though this might sound a little like a Kentucky-style version of *Party of Five* or a hillbilly *Beverly Hills 90210*, Payne manages through his writing to make the situation feel both genuine and convincing.

The characters are often intriguing, particularly Serena, her preacher father (one of the few tolerable preachers in literature), and her at times irritating boyfriend Robbie. Payne often uses indirect discourse, his narrative voice becoming effectively colored with the words and thoughts of his characters. There is a sense as well of oral wisdom and closeness to the land that surfaces at times in brief inset narratives. However, Payne's narrative skills seem to shine out most strongly with his minor characters. His ability to depict a farmer or to portray the younger sister of Serena's roommate in a few strokes is as masterful as anything in the book.

Though not a book that is likely to push literature in a new direction, *Chalk Lake* is an effective narrative about the ways lives and dreams both collapse and come to be reborn. It is a promising first novel. [Brian Evenson]

Michael Krekorian. *Channel Zero*. Plover Press, 1996. 121 pp. $17.95.

"Mockingbirds," notes Michael Krekorian, "repeat the white noise of the urban environment." So call Krekorian a mockingbird who's singing just for you in a novel as complex as the internet yet brief as a word from our sponsor. If Zero Coupon, "hero" of *Channel Zero*, is not that sponsor, he works for him/it—as adman, photographer of cheeseburgers strump-dilly-icious as centerfold cheesecake, purveyor of country-fried iguana, the P. T. Barnum of rain forest as theme park, and the one who knows what he sees at the scene of each crime: those "big electro-echo fast lane, on-line one liners" whose tribal name in the global village is "average Americans."

Channel Zero is the evening news gone haywire, a VH-1 video of life as early buyout in the midst of a hostile takeover. Call this virtual realism. Or change the channel and call it a systems novel (one that shows how individual lives are entangled in the larger systems of science, mass media, and the like). Owing something to Don DeLillo's *White Noise* ("IBM, Coca-Cola, Sony," one character chants; "Porche, McDonalds, and Disney"), *Channel Zero* is similarly fascinated by a world in which surface seems all the depth we possess, possession is nine-tenths of the law, and behind which surface the real sealers of our fate bark, a world in which characters are "free market holograms," and where appropriation, distraction, manipulation, irreverence, and amnesia are what's for sale. It is a "new age" wherein parents "cannot teach their own children anything," people "wear their products on their sleeve," and "the prevailing look, it will be natural."

Channel Zero does its necessary knife-work through a series of (seemingly) loosely connected chapters, each a series of (seemingly) loosely connected paragraphs, each of which is in turn a sequence of (seemingly) loosely . . . : "Win one thousand dollars. Funny things are better two thirds of the time. Youth: a pleasant pastime. Are credit cards out of hand? Call the White House." Such prose can prove wearing, and some readers, not all of them named Martini, will find themselves "shaken but not stirred." Others will be appropriately ambivalent, uncertain about what it is they hear in Krekorian's paternosters to nylon, his Maalox mantras, his just-wanna-be-like-you jeremiads. To them, this: "Do not wait for Zero Coupon to explain." [Brooke Horvath]

Gordon Lish. *Epigraph*. Four Walls Eight Windows, 1996. 163 pp. $22.00.

Near the end of his life, eighteenth-century writer Tobias Smollett confessed that his greatest difficulties had resulted from his being both a writer and an editor—those he offended with editorial decisions were always more than willing to take their frustrations out against his novels. Gordon Lish, whom Don DeLillo has called a man "famous for all the wrong reasons," has perhaps had similar difficulties, his operations as an editor obscuring and sometimes injuring his reputation as a writer. Nevertheless, though currently still known for all the wrong reasons, with *Epigraph* Lish has a shot of becoming recognized for the right ones.

In *Epigraph* a character by the name of Gordon Lish (not to be confused either with the real Gordon Lish or with the Lishes of Lish's earlier books, despite biographical similarities) struggles to avoid facing the fact of his wife's demise after a long, difficult illness. In partial recoil he becomes fixated on the events surrounding his wife's death and with justifying his own actions. When these events threaten to became too revealing he falls back to the relative safety of querying hyphenation and points of grammar, looking closely at the language so as to avoid understanding too closely what the language unveils. Spending his time reclined in the machine in which his wife died, he writes letters to the quasi-religious organizations which have helped him with her illness, tries by mail to hit on his wife's nurses, responds to the court's repeated request that his deceased wife report for jury duty. As all his repressions surge to the surface, he quickly writes himself mad.

The writing here is careful and consummate, the situation at once moving and shocking: the literary equivalent of simultaneously blessing and desecrating a grave. As the novel approaches its close, there begins to develop an erratic dance of guilt and madness, with Lish threatened by all that wells up from both immediate and distant past. In such an erratics, however, lies the only sort of salvation possible to a character such as Lish: to move through madness and burst through to the other side, to continue to write letters with a little more (perhaps temporary) calm, and to proceed forward fully in the face of death. Whatever one thinks of Lish as an editor, *Epigraph* is a powerful novel. [Brian Evenson]

Wang Ping. *Foreign Devil.* Coffee House Press, 1996. 287 pp. $21.95.

Wang Ping grew up in mainland China but for more than a decade has lived in the U.S. where she has been establishing herself as a writer in English. Consequently, she might be taken as belonging to both contemporary Chinese and Chinese-American writers, and those familiar with either sorts of fiction will encounter much in *Foreign Devil* that they have read before: an autobiographical mode with particular emphasis on a female perspective, the historical backdrop of the Cultural Revolution and its immediate aftermath, a narrative of discovering identity and the struggle to retain a sense of self within a cultural and historical context that would deny, even annihilate the individual. As with so much recent Chinese fiction, considerable emphasis is laid on sexuality in reaction to the pervasive repression, both public and psychological, of Chinese society. The title refers to the fact that the protagonist, Ni Bing, feels and is seen by those around her as odd, not fitting into Chinese expectations and society, and indeed at the center of the narrative is Ni's torturous path toward a chance to pursue her own life in the U.S. The novel ends rather predictably with the plane taking off on her journey to New York and the "foreign devil" about to become in fact a foreign devil in an alien country that holds out the promise of self-determination.

Wang Ping writes a very fluid and readable prose and for the most part skillfully interweaves the multitudinous narrative threads of the protagonist's memories. For readers who have yet to experience recent Chinese and especially Chinese-American fiction, this novel is certainly a good introduction. For others, however, much of the tale is likely to strike one as mining an overworked vein complete with the obligatory foot-binding scene, a difficult mother-daughter relationship which nonetheless ends in mutual acceptance and understanding, typical horrors of the Cultural Revolution, the psychological ravages of China's social repression, and so on. Ni's search for identity culminates, rather too literally, in a melodramatic revelation of her actual parentage, and a vision of universal forgiveness of all those whom she has struggled against to maintain her selfhood, not least of all her native culture, which comes across just a bit too neatly as she is leaving everything behind to fly off to the land of promise. I hope these are the weaknesses of a first novel and the latent promise of Wang Ping's talents will manifest themselves more consistently in future efforts. [Jeffrey Twitchell-Waas]

Ana Castillo. *Loverboys*. Norton, 1996. 224 pp. $21.00.

As one of the more accomplished of Latina writers, Castillo is often able to paint a vivid image of characters and the way in which they are affected by their sense of who they are and what their cultures tell them to be. Nevertheless, despite the fact that many of its individual stories are successful, *Loverboys* is interesting less for the stories taken separately than for the resonances that begin to become established between stories.

As intriguing as the book's culture depictions is the complex way in which gender and desire are figured and refigured from story to story. We have desire of all types, heterosexual and homosexual, from women who flirt with other women despite feeling themselves largely heterosexual, to the lesbian in the title story who finds herself drawn irresistibly to a young man. With the stories often showing passage from gay to straight relationships or vice versa, with the characters often torn between different desires, sexuality is envisioned as fluid. Sometimes this is echoed culturally when characters seem to experience similar fluidity in terms of possessing a social identity that makes multiple claims on the individual.

In addition to providing a number of stories that fit fairly snugly into our sense of what a conventional story is or does, Castillo also offers some that quietly test the boundaries. The three paragraph "A Kiss Errant," for instance, reduces a relationship to a single gesture. Others, like "Crawfish Love," seem to break off just as the story is beginning. "If Not for the Blessing of a Son" ends where it begins, the story cyclic in a way that suggests its enormous hidden secret. While some of the stories stumble—such as "Who Was Juana Gallo?" which telegraphs its ending or "A Lifetime" which risks sentimentality—few fall on their faces, and the other, stronger stories keep the collection moving forward. [Brian Evenson]

Tom LeClair. *Passing Off*. Permanent Press, 1996. 174 pp. $22.00.

The author of *In the Loop: Don DeLillo and the Systems Novel* and *The Art of Excess: Mastery in Contemporary American Fiction*, Tom LeClair is also a former point guard who now spends part of each year playing basketball in Greece. *Passing Off*, his first novel, draws upon such experiences to do for roundball what Don DeLillo, in *End Zone*, did for football: to take us deep into the sport itself while also reading it as a synecdoche of the cultural complexity—here, American and Greek—of which it is a part, as one system among many where the means to and definition of all sorts of mastery are contested and in which web of interconnecting systems the individual is always already implicated.

Plotwise by sodium-vaporlight, *Passing Off* concerns former CBA All-Star Michael Keever. A playmaker—hence the center of on-court knowledge and control—Keever's best was never good enough to land him a permanent spot in the NBA, but, jumped to Greece, he stars as the "funnel point" for Panathinaikos in the Greek Basketball Association. All that was necessary was to relocate to Athens, get used to some cultural differences, and feign Greek ancestry, which Keever, metamorphosed into Mikhalis Kyvernos, manages successfully until his hoax is uncovered and he is blackmailed into an off-court assist—helping stage an act of ecoterrorism to dramatize the ecological nightmare awaiting us all and foreshadowed during Keever's year in Athens by water shortages and a "thermal inversion" whose stagnant, heavily polluted air leaves dozens dead.

While the novel knowledgeably re-creates a season of Greek ball and entertainingly sketches daily life in Greece—its tavernas and storied ruins, traffic jams and vagetable toting fans—LeClair exposes basketball's defining characteristics as illustrative of how, today, one must necessarily be in this world, both "injecting information deep into [one's] body" and "recovering knowledge from that source, recognizing how the crowded and collaborating inside overlaps with . . . the crowded, collaborating, competing outside world."

If LeClair owes a debt to DeLillo—in his fascination with crowds, technologically mediated experience, word-driven worlds, banal surfaces betrayed by their engimatic, sinister undersides—he has made such material his own, deftly peeling back the overlapping overlays—tourism and terrorism, ecology and history, economics and politics, language and aesthetics—that "anywhere, nowhere, or everywhere" infiltrate and affect us. Moreover, no one writes better about basketball as seen through the eyes of a player in action ("all filmy memory, fuzzy logic, informed estimation, exact guesswork") or understands more suasively both the limits of words even in a world where language seems always not only to precede but to determine events, and the need, in such a world, to feel "like an athlete outside, as well as inside, the gym." [Brooke Horvath]

Agnes Owens. *People Like That*. Bloomsbury, 1996. 176 pp. £13.99.

They're found in the gutted rooms of condemned buildings, the streets of decaying villages, and the servants' quarters of seedy hotels—"We have them in here all the time," a clerk says offhandedly, "people like that." These are the welfare state's leftovers: drug addicts, the elderly, the insane, and the occasional decent person trying but not succeeding in the lousiness of just getting by.

Agnes Owens is a definite success, part of the famous Glasgow literary enclave, friend and collaborator to the likes of James Kelman and Alasdair Gray (who did the jacket illustrations). Like her previous books—*Gentlemen of the West, A Working Mother*, and *Like Birds in the Wilderness*—the bare-bones, unsentimental, and heavily accented stories in *People Like That* examine the nooks and crannies of Scottish life, particularly as it's lived in the dysfunctional working-class family. When a father abandons his wife and children, the narrator of "The Marigold Field" writes flatly, "Mother said she couldn't bear to go back to that place where she had once been so happy." But even among the marigolds, theirs has been a strange sort of happiness; coaxing his children into giving the camera a smile, the brutal parent calls them "the most miserable kids I've ever seen." It's all a tangle of addictions and accusations, and the narrative gaze is tough and unrelenting throughout; Owens refuses to put any stock in the daydreaming that might transform bitter experiences. Triumph, when it comes, is sure to seem perverted, the result of finally giving in to the dark side, as in the "accident" that concludes "The Castle"—a combination psychological thriller and comedy of manners, in which two sisters recently bereft of their father take a consoling trip to France and let their petty grievances tailspin into (gleeful) tragedy.

Owens's stories almost invariably end with this sort of surprise: there's a rape,or a secret is revealed or someone dies. The barrage of shock endings may exhaust the most willing reader's suspension of disbelief—and perhaps that is Owens's intention, the grand theme drawing her disparate narratives together: life is full of surprises, but in the end even they amount to very little. The shock, in fact, drifts quietly away into disaffection, as in "The Lighthouse" (a wicked update of the Woolf novel): after the swift and shattering climax, we watch a body make a hollow for itself in the sand, unobserved on a lonely beach: "No one came by that day and in the evening when the sun went down she was gone with the tide."

One of the greatest surprises is that Owens is also, as Montaigne would say, the matter of her own book. The final piece appears at first to be another short story, but it's really the abbreviated account of her life—how she went from squatter to author. Her terse account of raising babies by the light of a kerosene lamp under a canvas tent is easily as powerful as anything in the fictions, and it can serve as a metaphor for the writing process itself: a desperate attempt to nurture and thrive in a dimly perceived world, to make something out of unpromising surroundings. This piece and the best stories in the collection indicate that the author may have surprised herself more than anyone, perhaps even has found a version of the contentment that—like the lighthouse, the marigold field, and the castle—has eluded her characters. [Susann Cokal]

James Chapman. *In Candyland It's Cool to Feed on Your Friends*. Fugue State Press, 1997. 190 pp. Paper: $8.00.

The premise behind James Chapman's latest book is that one of the putative (and perhaps real) author's previous novels exploited a situation two of his best friends were suffering through and that now the friends won't talk to him. As a response, the author takes up the situation again, this time in the form of a narrator by the name of Jim Chapman (not to be confused with James Chapman) and his relationship with his two friends, Dinah and David.

On one level, it doesn't matter if this frame is true or not; on another level, it's more fun to read the book if you can think it is true. The book itself, however, concerns itself little with issues of plot or truth, events tumbling onto one another, the whole narrative functioning like a sort of combination of imagism and experimental film. What one can gather is that something is wrong between the narrator and his friends, that the narrator is involved in a relationship with a female doctor whom he seems to exploit, that he is friends with a performance artist, Albion, who chooses to make his art out of the death of someone close to him, and that the narrator seems—perhaps mainly as a result of his artistic stance—to be suffering stomach problems. The novel is about indigestion and eating, both metaphorically and literally, with potatoes gaining a strange importance, but it is equally a meditation on the nature of art. Indeed, for Jim, photography is a means of taking apart other people, of doing violence to them.

In addition to larger formal displacements of the conventions of fiction, Chapman employs slight dislocations and compressions of language while still maintaining a manageable sentence. Sometimes, however, his dislocations make the sentences read a little like 1940s Hollywood trying to do Japanese and Chinese characters.

Better and more lucid than his previous book *Our Plague*, *In Candyland* seems a positive step for Chapman. He's a little more relaxed, a little more aware of the shape of the book. Though, as in most experiments, there's a certain risk of failure and not everything comes off, Chapman writes well enough to keep readers with him. [Brian Evenson]

Abdulrazak Gurnah. *Admiring Silence*. The New Press, 1996. 224 pp. $19.95.

"Every several months she would send me a few words about everyone's health and regards and best wishes, and some months later I would send something back."

The narrator would frequently speak like this, generally, flatly, with little specificity of incident. He would go to the doctor and then he would go home. He would do this and he would do that. The narrator would think about being from Zanzibar and compare the experiences. At home he would keep his ailment secret from his child and wife. Then he would remember his in-laws and the first time he met them. His English in-laws would always have some strong opinions about his being from Zanzibar. He would tell them, the father especially, exaggerated stories about life there. He would tell his stories in such a way that they confirmed every stereotype held about Zanzibar. He and the in-laws would mourn the chaos England left when it loosened its colonial hold. If the reader misses that the narrator would be ironic in his mourning, would that it were because Abdulrazak Gurnah provided some element of uncertainty. Instead, the narrator speaks in motives that are more explicit than human: "Emma glaring at me! Demanding that I take the blame for my ineffectual love for a daughter willingly overwhelmed by the gloating self-assurance of the culture that had nurtured her." And "This was where my narcissism lay, I suppose, in my desire to insert myself in self-flattering discourse which required that England be guilty and decadent, instead of playing my part as well and as silently as Pocahontas." These examples are the wreckage left over after Vienna's main intellectual export and poststructuralism get hold of a writer who is both eluded by their syntax and bettered by their ideas.

Whole sections of this novel are in the habitual past, a tense which most anyone who works at writing would tell you is strong poison, a writer's Kryptonite. I've tried to write this review in the habitual past and the effort has just about done me in. The tense has been known to induce symptoms of flatness, generality, and sloppiness. Consider the charged situation between the narrator and his in-laws. The reader of *Admiring Silence* never hears the relatives' comments; hearing that they *would* make these comments is a pale substitute.

When the narrator returns to his family in Zanzibar, for a few pages, he's actually observing. Specificity happens. The change of scenery knocks something loose in the narrator or demands more attention from Gurnah. In these pages Gurnah miraculously halts the novel's slow nosedive. He finds a way to combine his sociological observations about place and people with a specific scene and characters.

His solution is short-lived. For whatever reason, the habitual past returns. Much of *Admiring Silence* reads like a struggle between the methodologies of a sociologist and a conventional novelist. I don't believe one necessarily is the enemy of the other, especially if one takes the fine middle of this novel as any indication. In *Admiring Silence*, however, Gurnah relies on the sociologist and a boxful of lazy habitual generalities to carry his novel. Would that it were otherwise. [Paul L. Maliszewski]

William F. Van Wert. *Stool Wives*. Plover Press, 1996. 209 pp. $20.00.

It is there and it isn't there. The Africa that William Van Wert creates in *Stool Wives* is an Africa of words, an Africa where characters may speak in anagrams or lob puns like grenades or be named after great wordsmiths like Achebe and Ngugi. A level of satire and social realism does exist here—this is not merely a work about language, and one can, with a healthy dollop of imagination, discern a tangible, flesh-and-blood African reality through the language—but the great appeal of this fiction is the humor, irony, and surprisingly powerful emotion released by and through words. Plover Press calls this work a "nivola," and it certainly is something new under the sun. *Stool Wives* might be best envisioned as a *Things Fall Apart* written by a Nabokov, Barthelme, or Coover, a work in which we have the twin pleasures of reading a dramatic narrative about a distant and different place and knowing that we are reading a dramatic narrative about a distant and different place.

The story is at once mythic and mythical. In rural Nigeria a tall young man named Kimbene thirsts for glory, and his best chance of it is in growing tall enough—or at least seeming to grow tall enough—to overshadow the current rural king and assume his position. With the help of his devious Shakespeare-loving friend Ngugi, he becomes rural king and presides over a growing group of "stool wives," wives whose function is to sit behind the king as he feasts, to bear him children, and to raise them. Through the twists and turns of fate and Van Wert's narrative, Kimbene is forced to an awareness of a larger existence, to the knowledge that there are realities beyond feasting and sexing his stool wives. He must engage other tribes through warfare or statecraft and must confront directly the outside world in the persons of a Texas oilman, a melancholy Briton, a Finnish soap dealer, a group of Japanese businessmen, and an Italian journalist named Caruso. At length he becomes something both more and less than what he was when he aspired to kingship, and at the end of the story, he literally and figuratively disappears. The work concludes with the thoughts of Kimbene's wives, who discuss the nature of men and power and love, and we are left to try and make some sense of our reading experience with their help.

This conclusion and the title of the fiction seem appropriate, since, as one of the wives points out, in Africa (and elsewhere, perhaps), men dream and women work: "Men like to be myths. . . . We are left to be the reality." While *Stool Wives* twists and turns and sometimes loves words so much that it hinders healthy digestion, it's a work well worth reading, not so much for what it can tell us about African reality, but for the sheer joy of language and the moments of connection with word-created humanity. [Greg Garrett]

Robert Shapard and James Thomas, eds. *Sudden Fiction (Continued)*. Norton, 1996. 311 pp. $25.00.

How to marry a millionaire? How to steal a million? (Or for that matter, How to stuff a wild bikini?) How to review in less than 400 words sixty short-short stories? One of the above is in Sam Goldwyn's pithy phrase, "In two words Im-POSSIBLE." The others are Im-PROBABLE. However, five stories are noteworthy. Thomas McGuane's "War and Peace" is brilliantly evocative of life aboard a Navy light cruiser in and around the Solomon Islands: "Bodies were always floating past us, Japs and Americans, just bobbing meatballs that used to have moms and home towns." Ron Carlson's "The Tablecloth of Turin," like Robert Benchley's well-known comic lectures, is a spoof about Leonard Christofferson's change from an insurance investigator to a zealous lecturer on the Tablecloth of Turin, sold to him on a trip to Italy by Antony Cuppolini, who works in his brother's restaurant. It is pure tongue in cheek, related as it is to the Shroud of Turin and other variations of the true cross. Mostafa Abd el-Salaam, in Allen Hibbard's "Crossing to Abbassiya," has a simple task: to transfer a group of madmen by truck from one side of Cairo to the other. His mind wanders and he finds himself in a café with friends. When he remembers the truck outside, he goes out to find that his charges have escaped. With practical Arab logic he collects the first dozen men who accept a ride to a promised job; he delivers them to the asylum where they are taken in and processed amid their howls and cries. Mustafa returns home! Traci L. Gourdine's "Graceful Exits" repeats the theme of *Summer of '42*, but without the *Tea and Sympathy* ending. When the young man leaves, both parties are relieved. Arnie Watson (Barry Peters's "Arnie's Test Day") has five tests on Friday. Misusing his natural ingenuity, he turns himself into a human "crib": the bill of his Bulls cap contains twenty Spanish words, abbreviated versions of the amendments go on the inside of his Reebok polo shirt, notes for *The Great Gatsby* are entered on the inside of his belt and the pale blue inside of his jeans, quantum physics formulas on the outside of his polyester white socks, and finally "trigonometry notes on the bottom white soles of his Air Jordan basketball shoes." This is the generation politicos are worried about? This is the third collection of short-short stories by Shapard and Thomas. The majority of these stories are excellent examples of the form. [Jack Byrne]

Elizabeth McCracken. *The Giant's House*. Dial Press, 1996. 259 pp. $19.95.

I'm sure I'm not the only one who found it odd that Elizabeth McCracken should be nominated one of the twenty-five "Best Young Novelists in America" by *Granta* in their recent issue of the same name: at the time the nominations were submitted, McCracken had not yet published a novel—

would you award an Oscar to a movie that no one had seen? (To be fair, her short story collection, *Here's Your Hat, What's Your Hurry,* received considerable acclaim a few years ago.) Somewhat skeptical, I sat down with the published excerpt from *The Giant's House;* the next time I got out of that chair it was to jump on a late-night bus, make three transfers, and endure the sullen indignity of closing-shift bookstore employees in order to get my hands on this stunning first novel.

Ostensibly the memoirs of Peggy Cort, retired librarian of Brewsterville, Cape Cod, the elegantly drawn tale which unfolds across the book's (physically) tall pages is much more than fictional reminiscence; an often profound meditation on the quietest sort of love, McCracken's novel insists upon the dignity of its characters, all of whom are as fully alive, as fully hopeful, as they are damaged. Peggy never once questioned her choice of vocation—"I was to the library born," she tells James Sweatt, the tallest boy in the world. It's the perfect profession for the shy, self-styled misanthrope, who not only watches James grow from a boy to a man but gradually falls in love with him as well. She really is one of my favorite characters in recent fiction, unapologetically self-absorbed but in every way likeable—the brief, poignant flashbacks to her clumsy college years, for example, coax you to fall in love with her as you recognize the fragility of her carefully constructed self-assurance. James, fourteen years Peggy's junior, is equally memorable: a sad, gentle boy who grows up to be a sad, gentle man, the fact of his tallness is eclipsed only by the greatness of his heart. The long, nearly pantomimic courtship between these two misfits, including its intersections with McCracken's wonderful secondary characters, constitutes the plot of the novel entire.

Which is not to say nothing happens—a lot does. In fact, upon second reading, I was repeatedly impressed by McCracken's intricate, seamless plotting. The ending of this wholly original novel, fantastic to the point of improbable, reads as anything but. For McCracken to be named as one of our best seems, then, not odd at all. [Joseph Allen O'Rear]

Back in Print

• These were never out of print but are well worth noting. Under the book imprint of State Street Books, Borders has begun a series that parallels Modern Library and Everyman, but at a much cheaper price. While the quality of production is in fact superior to that of Modern Library and Everyman (State Street has completely reset its books so that the print is clear and crisp), these hardback uniform editions are in the $10-12 price range. Among the initial volumes are: Henry David Thoreau's *Citizen Thoreau* (which includes *Walden, Civil Disobedience,* and other writings, 442 pages, $11.00); Henry James's *Portrait of a Lady* (759 pages, $12.00), and Jane Austen's *Pride and Prejudice* (443 pages, $9.95).

- Library of America continues its splendid uniform reissues of the works of major American writers. Three new volumes are devoted to Vladimir Nabakov: *Novels and Memoirs 1941–1951* (which includes *The Real Life of Sebastian Knight, Bend Sinister,* and *Speak Memory,* 710 pages, $35.00); *Novels 1955–1962* (*Lolita, Pnin, Pale Fire, Lolita: A Screenplay,* 904 pages, $35.00), and *Novels 1969—1974* (*Ada, Transparent Things, Look at the Harlequins,* 824 pages, $35.00). For Nabakov enthusiasts and scholars, these are the volumes to get, now beautifully produced in this distinguished series.
- Shortly after his death, Stanley Elkin won the National Book Critics Circle Award for his novel *Mrs. Ted Bliss,* which is now available from Avon ($12.00). In bringing out in paperback Elkin's last novel, Avon also has reissued three previous Elkin novels: *The Living End* ($12.00), *George Mills* ($14.00), and *A Bad Man* ($12.00). All are vintage Elkin, and one hopes that they will stay in print.
- In 1995 Knopf brought out a newly translated two-volume hardback translation of Robert Musil's *The Man without Qualities.* Vintage has now issued a two-volume paperback edition (all 1,774 pages of it!) of this modern German masterpiece. Volume 1 is $20.00, and volume 2 is $22.00. This is a major work, wonderfully translated, of the twentieth century and, despite the steep price, a bargain. As with the Elkin books above, one hopes that this novel will stay in print.

From the School of Stupidity

This is an ongoing feature in the Review *that will record some of the more glaring acts of stupidity by critics and scholars.*

To make this award only three times each year is quite difficult given the vast competition for it. For instance, the fiction committee of the National Book Award could and should be given it every year, and yet such annual recognition would not seem fair to everyone else who is deserving (as we now know, the committee has once again lived up to its customary brilliance, proving that mediocre committees can with utter precision chose mediocre books). In any event, my feeling is that the recognition of glaring stupidity should go to an individual rather than to a group or committee, and therefore will not chose the NBA fiction committee, no matter how meritorious their efforts may be.

Instead, the award this time goes to Thomas Christensen for his review of Fernando del Paso's novel *Palinuro of Mexico* for the 6th October 1996 issue of the *San Francisco Chronicle.* Like the Surgeon General, Mr. Christensen provides the health warning that this massive experimental tome is "not for the timid reader," among whom Mr. Christensen apparently counts himself. Why not for the timid reader? Well, there are the hints of Joyce and Rabelais in the book. In other words, this is a bookish book which has "almost completely expunged character and plot" and has inserted in their place "linguistic play" (the equivalent in a review such as this as identifying high levels of tar and nicotine). Mr. Christensen apparently found no humor in this comic novel, nor does he even suggest that it *is* a comic novel. Oh, well, comedy, like intelligence, is a very personal matter. Laurence Sterne should be relieved that he wrote the great *Tristram* a very long time ago, so as not to have taxed Mr. Christensen's sense of humor or taste. Mr. Christensen also has a particular problem with *Palinuro's* use of time (it has "little connection either to real time or to novelistic conventions"—just what "conventions" does Mr. Christensen have in mind? Proust's? Joyce's? Faulkner's? Let it pass).

Rather than being completely dismissive of Mr. Christensen, I should point out that he is the translator of *Like Water for Chocolate*, that most beloved and easily understood of Mexican novels, one that brought a tear to the eye of even the least sophisticated of readers, one that will live on in the hearts and minds for at least, well, a year. On the other hand, I should point out one minor problem that Mr. Christensen has with time, and this with a man who not only understands "real" but also "novelistic" time! As he shrewdly points out, the novel was first published in Spanish in 1980, but then he says that "it has taken decades for this English version to appear." Now let me see, using fingers and toes, I come up with . . . but then I do not have the understanding of "real" time that Mr. Christensen has. But Dalkey Archive's edition is not the first English edition; the first English edition was published by Quartet in England in 1989, which would make nine years, but who am I to question the translator of *Waterford Chocolates*?

So, it is with great humility and appreciation that I award Thomas Christensen lifetime membership in the School of Stupidity.

Books Received

Aksyonov, Vassily. *The Winter's Hero*. Random House, 1996. $27.50. (F)

Alter, Robert. *Genesis*. Norton, 1996. $25.00. (NF)

Amerson, Robert. *From the Hidewood: Memories of a Dakota Neighborhood*. Minnesota Historical Society, 1996. Paper: $17.95. (F)

Anscombe, Roderick. *Shank*. Hyperion, 1996. $22.95. (F)

Arden, John. *Jack Juggler and the Emperor's Whore*. Minerva, 1996. Paper: £8.99. (F)

Armitt, Lucie. *Theorising the Fantastic*. Arnold, 1996. $59.95. (NF)

Baudrillard, Jean. *The Perfect Crime*. Trans. Chris Turner. Verso, 1996. Paper: $16.00. (F)

Bell, Madison Smartt. *Ten Indians*. Pantheon, 1996. Paper: $23.00. (F)

Berkéwicz, Ulla. *Angels Are Black and White*. Trans. Leslie Willson. Camden House, 1996. No price given. (F)

Bevilacqua, Alberto. *Eros*. Trans. Ann McGarrell. Steerforth, 1996. $20.00. (F)

Bishop, Michael. *At the City Limits of Fate*. Edgewood, 1996. Paper: $14.00. (F)

Bloom, Claire. *Leaving a Doll's House*. Little, Brown, 1996. $23.95. (NF)

Boyd, Greg. *Sacred Hearts*. Hi Jinx, 1996. Paper: $13.00. (F)

Bradbury, Malcom. *Dangerous Pilgrimages*. Viking, 1996. $29.95. (NF)

Breton, André. *The Lost Steps*. Trans. Mark Polizzotti. Nebraska, 1996. $30.00. (NF)

Bruccoli, Matthew J., ed. *F. Scott Fitzgerald: On Authorship*. South Carolina, 1996. $29.95. (NF)

——. *The Only Thing That Counts: The Ernest Hemingway–Maxwell Perkins Correspondence*. Scribner, 1996. $35.00. (NF)

Burwell, Rose Marie. *Hemingway: The Postwar Years and the Posthumous Novels*. Cambridge, 1996. $54.95. (NF)

Butler, Robert Olen. *Tabloid Dreams*. Henry Holt, 1996. $22.50. (F)

Calder, Richard. *Dead Things*. St. Martin's, 1997. $20.95. (F)

Carrington, Leonora. *The Hearing Trumpet*. Exact Change, 1996. Paper: $15.95. (F)

Cervantes, Miguel de. *Don Quijote*. Trans. Burton Raffel. Norton, 1996. Paper: $18.00. (F)

Chapman, Stepan. *Danger Music*. The Ministry of Whimsy, 1996. Paper: $2.99. (F)

Clark, Geoffery. *Jackdog Summer*. Hi Jinx, 1996. Paper: $15.00. (F)

Codrescu, Andrei. *Alien Candor*. Black Sparrow, 1996. Paper: $15.00. (Poetry)

Cohen, Garnett Kilberg. *Lost Women: Banished Souls*. Missouri, 1996. Paper: $16.95. (F)

Cohn, Nik. *Need*. Secker & Warburg, 1996. £15.99. (F)

Coleman, Wanda. *Native in a Strange Land: Trials and Tremors*. Black Sparrow, 1996. Paper: $15.00. (F)

Conley, Katherine. *Automatic Woman: The Representation of Woman in Surrealism*. Nebraska, 1996. $35.00. (NF)

Conn, Peter. *Pearl S. Buck: A Cultural Biography*. Cambridge, 1996. $29.95. (NF)

Crant, Phillip A. *Hervé Bazin: Social Reflections in Fiction*. New Paradigm, 1995. Paper: $21.95. (NF)

Crevel, René. *Babylon*. Trans. Kay Boyle. Sun & Moon, 1996. Paper: $12.95. (F)

D'Ambrosio, Charles. *The Point*. Little, Brown, 1995. $19.95. (F)

De Rosa, Tina. *Paper Fish*. Feminist, 1996. Paper: $9.95. (F)

Desai, Anita. *Journey to Ithaca*. Minerva, 1996. Paper: £6.99. (F)

Di Piero, W. S. *Shooting the Works*. Northwestern, 1996. Paper: $14.95. (NF)

Dijkstra, Bram. *Evil Sisters*. Knopf, 1996. $30.00. (NF)

Dodic, N. J. *Muck*. Gutter, 1996. Paper: $11.95. (F)

Doyle, Roddy. *The Woman Who Walked into Doors*. Viking, 1996. $22.95. (F)

Eco, Umberto. *The Island of the Day Before*. Trans. William Weaver. Minerva, 1996. Paper: £6.99. (F)

Eldredge, Sears A. *Mask Improvisation for Actor Training and Performance*. Northwestern, 1996. No price given. (NF)

Ellison, Ralph. *Flying Home and Other Stories*. Ed. John F. Callahan. Random House, 1996. $23.00. (F)

Erickson, Steve. *Arc d'X*. Owl, 1996. Paper: $14.00. (F)

Ferrari, Rita. *Innocence, Power, and the Novels of John Hawkes*. Pennsylvania, 1996. $34.95. (NF)

Fitzpatrick, Kevin. *Rush Hour*. Midwest Villages & Voices, 1997. Paper: $9.00. (Poetry)

Ford, Glyn, Glenys Kinnock, and Arlene McCarthy, eds. *Changing States: A Labour Agenda for Europe*. Mandarin, 1996. Paper: £7.99. (NF)

Foster, David. *The Glade within the Grove*. Fourth Estate, 1996. £16.99 (F)

Franklin, Benjamin V., ed. *Recollections of Anaïs Nin by Her Contemporaries*. Ohio, 1996. $29.95. (NF)

Friedman, Bruce Jay. *A Father's Kisses*. Donald I. Fine, 1996. $22.95. (F)

Gates, Henry Louis, Jr., and Nellie Y. McKay, ed. *The Norton Anthology: African American Literature*. Norton, 1996. $49.95. (F)

Gatt-Rutter, John. *Oriana Fallaci: The Rhetoric of Freedom*. Berg, 1996. Paper: $16.95. (NF)

Gelman, Peter. *Flying Saucers over Hennepin*. Permeable, 1997. Paper: $12.00. (F)

Glazner, Greg. *Singularity*. Norton, 1997. $19.00. (Poetry)

Gluzman, Michael, and Naomi Seidman, eds. *Israel: A Traveler's Literary Companion*. Whereabouts, 1996. Paper: $12.95. (F)

Goldman, Francisco. *The Ordinary Seaman*. Atlantic Monthly, 1997. $23.00. (F)

Gozzano, Guido. *Journey to the Cradle of Mankind*. Trans. David Marinelli. Northwestern, 1996. Paper: $14.95. (F)

Grant, Richard. *Tex and Molly in the Afterlife*. Avon, 1996. $24.00. (F)

Graves, Robert. *Complete Short Stories*. ed. Lucia Graves. St. Martin's, 1996. $39.95. (F)

Green, Julian. *The Stars of the South*. Marion Boyars, 1996. $29.95. (F)

Guibert, Hervé. *Blindsight*. Trans. James Kirkup. George Braziller, 1996. $20.00. (F)

Hawke, Ethan. *The Hottest State*. Little, Brown, 1996. $19.95. (F)

Heberlein, L. A. *Sixteen Reasons Why I Killed Richard M. Nixon*. Livingston, 1996. Paper: $11.95. (F)

Henry, Richard. *Pretending and Meaning: Toward a Pragmatic Theory of Fictional Discourse*. Greenwood, 1996. $55.00. (NF)

Høeg, Peter. *The Woman and the Ape*. Trans. Barbara Haveland. Farrar, Straus & Giroux, 1996. $23.00. (F)

Hogan, Ed, ed. *From Three Worlds: New Ukranian Writing*. Zephyr, 1996. Paper: $13.95. (F)

Howell, Stokes. *The Sexual Life of Savages and Other Stories*. St. Martin's, 1996. $20.95. (F)

Hughes, Langston. *Short Stories*. Ed. Akiba Sullivan Harper. Hill and Wang, 1996. $25.00. (F)

Humphreys, Emyr. *Unconditional Surrender*. Dufour, 1996. $24.95. (F)

Hunt, D. Trinidad. *The Operator's Manual for Planet Earth*. Hyperion, 1996. $19.95. (F)

Jarry, Alfred. *Exploits & Opinions of Dr. Faustroll, Pataphysician*. Exact Change, 1996. Paper: $13.95. (F)

Jeal, Tim. *For God and Glory*. William Morrow, 1996. $25.00. (F)

Jones, Jordan, ed. *Bakunin*. Coyote, 1997. Paper: $10.00. (F)

Kamau, Kwadwo Agymah. *Flickering Shadows*. Coffee House, 1996. $21.95. (F)

Kenny, Seán. *The Hungry Earth*. Wolfhound, 1995. Paper: £6.99. (F)

Khoury, Elias. *The Kingdom of Strangers*. Trans. Paula Haydar. Arkansas, 1996. Paper: $16.00. (F)

Kissel, Susan S. *Moving On: The Heroines of Shirley Ann Grau, Anne Tyler, and Gail Godwin*. Popular, 1996. Paper: $19.95. (NF)

Kleiner, Gregg. *Where River Turns to Sky*. Avon, 1996. $23.00. (F)

Lappin, Elena, ed. *Daylight in Nightclub Inferno: Czech Fiction from the Post-Kundera Generation*. Catbird, 1997. Paper: $15.95. (F)

Larsen, Jeanne. *Manchu Palaces*. Henry Holt, 1996. $25.00. (F)

Larsen, Michael. *Uncertainty*. Trans. Lone Thygesen Blecher and George Blecher. Harcourt Brace, 1996. $22.00. (F)

Lawrence, Margaret. *Hearts and Bones*. Avon, 1996. $23.00. (F)

Lê, Linda. *Slander*. Trans. Esther Allen. Nebraska, 1996. Paper: $14.00. (F)

Le Carré, John. *The Tailor of Panama*. Knopf, 1996. $25.00. (F)

Leithauser, Brad. *The Friends of Freeland*. Knopf, 1997. $26.00. (F)

Logue, Mary. *Halfway Home: A Granddaughter's Biography*. Minnesota Historical Society, 1996. Paper: $14.95. (NF)

London, John, ed. *The Unknown Federico García Lorca*. Atlas, 1996. Paper: £7.99. (NF)

MacLaverty, Bernard. *Walking the Dog and Other Stories*. Norton, 1996. Paper: $11.00. (F)

Mahdi, Muhsin, ed. *The Arabian Nights*. Trans. Husain Haddawy. Norton, 1996. Paper: $14.95. (F)

Marínex, Tomás Eloy. *Santa Evita*. Trans. Helen Lane. Knopf, 1996. $23.00. (F)

Martin, Emer. *Breakfast in Babylon*. Wolfhound, 1995. Paper: £6.99. (F)

Martinez, Dionisio D. *Bad Alchemy*. Norton, 1996. Paper: $12.00. (Poetry)

Maso, Carole. *Aureole*. Ecco, 1996. $22.00. (F)

Mazza, Cris, Jeffrey DeShell, and Elisabeth Sheffield, eds. *Chick-Lit 2*. FC2, 1996. Paper: $11.95. (F)

McCaffery, Larry. *Some Other Frequency*. Pennsylvania, 1996. Paper: $19.95. (NF)

McClanahan, Ed. *A Congress of Wonders*. Counterpoint, 1996. $21.00. (F)

Michael, Magali Cornier. *Feminism and the Postmodern Impulse*. SUNY, 1996. Paper: $21.95. (NF)

Mongia, Padmini, ed. *Contemporary Postcolonial Theory: A Reader*. Arnold, 1996. $59.95. (NF)

Moriarty, Laura. *Symmetry*. Avec Books, 1996. Paper: $9.95. (Poetry)

Morrow, Bradford, ed. *Conjunctions: The Archipelago: New Carribean Writing*. Bard College, 1996. Paper: $12.00. (NF)

Mulisch, Harry. *The Discovery of Heaven*. Trans. Paul Vincent. Viking, 1996. $34.95. (F)

Müller, Herta. *The Land of Green Plums*. Trans. Michael Hofmann. Henry Holt, 1996. $23.00. (F)

Munro, Alice. *Selected Stories*. Knopf, 1996. $30.00. (F)

Mustafa, Fawzia. *V. S. Naipaul*. Cambridge, 1995. $54.95. (NF)

Nadir, Shams. *The Astrolabe of the Sea*. Trans. C. Dickson. City Lights, 1996. Paper: $9.95. (F)

Nerval, Gérard de. *Aurélia & Other Writings*. Trans. Geoffrey Wagner, Robert Duncan, and Marc Lowenthal. Exact Change, 1996. Paper: $15.95. (F)

Norfolk, Lawrence. *The Pope's Rhinoceros*. Harmony, 1996. $25.00. (F)

North, Sam. *By Desire*. Secker & Warburg, 1996. £12.99. (F)

Novarina, Valère. *The Theater of the Ears*. Trans. Allen S. Weiss. Sun & Moon, 1996. Paper: $13.95. (F)

Olsen, Lance. *Burnt*. Wordcraft, 1996. Paper: $11.95. (F)
———. *Time Famine*. Permeable, 1996. Paper: $12.95. (F)
Paasilinna, Arto. *The Year of the Hare*. Trans. Herbert Lomas. Peter Owen, 1996. Paper: £9.50. (F)
Parker, Hershel. *Herman Melville, A Biography: Volume 1 1819-1851*. Johns Hopkins, 1996. $39.95. (NF)
Parshchikov, Alexei. *Blue Vitriol*. Trans. John High, Michael Molnar, and Michael Palmer. Avec Books, 1994. Paper: $9.50. (Poetry)
Pearson, Ridley. *Beyond Recognition*. Hyperion, 1997. $22.95. (F)
Pell, Derek. *The Marquis de Sade's Elements of Style*. Permeable, 1996. Paper: $5.95. (F)
Perloff, Marjorie. *Wittgenstein's Ladder*. Chicago, 1996. $27.95. (NF)
Pfeiffer, Peter C., and Laura García-Moreno, eds. *Text and Nation*. Camden House, 1996. $58.00. (NF)
Poniatowska, Elena. *Tinisima*. Trans. Katherine Silver. Farrar, Straus, & Giroux, 1996. $25.00. (F)
Price, Charles F. *Hiwassee: A Novel of the Civil War*. Academy Chicago, 1996. $20.00. (F)
Rabaté, Jean-Michel. *The Ghosts of Modernity*. Florida, 1996. $49.95 (NF)
Rabin, Arnold. *The Rat and the Rose: A Naughtobiography*. Black Heron, 1996. Paper: $12.95. (F)
Richards, John. *Working Stiff*. Hi Jinx, 1996. $15.00. (F)
Richards, Thomas. *Zero Tolerance*. Farrar, Strauss, and Giroux, 1997. $23.00. (F)
Robinson, Eden. *Traplines*. Metropolitan, 1996. $23.00. (F)
Rohrer, Matthew. *A Hummock in the Malookas*. Norton, 1995. Paper: $11.00. (Poetry)
Romyn, Mark. *Flyscraper*. Carolina Vegas Starr. *Toxic Shock Syndrome*. Permeable, 1996. Paper: $8.00. (F)
Rossel, Sven H., and Bo Elbrønd-Bek, eds. *Christmas in Scandinavia*. Trans. David W. Colbert. Nebraska, 1996. $30.00. (F)
Ruff, Shawn Stewart, ed. *Go the Way Your Blood Beats*. Henry Holt, 1996. $30.00. (F)
Satie, Erik. *A Mammal's Notebook*. Ed. Ornelia Volta. Trans. Antony Melville. Atlas, 1996. Paper: $24.99. (F)
Schein, Lorraine. *The Raw Brunettes*. Wordcraft, 1996. $6.00. (F)
Schneider, Peter. *Couplings*. Farrar, Strauss, and Giroux, 1996. $24.00. (F)
Sepúlveda, Luis. *The Name of a Bullfighter*. Trans. Suzanne Ruta. Harcourt Brace, 1996. $21.00. (F)
Shreve, Anita. *The Weight of Water*. Little, Brown, 1997. $22.95. (F)
Simpson, Mona. *A Regular Guy*. Knopf, 1996. $25.00. (F)
Skarmeta, Antonio. *Love-Fifteen*. Latin American Literary Review, 1996. Paper: $13.95. (F)
Skemer, Arnold. *B*. Phrygian, 1996. Paper: $6.00. (F)

————. *The Occupation*. Phrygian, 1996. Paper: $10.00. (F)

Smiley, Jane. *The Greenlanders*. Fawcett Columbine, 1996. Paper: $14.00. (F)

Smith, Charlie. *Cheap Ticket to Heaven*. Henry Holt, 1996. $25.00. (F)

Sobieszek, Robert A. *Ports of Entry: William S. Burroughs and the Arts*. Los Angeles County Museum of Art, 1996. Paper: $24.95. (NF)

Spoerri, Daniel. *An Anecdoted Topography of Chance*. Atlas, 1996. Paper: $24.99. (NF)

Steppling, John. *Sea of Cortez and Other Plays*. Sun & Moon, 1996. Paper: $14.95. (F)

Stracher, Cameron. *The Laws of Return*. Morrow, 1996. $23.00. (F)

Toer, Pramoedya Ananta. *House of Glass*. Trans. Max Lane. William Morrow, 1996. $26.00. (F)

Trevor, William. *After Rain*. Viking, 1996. $22.95. (F)

Trinidad, David. *Answer Song*. High Risk, 1994. Paper: $10.99. (Poetry)

Vachss, Andrew. *False Allegations: A Burke Novel*. Knopf, 1996. $23.00. (F)

VandenBroeck, André. *Breaking Through: A Narrative of the Great Work*. City Lights, 1996. Paper: $15.95. (F)

Vandermeer, Jeff. *The Book of Lost Places: The Selected Works of Jeff Vandermeer*. Ed. Mike Olson and Joe Morey. Dark Regions, 1996. Paper: $8.95. (F)

Ventura, Michael. *The Death of Frank Sinatra*. Henry Holt, 1996. $22.50. (F)

Vircondelet, Alain. *Marguerite Duras: Vérité et légendes*. Editions du Chêne, 1996. No price given. (NF)

Voien, Steven. *Black Leopard*. Knopf, 1997. $23.00. (F)

Voigt, Ellen Bryant. *Kyrie*. Norton, 1995. Paper: $11.00. (Poetry)

Waldrop, Keith. *The Locality Principle*. Avec Books, 1995. Paper: $9.95. (Poetry)

Wallace, David Foster. *A Supposedly Fun Thing I'll Never Do Again*. Little, Brown, 1997. $23.95. (NF)

Watson, Wallace Steadman. *Understanding Rainer Werner Fassbinder*. South Carolina, 1996. $39.95. (NF)

Welch, Denton. *A Voice Through a Cloud*. Exact Change, 1996. Paper: $15.95. (F)

Whalen, Tom. *Roithamer's Universe*. Portals, 1996. Paper: $12.00. (F)

Wieners, John. *707 Scott Street*. Sun & Moon, 1997. Paper: $12.95. (NF)

Wiggins, Todd. *Zeitgeist*. Henry Holt, 1996. $17.95. (F)

Williams, John. *Fiction as False Document: The Reception of E. L. Doctorow in the Postmodern Age*. Camden House, 1996. $52.95. (NF)

Williams, Marie Sheppard. *The Worldwide Church of the Handicapped and Other Stories*. Coffee House, 1996. Paper: $12.95. (F)

Willson, A. Leslie, ed. *Contemporary German Fiction*. Continuum, 1996. $29.50. (NF)

Wilson, A. N. *A Watch in the Night.* Norton, 1996. $23.00. (F)

Wirth-Nesher, Hana. *City Codes: Reading the Modern Urban Novel.* Cambridge, 1995. $49.95. (NF)

Wolff, Tobias. *Back in the World.* Vintage, 1996. Paper: $12.00. (F)

Wurlitzer, Rudolph. *Nog.* Serpent's Tail, 1996. Paper: $11.99. (F)

Yau, John. *Forbidden Entries.* Black Sparrow, 1997. $25.00. (Poetry)

Zinik, Zinovy. *One-Way Ticket.* New Directions, 1996. $19.95. (F)

Contributors

MARIA NEMCOVA BANARJEE is Professor of Russian and Comparative Literature at Smith College. She is the author of *Terminal Paradox: The Novels of Milan Kundera* (1990).

LARISA CHADDICK, born in Oklahoma, received her M.A. in Latin American Literature at the University of Maryland. Her translations include poetry, essays, and fiction by such Peruvian authors as Blanca Varela, Gregorio Martínez, Carmen Ollé, Magdalena Chocano, and Alberto Bravo de Rueda. She is currently working on her Ph.D. at King's College, London.

ELIZABETH DIPPLE is Professor of English at Northwestern University. Her primary interests are Shakespeare, Renaissance studies, the history of fiction, and contemporary fiction. She is the author of *Plot, Iris Murdoch: Work for the Spirit*, and a study of international contemporary fiction, *The Unresolvable Plot*.

LUBOMIR DORUZKA collaborated with Josef Skvorecky on translations of Henry James, William Faulkner, and Ernest Hemingway, on various radio programs about American literature and jazz, and on the book to a musical adaptation of *The Rivals*. He is the author of several books on jazz and pop music and has served as president of the European Jazz Federation.

EDWARD L. GALLIGAN, Professor Emeritus of English at Western Michigan University, is the author of *The Comic Vision in Literature* (1984) and of numerous articles and essays in the *Sewanee Review.*

JAMES GROVE is Chair of the English department at Mt. Mercy College in Cedar Rapids, Iowa. In 1989–1990 he was a Fulbright lecturer at Palacky University in Olomouc, Czechoslovakia. His publications include articles in *The Best from "American Literature"*: *Mark Twain*, the *New England Quarterly*, and *Critique*. He has also published an interview with the Czech poet Sylva Fischerova in the *Prairie Schooner.*

STEVEN HOROWITZ teaches in the Rhetoric Department at Coe College in Cedar Rapids, Iowa. He has published several articles on Eastern European and literary topics and served as a Fulbright lecturer in American Studies at Joszef Atilla University in Szeged, Hungary. He is also Arts and Entertainment Editor of the alternative weekly, *Icon.*

JOSEF JARAB has recently completed his seven-year tenure as Rector of Palacky University (Olomouc, Czech Republic). He became rector in

1989, after being very active in the Velvet Revolution. Previously, Dr. Jarab was professor of English and American Literary Theory at Palacky University. He has published six books and many articles on Czech, English, and American literature. In 1992 he was awarded the Commenius Award by the Czech Republic.

DANE JOHNSON is Assistant Professor of World and Comparative Literature at San Francisco State University. He is currently at work on a book entitled *Which Difference Makes a Difference: William Faulkner, Gabriel García Márquez, Toni Morrison, and the Creation of Literary Value in the United States since 1929.*

HELEN KOSEK is the author of *Hledani ztracene generace* (Searching for the Lost Generation, 1987). She lives in Sweden.

EFRAÍN KRISTAL teaches in the Department of Spanish and Portuguese at the University of California—Los Angeles.

JOHNNY PAYNE's novel *Chalk Lake* has just been published by Limited Editions Press (reviewed on p. 198). His musical play *The Devil in Disputanta* was produced by Loyola University in October 1996 and will be produced by Barter Theater in 1997. His other books include *The Ambassador's Son, Conquest of the New Word: Experimental Fiction and Translation in the Americas,* and the creative writing textbook *Voice and Style.* He teaches at Northwestern University.

LUIS REBAZA-SORALUZ, born in Lima, Peru, has published three collections of poetry since 1978. His most recent volume, *Del reino y la frontera* (Of the Kingdom and the Frontier) was published in 1992. His creative work has appeared in the *Washington Review, Delos, Boulevard,* and the *Plum Review.* He received his Ph.D. in Latin American Literature from the University of Maryland. He currently teaches and resides in London.

MÍLA ŠAŠKOVÁ-PIERCE, who teaches at the University of Nebraska, is co-author of *Czech for Communication* and the author of numerous articles on the Czech American experience and minority language disappearance.

PHYLLIS SILVERSTEIN is currently translating Teresa Porzecanski's *Perfumes de Cartago.* She is a graduate student in English at the University of Chicago.

SAM SOLECKI is Professor of English at the University of Toronto. He is the author of *Prague Blues: The Fiction of Josef Skvorecky* (1990) and has edited *Spider Blues: Essays on Michael Ondaatje* (1986), Josef Skvorecky's *Talkin' Moscow Blues* (1988) and *The Achievement of Josef Skvorecky* (1994).

MARGARET WEHR is a writer and critic with a long history of working with arts foundations and independent publishers in the Pacific Northwest. For several years she has served as a consultant to small presses in the areas of financial planning, marketing, and fundraising.

ALEX ZISMAN, a Peruvian critic living in Toronto, co-edited Mario Vargas Llosa's *La guerra del fin del mundo* (Seix Barral, 1981). Most recently he and María del Carmen Ghezzi supervised the revision of Vargas Llosa's memoir, *Un pez en el agua* (Seix Barral, 1993). He is the editor of *Quiebre*, a Toronto-based magazine that showcases the work of Spanish-speaking writers and artists living in Canada.

 High Plains Literary Review

"A rich blend of intelligent
new voices" — **Choice**

Rita Dove • Tony Ardizzone • Marilyn Krysl
Joyce Carol Oates • Richard Currey
Ron Carlson • Malcolm Glass • Nancy Lord
John Domini • Julia Alvarez • Floyd C. Stuart
Cris Mazza • Michael Marrone • Njabulo
S. Ndebele • Darrell Spencer • Askold Meinyczuk

Fiction • Poetry • Essays • Interviews • Criticism

180 Adams Street, Denver, CO 80206

$7.00 / issue $20 / year

We're Back

Gargoyle Magazine
20th Anniversary Issue

"I get a lot of literary magazines. There are some I save to read later.
Gargoyle is the only one I'll pick up right away. What I like is how eclectic it is.
I love the stories because they take chances; occasionally, I find myself
thinking about them long after. I don't have that reaction to other magazines."
--Rita Dove in the *Washington Post*

S T O R Y Q U A R T E R L Y 32

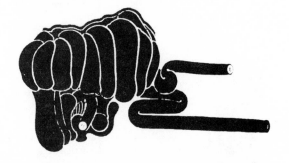

Single Issue $5
P.O. Box 1416, Northbrook, IL 60065

Prairie Schooner

may be 70 years

old, but we're still

running strong.

What's the secret? Well, it has to do with horsepower.

Prairie Schooner is still one of the leading literary magazines today because we haven't changed the essential fuel that makes us run.

Excellence.

Prairie Schooner publishes the best contemporary poetry, fiction, essays, and reviews four times a year. While hundreds of other magazines have sputtered and died, *Prairie Schooner* continues to collect kudos from the likes of Best American Short Stories, Essays, and Pushcart Prize anthologies.

Contribute to a natural resource. Subscribe to *Prairie Schooner*.

Send $22.00 for a one-year subscription (4 issues) to:
Prairie Schooner, 201 Andrews Hall, University of Nebraska, Lincoln, NE 68588-0334 (make checks payable to *Prairie Schooner*)

Studies in Twentieth Century Literature

Volume 21, No. 1 (Winter, 1997)

A journal devoted to literary theory and practical criticism

A Special Issue on
Contemporary German Poetry
James Rolleston, Guest Editor

Contributors include:

Nora M. Alter . . . und Fried . . . und . . .: The Poetry of Erich Fried and the Structure of Contemporaneity

Amy Colin Writings from the Margins: German-Jewish Women Poets from the Bukovina

Christine Cosentino "An Affair on Uncertain Ground": Sarah Kirsch's poetry Volume *Erlking's Daughter* in the Context of Her Prose After the "Wende"

Neil H. Donahue The Intimacy of Internationalism in the poetry of Joachim Sartorius

Elke Erb Fundamentally Grounded

Erk Grimm Mediamania? Contemporary German Poetry in the Age of New Information Technologies: Thomas Kling and Durs Grünbein

Barbara Mabee Footprints Revisited or "Life in the Changed Space that I don't Know": Elke Erb's Poetry Since 1989

Charlotte Melin Improved Versions: Feminist Poetics and Recent Work by Ulla Hahn and Ursula Krechel

Jonathan Monroe Between Ideologies and a Hard Place: Hans Magnus Enzensberg's Utopian Pragmatist Poetics

Leonard Olschner A Poetics of Place: Günter Kunert's Poem Sequence "Herbstanbruch in Arkadien"

James Rolleston Modernism and Metamorphosis: Karin Kiwus' *Das Chinesische Examen*

and **New Poetry** by **Gerhard Falkner** and **Günter Kunert**

Also in preparation: *Illness and Disease in Twentieth-Century Literature*—Sander L. Gilman, Guest Editor

Subscriptions: Douglas Benson email: bensonml@ksu.ksu.edu

MSS in French and German—Marshall Olds, Editor: molds@unlinfo.unl.edu
MSS in Spanish and Russian—Silvia Sauter, Editor: silviae@ksu.ksu.edu

VQR

The Virginia
Quarterly Review

*A National Journal of
Literature and Discussion*

JOHN DOS PASSOS,
1896-1970: MODERNIST
RECORDER OF THE
AMERICAN SCENE
Townsend Ludington

—

MARY LEE SETTLE:
THE LIONESS IN
WINTER
Mariflo Stevens

—

REMEMBERING *THE
BEST YEARS OF
OUR LIVES*
Philip D. Beidler

—

FICTION
*Elaine Fowler Palencia
William Hoffman
Brad Barkley
Barbara Haas*

—

POETRY
*Mary Winifred Hood
Susan Imhof
Sam Witt
Edward Kleinschmidt
Doug Anderson
Yehuda Amichai*

—

THE GREEN ROOM
NOTES ON
CURRENT BOOKS
REPRINTS &
NEW EDITIONS

AUTUMN 1996

Volume 72, Number 4

Five Dollars

Two Literary Giants

JOHN DOS PASSOS

MARY LEE SETTLE

The Virginia Quarterly Review
One West Range
Charlottesville, VA   22903

Dalkey Archive Press
New & recent titles

God Head   by Scott Zwiren

Collected Stories   by Arno Schmidt

Poundemonium   by Julián Ríos

Lyric of the Circle Heart   by William Eastlake

Spleen   by Olive Moore

The Complete Fiction   by W. M. Spackman

The Fountains of Neptune   by Rikki Ducornet

Collected Fiction   by Louis Zukofsky

A Night at the Movies   by Robert Coover

Reader's Block   by David Markson

"A powerful, harrowing account of manic-depressive illness. It captures both the horrors and ecstasies with extraordinary force."
—Kay Redfield Jamison, author of *An Unquiet Mind*

$10.95
1-56478-130-5

God Head
S c o t t   Z w i r e n

In *God Head*, Scott Zwiren boldly and courageously records the terrifying, destructive experience of manic depression. From a promising young college student to mental hospitals to a confined, out-of-control, roller-coaster life on New York City's Upper West Side, Zwiren's narrator traces from the inside the horrors of an existence that swings between numbing depression and exalting highs.

"Zwiren writes from so deeply inside the point of view of his protagonist that we feel, along with him, the disorientation and sadness of someone with a terrible disease. . . . [An] important and powerful novel."—*Los Angeles Times*

"A must for anyone interested in the nature of mental illness as seen from the inside."—*Kirkus*

"A powerful, fascinating work."—*Library Journal*

"Once in a while you discover a piece of writing that stands out by virtue of its great originality, its ability to transform experience in a way you've never seen. And that reaffirms your faith in the entire literary enterprise, reminding you of why it is exactly that you read. *God Head*, the first novel by 32-year-old Scott Zwiren, is just sech a book."
—*Newsday*

Dalkey Archive Press

"That rarest of rarities: an experimental writer who's actually fun to read."—*Kirkus*

$13.50
1-56478-134-8

Collected Stories,
A r n o   S c h m i d t

The thirty-five stories collected here—described by *Library Journal* as "the perfect introduction" to Arno Schmidt—range from Schmidt at his most inviting and whimsical to Schmidt at his most cerebral and complex. In addition to *Collected Stories*, Dalkey Archive has previously published Schmidt's *Collected Novellas* and *Nobodaddy's Children*.

"Schmidt has gone all out to rewrite the rules of fiction. . . . [He] represents a refreshing voice in modern German literature that is neither radical nor slavishly patriotic . . . a unique explorer of the literary universe."—Philip Brantingham, *Chicago Tribune*

"Perplexing, terrifying and lyrical pages so rich in literary allusion and the exact evocation of nature that anyone unwilling to be addicted should be warned away from them."—D. J. R. Bruckner, *New York Times*

"Schmidt's imaginative descriptions and clever, sarcastic voice make this collection a joy to read."—*Publishers Weekly*

Dalkey Archive Press

"Julián Ríos's texts are very important . . . they are an assimilation of the most radical traditions."—Octavio Paz

$13.50
1-56478-138-0

Poundemonium
Julián Ríos

Just as Ezra Pound wrote a "Homage to Sextus Propertius" to pay tribute to an important influence, Julián Ríos offers in his new novel a "Homage to Ezra Pound" (as the original Spanish edition is subtitled). On November 1, 1972, news of Pound's death in Venice reaches three Spanish bohemians in London, passionate admirers of "il miglior fabbro" ("the better craftsman," as Eliot called him), who decide to honor Pound's memory by visiting various sites in London associated with him. Filled with allusions to Pound's life and works and written in a style similar to *Finnegans Wake*, *Poundemonium* is the second volume in Ríos's projected five-novel cycle called *Larva*. Dalkey Archive published the first volume, *Larva: Midsummer Night's Babel*, in 1990.

"*Poundemonium* invites us to a prodigious pilgrimage through the London of Pound that is also a no less prodigious journey through Julián Ríos' prose."—Octavio Paz

"Wonderfully translated into an English that preserves much of the original humor."—*Kirkus*

"Lots of fun and beautifully translated."—*Library Journal*

"A Baedeker of modernism."—*Publishers Weekly*

Dalkey Archive Press

"Eastlake's prairie-hard prose is as pure and clean as the wind-sanded land that fosters it."—Ken Kesey

$14.95
1-54678-136-4

Lyric of the Circle Heart
William Eastlake

Long before Cormac McCarthy and even long before Tom Robbins, William Eastlake invented an American Southwest whose comic and tragic dimensions, as well as its hard beauty, encapsulates American myths and nightmares. Against a background of New Mexico that transcends regional space, Eastlake explores race, greed, and tradition, evoking stereotypes for the sake of exploding them and laying bare an american reality that is a strange mix of pop culture, zany humor, biting satire, and a deep-seated respect for and love of the land.

All three of the novels collected here, *Go in beauty*, *The Bronc People*, and *Portrait of an Artist with Twenty-six Horses*, face head-on the reality of the American Indian—the last great taboo in an American culture that would prefer not to think about the invasion of a land and destruction of a native people in the name of religion and political freedom.

"Eastlake's novels are a pleasure to read, easily accessible on many levels. The wit is balanced by irony, the comedy and fantasy rooted in an honest avowal of the harshness, cruelty, and sometimes ugliness of the modern world. Eastlake tells the truth. And that truth is informed by sympathy for the wounded, by hatred for injustice, by scorn for the powerful, by love for the good and the beautiful."—Edward Abbey

Dalkey Archive Press

"A dramatic page-turner . . . among this century's most original and provocative novels of ideas."—*Chicago Tribune*

$10.95
1-56478-148-8

Spleen
O l i v e   M o o r e

Dalkey Archive Press first introduced readers to this "best-kept secret" of the British literature with the hardback *Collected Writings of Olive Moore* in 1992. *Spleen,* the best of the author's three novels, tells the disturbing story of a woman who goes into self-imposed exile to an island off the coast of Italy after giving birth to a deformed child. Filled with self-reproach and guilt about her son and her life (having yearned to give birth to something "new and rare," she blames herself for her son's deformity), Ruth broods on what it means to be a woman ("nature's oven for nature's bun") and the inequalities between the sexes.

Filled with the colors and beauty of the Italian countryside and in a style similar to Virginia Woolf's, *Spleen* challenges the assumption that women can't help but be tender and maternal, that their heads are only "ever-enlarging hearts."

"A redemptive and often witty novel."—*Belles Lettres*

"There's something fascinating about the fiction here—the ghostly, disturbing echo of a youthful voice, a voice at once secretive and exhibitionistic, reckless and self-protective, lyrical and satiric."—*Washington Post*

Dalkey Archive Press

"Spackman's highly elegant and original style turns sentences inside out and makes a leaping torrent of stream-of-consciousness."—*Chicago Tribune*

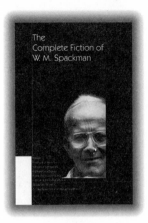

$16.95
1-56478-137-2

The Complete Fiction
W.   M.   S p a c k m a n

Described by Stanley Elkin as "this country's best-kept literary secret" and "a lost American classic," W. M. Spackman might well be one of the finest and most entertaining writers of the century. This omnibus edition includes all five of the author's previously published novels: *Heyday*, published by Ballantine in 1953 (and here presented with revisions the author made shortly before his death); and the critically acclaimed novels Knopf published between 1978 and 1985: *An Armful of Warm Girl* (1978), *A Presence with Secrets* (1980), *A Difference of Design* (1983), and *A Little Decorum, for Once* (1985). The novel *As I Sauntered Out, One Midcentury Morning* is published here for the first time, as well as the author's only two short stories.

"Wonderful! Absolutely delicious, a total delight. . . . So much fun to read that you forget how much skill has to go into such control, such perfect pitch."—Alice Adams

"On finishing *A Presence with Secrets*, I turned right back to page 1 to read it again."—*Newsweek*

"He has the power to make you believe you are engaged in an important act merely by reading him."—Stanley Elkin

Dalkey Archive Press

"An extraordinary work of the imagination . . . her best so far."
—Robert Coover

$12.95
1-56478-155-0

The Fountains of Neptune
R i k k i   D u c o r n e t

Rikki Ducornet's third novel, *The Fountains of Neptune*, is a haunting story of obsession and memory, spanning both world wars.

Rikki Ducornet skillfully conjures a world of darkness and light, innocence and depravity. Sensual and slyly comic, *The Fountains of Neptune* investigates the effects of terror, the roots of myth, and the wellsprings of memory. At the novel's heart is a moving story of personal discovery.

"In the bizarre world of Rikki Ducornet's fiction, laughter and terror hold hands in an uneasy truce and almost anything can happen." —Richard Burgin, *Washington Post*

"Linguistically explosive and socially relevant, [Ducornet's] works are solid evidence that [she] is one of the most interesting American writers around."—Charlotte Innes, *Nation*

"A sensual and voluptous feast. . . . A profound work, enchanting and psychologically complex."—*Toronto Star*

"She writes like a stunned time-traveler, testifying in breathless fragments to exotic ages that have gone or never were."—*Chicago Tribune*

Dalkey Archive Press

"*Little*'s plot is intriguing, its details consistently enjoyable. Its puns, puzzles, and word games are genuinely funny. . . ."
—*Saturday Review*

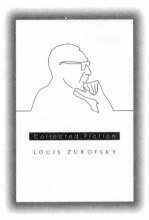

$13.50
1-56478-156-9

Collected Fiction
L o u i s Z u k o f s k y

Best known as one of the most significant poets of the 20th century, Louis Zukofsky was also an accomplished writer of fiction, all of which is collected here. Included is his only novel, *Little* (1970), which John Leonard in the *New York Times* called "an odd, playful, thoroughly charming novel about a child prodigy." (The novel is very autobiographical and Zukofsky's son, violin virtuoso Paul Zukofsky, has written an afterword for this edition.) Also included are the four stories comprising *It Was*, published in 1961 in a limited edition and virtually unobtainable for years.

"[*Little*] is a gnomic and gnomelike amusement, privy to prodigies, a careenager's tale, a fiddler's playful family tale, acrid and affectionate, stuck with proper names like cloves."—Robert Fitzgerald

"Anyone who has responded to Kafka or Walser or Borges or Donald Barthelme will recognize [in Zukofsky's short fiction] a similar breathtaking deftness of narration, and feel something of their remoteness from the interchangeable themes and styles of the large part of current fiction."—Guy Davenport, *New York Times*

Dalkey Archive Press

"A brilliantly malicious tribute to the mesmeric powers of film."
—*The Observer*

$11.95
1-56478-160-7

A Night at the Movies
R o b e r t   C o o v e r

In an alarmingly inventive collection of short fictions, Robert Coover offers us A *Night at the Movies*, complete with previews of coming attractions, cartoons, the weekly serial, a travelogue, a musical inter-lude, other selected short subjects, and three full-length features cover-ing that movie-poster spectrum of "the sum total of all human emo-tions": from *Adventure!* to *Comedy!* to *Romance!* There is even an inter-mission—though, as always with this master of metafiction, things are not always what they seem. "You can," as the movie advertisements used to say, "expect the unexpected."

"Robert Coover has made literary art out of a total immersion in the movies . . . enlarging his literary technique by forcing it to assimilate cinematic conventions and to approximate filmic style. . . .Vivacious and entertaining."—Edmund White, *New York Times*

"Brazenly witty."—*Times Literary Supplement*

"All our darkest wants, fears, dreams and myths are here in that mag-nificent celluloid palace no VCR will ever replace."—*Cleveland Plain Dealer*

"Coover's skill as a parodist is breathtaking."—*Kansas City Star*

Dalkey Archive Press

"Exhilarating, sorrowful and amazing. Indeed, a minor masterpiece."
—Michael Dirda, *Washington Post*

$12.95
1-56478-132-1

Reader's Block
David Markson

David Markson, critically acclaimed author of *Wittgenstein's Mistress* (Dalkey, 1988), electrifies his latest novel with unbearable emotional force. In this spellbinding, utterly unconventional fiction, an aging author identified only as Reader contemplates writing a novel. As he does, other matters insistently crowd his mind—literary and cultural anecdotes, endless quotations, attributed and not, scholarly curiosities— the residue of a lifetime's reading which is apparently all he has to show for his decades on earth.

Out of these unlikely yet incontestably fascinating materials— including innumerable detail about the madness and calamity in many artists' and writers' lives, the eternal critical affronts, the startling big- otry, the countless suicides—David Markson has created a novel of extraordinary intellectual suggestiveness.

"A comically despondent hymn . . . that comes off as an inspired scrawl of American graffiti."—Bill Marx, *Boston Globe*

"Best Books of '96."—*Publishers Weekly*

Dalkey Archive Press

Order Form

Individuals may use this form to order Dalkey titles at a
10-20% discount directly from our distributor,
the Chicago Distribution Center.

Title	ISBN	Quantity	Price

(10% on orders of one book, 20% on orders of two or more books)

Subtotal _____

Less discount _____

Subtotal _____

($3.50 for the first book, $.75 for each additional) Plus domestic postage _____

($4.50 for the first book, $1.00 for each additional) Plus foreign postage _____

Total _____

Ship to:

_____

_____

_____

_____

mail or fax this form to:
Dalkey Archive Press
c/o Chicago Distribution Center
11030 S. Langley Ave.
Chicago, IL 60628
fax: 773.660.2235 *tel:* 773.568.1550

Credit card payment ❏ Visa ❏ Mastercard

Acct # _____ Exp. Date _____

Name on card _____

Phone Number _____

Please make checks (in U. S. dollars only) payable to *Chicago Distribution Center*